White County, Tennessee

DEED ABSTRACTS
1801–1820

Abstracts of

DEED BOOKS
Volumes A, B, C, D, E and F

Abstracted by
Joyce Martin Murray

Index System by
Martin Richard Murray

Heritage Books
2024

HERITAGE BOOKS

AN IMPRINT OF HERITAGE BOOKS, INC.

Books, CDs, and more—Worldwide

For our listing of thousands of titles see our website
at
www.HeritageBooks.com

Published 2024 by
HERITAGE BOOKS, INC.
Publishing Division
5810 Ruatan Street
Berwyn Heights, MD 20740

International Standard Book Number
Paperbound: 978-0-7884-9064-4

Dedicated
to the

CARRICK
LOWERY
VANCE
and
BARGER

Families
of White County, Tennessee

Whose descendant was my Grandmother

ANN CARRICK MARTIN
(Born in White Co, TN and
Died in Ellis Co, TX)

INTRODUCTION

Present White County was a part of the Indian Lands (Cherokee) at the times of the 1790 and 1800 censuses. In 1806 White County was formed out of the previously designated counties of Overton (1806), Jackson (1801) and Smith (formerly part of Sumner County, formed in 1786). As first laid out, White County included portions of the present counties of Van Buren (1840), DeKalb (1837-8), Putnam (1854), and Cumberland (1856). Its current boundaries were reached by the time of the 1860 census.

For additional reading, the book HISTORY OF WHITE COUNTY, TENNESSEE, by Monroe Seals, would be of interest. The county is named for a Revolutionary War veteran and early settler in the area, John White, of Amelia County, Virginia, who is said to have come in 1789.

Many references to indentures (deeds) and other transactions that took place in the later 1700's will be found, and the areas of residence listed reflect former North Carolina, Virginia, Maryland, Pennsylvania, South Carolina, Georgia and other migratory origins. Be sure to check the PLACE INDEX for references to neighbors.

I am grateful to the Tennessee State Library for providing the microfilm which I used. I have tried to read accurately the many names in the handwritten documents, checking my interpretations when possible by the names in books and printed census lists. I have usually not listed more than one time the names of Clerks, Surveys, Judges and other officials. I do not list the county of residence of persons unless they do not live in White County, or understanding will be helped. I do try to include all other residences referred to. Most properties described lay within the boundaries of White County, but there is an exciting treasure trove (for the genealogist) of other counties and states.

ABBREVIATIONS USED:
ack-acknowledged, tr-tract, certif-certificate, adj-adjoining, clk-clerk, orig-original, admr-administrator, admx-administratrix, decd-deceased, cor-corner, beg-beginning, dist-district, sur-survey/surveyed, senr-senr, junr-junior, NP-Notary Public, sd-said, assee-assignee, wit-witness, co-county, conv-conveyed, CClk-County Clerk, CC-County Court, undiv-undivided, bdy-boundary, preemp-preemption, N-north, S-south, E-east, W-West, DS-Deputy Surveyor, CC-chainman, Warr-warrant.

DEED & TRUST DEED RECORDS

Volume A
Feb 1801 - Sept 1809

(No page number - seems to be odd sheet inserted in front of book)
Indenture 10 Feb 1801   ANDREW WADE, Anson Co, NC, and ELIJAH CHISUM,
Grainger Co, TN, $1550 paid, tr in Middle District of State of Tennessee on
head of Caney fork of Cumberland River, 5000 acres by virtue of his title
from JOSHUA PRONT _____, (incomplete).

Page 1 Indenture 25 Sept 1806   JOHN WRIGHT, Junr, Anson Co, NC, and
MOSES GUEST of White Co, TN, $100 paid, tr on headwaters of Caney fork of
Cumberland River, beg at NW cor 200 acre whereon Guest now lives, and being
60 acres. Wit: WILLIAM CHISUM, DAVID MAY. Clerk of Jan Term 1807 is JOS
TERRY. (Name of Grantee herein is also spelled MOSES GUIST.) JOHN DIRGA
is Registrar.

Page 3 Indenture 25 Sept 1806   Grantor as above, to DAVID MAY, White Co,
TN, $600 paid, tract on Mays fork, one of headwaters of Caney fork of
Cumberland River abutting at one point upper cor of THOMAS MAY, 400 acres.
Wit: WILLIAM CHISUM, Jr, THOMAS MATTHEWS. Certif by JOSEPH TERRY, Clk of
Court of Pleas. JOHN DIRGAN, Reg.

Page 5 Indenture 19 Oct 1804   ROBERT KING, Roane Co, TN, and WILLIAM
KING, Sullivan Co, TN, (relationship not stated), $600 paid, parcel of land
in Smith County (formerly Hawkins) in Calf Killers Valley on Caney fork,
640 acres granted by North Carolina at Newbern on 17 July 1794 to sd
Robert King, #2385. Wit: TOWNLEY DEAKINS. Ack before JNO OVERTON (?),
JSC DC for sd state.

Page 6 Indenture 14 Jan 1806   Grantor as above, and JACOB BROWN,
Washington Co, TN, $500 paid, tract of 333 1/3 acres in Smith County, it
being undiv moiety of land of 1000 acres patented to STOCKLY DONELSON,
WILLIAM TYRRELL, & ROBERT KING on water of Caney fork, including a lick &
on both sides of small creek called King & Co little lick creek. Wit:
EDMUND WALLAR, JACOB WART, JAS GORDON. Ack before DAVID CAMPBELL, a Judge
of Superior Ct for state.

Page 8 Indenture 10 Feb 1801   ANDREW WADE, Anson Co, NC, and ELIJAH
CHISUM, Grainger Co, TN, $1250 paid, tr in Mid dist of State of Tennessee
on headwaters of Caney fork, being 5000 acres, as Wade is authorized to do
by his title from JOSHUA PRANT. Wit: NIMROD DODSON, JOHN HOUND(?), ISAAC
SOME(?), Jurat. Reg in Grainger Co by AM YANCEY, Clk.

Page 9 Land Grant No 362   29 Jan 1798   STATE OF NORTH CAROLINA to
ROBERT KING, for 50 shillings for every hundred acres granted, 640 acres in
Sumner County on a branch of the Caney fork of Cumberland River. Signed by
SAMUEL ASHE, Esquire, our Governor, Captain and Commander in chief, at
Raleigh. WM HILL, D Secy.

Page 10 Will of GEORGE REEL   21 Nov 1806   ROBERT G ANDERSON appeared
before JOHN BRYAN, JP of White County, making oath that on 14 Nov he and
JAMES ANDERSON, his father, being at house of sd Reel, Reel being in low
state of health, heard his verbal will: to daughter SALLY (REEL), being

daughter by his first wife, a good feather bed & furniture, 1 cow, and to his wife & 3 children the property he now has, etc. Wit: JOHN BRYAN, Jr.

Page 12 Land Grant No 2935 22 Feb 1797 NORTH CAROLINA for signal bravery & persevering zeal of SAMPSON EADS(?), a private, entitled under act for relief of Officers & Soldiers of Continental line of the state, grants to JAMES COWAN, assee of Heirs of sd Sampson, 640 acres in Davidson County, lying on both sides of Murr's fork of Caney fork of Cumberland. Executed at Raleigh. DS THOMAS KING states he sur 640 acres for sd Cowan. Chain Bearers HENRY WARD, JONATHAN WOOD.

Page 13 Land Grant No 2966 NORTH CAROLINA to JOHN POGUE, a private, he being entitled under act for Relief of Officers & soldiers in the Continental line of this state, and thence to JAMES CUMMIN, ...

(Pages 14-17 are missing)

Page 18   (Remainder of Land Grant)   2 Mar 1797 640 acres in Middle Dist. Surveyor field notes attached. Surveyed 20 June 1796 by JOAB WOOD, DS. CC: SO BLAIR, T LEEPER.

Page 19 Land Grant No 2965 2 Mar 1790 (?-date is unclear) NORTH CAROLINA to WILLIAM FORSTERS, a private in Continental line of sd state, he being entitled to relief of officers and soldiers, his assee being JAMES COWAN, 640 acres in middle dist on N of Cumberland mountain on W of Caney fork of Cumberland river.

Page 20 Indenture 1 August 1806 EDWARD HARRIS, of Newbern, NC, Esq, and THOMAS STORM, Esq, of City of New York. Whereas WILLIAM BLOUNT, Esq, late of Knoxville, TN, and sd Storm were parties in deed of 2 July 1796, for $22,080, conveying tract of 44,160 acres granted by State of North Carolina to EDWARD HARRIS, being in Sumner County, in 69 different grants of 640 acres each numbered from 2612 to 2680. Tenants in common listed are JAMES MANNING, of City of New York, JOHN F LUYDAM, SAMUEL DENTON, HENDRICK J WICKOFF and JOHN LUYDAM, TIMOTHY GREEN, WILLIAM ROBERTSON, and SYLVERTER ROBERTSON, NICHOLAS COOK, STEPHEN TILLINGHART, LEBBINS LOOMIS, JONATHAN RUSSELL, DAVID GELSTON, all of sd city, JOHN MCLEAN of Boston, MA, SAMUEL BLAGGE, also of Boston, MOSES FISK, late a Tutor in Dartmouth College in New Hampshire. Wit: BENJN WOODS, JAS LEE GUION. Ack by GEORGE EVANS, CC, on first Monday of Aug 1800, in Pitt Co, NC. Certified by OLIVER SMITH, a justice of CC.

Page 27 Land Grant No 317 6 Dec 1796 NORTH CAROLINA for 10 pounds for every hundred acres hereby granted paid by THOMAS SAVAGE, grant to JOHN RUTLEDGE, assee of Savage, 5000 acres in our middle Dist on main fork of Elk river joining to a sur of sd Rutledge by Warrant No 1432. Surveyor's fieldnotes included, signed by STOCKLEY DONELSON, DS, and CC JOHN HUTCHINGS, WILLIAM DONELSON.

Page 30 Land Grant No 316 Date and parties and consideration as above, 5000 acres on main fork of Elk river adj a survey made for sd Rutledge. Surveyor's field notes attached.

Page 32 Land Grant No 319 Date, parties & consideration as above, John Rutledge being assee of ROGER SMITH, 5000 acres on main fork of Elk river.

Surveyor's field notes attached.

Page 35 Land Grant No 318 Date, parties & consideration as above, John Rutledge being assee of ALEXANDER FRAZER, Senr, and ALEXR FRAZER, Junr, and WM FRAZER, 5000 acres in our Middle Dist on a creek that empties into Findleston's creek, being the waters of Elk river & adj a sur of STOCKLEY DONELSON and WILLIAM TYRRELL that includes a large spring known by name of Fendleston spring. Field notes attached.

Page 38 Land Grant No 315 Same date and parties as in above deed, JOHN RUTLEDGE being in this case of JOSHUA WARD, 5000 acres in Middle Dist on a large creek the waters of Elk river. Field notes attached.

Page 41 Land Grant No 322 12 Dec 1796 NORTH CAROLINA to THOMAS WADE, tr of 5000 acres in Middle Dist on Caney fork of Cumberland river. Field notes attached.

Page 43 Land Grant No 324 Date, parties and consideration as above, 5000 acres on Caney fork of Cumberland. Field notes attached.

Page 46 Indenture 11 July 1801 JOHN MCVICKER and SAMUEL MANSFIELD of City of New York, Merchants, & __BBERN LOOMIS and STEPHEN TILLINGHART, late of City of New York, Merchants Bankrupt, first part, and THOMAS STORM of same City of New York, second part- by Articles of Agreement made at Philadelphia on 1 June 1796 between WILLIAM BLOUNT, lately Governor of SW Terr, and MOSES FISK(?), lately a Tutor in Dartmouth University in State of New Hampshire, as agent for THOMAS STORM, etc. (See Indenture on Page 20 for names of other persons involved - goes through page 54. Persons interested should order copies from the White County Clerk). Sworn to by SAMUEL JONES, Junr, Attorney in New York City on 26 June 1806. Ack before JAMES M HUGHES in sd city on 19 Sept 1801.

Page 55 Land Grant No 320 12 Dec 1796 NORTH CAROLINA to THOMAS WADE, 5000 acres on Caney fork of Cumberland river.

Page 56 Indenture 31 Dec 1803 JAMES COWAN, Raleigh, NC, and THOMAS DILLON, Davidson Co, TN, $4480 paid, 7 tracts of land in Tennessee, each one being 640 acres. Wit: JNO OVERTON, JAMES THOMPSON. Ack before DAVID CAMPBELL, a judge of Superior Ct for state.

Page 60 Power of Attorney 20 Apr 1807 Executed at Carthage. THOMAS DILLON, Davidson Co, TN, appoints Major ISAAC TAYLOR as his Attorney to contract some of the settlers who can obtain titles to 200 acres of land. Wit: JNO OVERTON, EDW SCOTT.

Page 62 Quitclaim Deed 26 Mar 1805 JOHN F SAYDAM, of City of New York, to SAMUEL DENTON his undivided 40th part of tract contracted for in Philadelphia. Wit: BENJAMIN MEAD, ISAAC B STRONG. Ack before PIERRE C VON WYCK, Esq, in New York, and WILLIAM L DARE.

Page 65 Deed of Gift 15 Dec 1806 RICHARD HORN, Senr, of Overton Co, TN, for love I bear for my following named children do convey to my daughter(s) SARAH EDGE, LETTUCE BREEDING, my son(s) RICHARD, WILLY and ZACHAUS the following property: one Negro man slave named JIM, one Negro woman slave named AMEY and her child named DILSEY, one Negro woman ALICE and her child named HANNAH, also 15 head of Horse Creatures, 3 cows, etc. Wit: S WILLIAMS, JACOB BAKER. Ack in Winchester Dist, TN, on 22 Apr 1807 by JIM OVERTON, one of Judges for state.

Page 66 Indenture 19 Apr 1810 TIMOTHY GREENE and MARY GREENE, his wife, and SAMUEL DENTON, all of City, County and State of New York, $840 paid, all our right in 1 undiv 10th part & also 1 undiv 20 part to Indenture of Contract made in Philadelphia on 1 June 1796 between WILLIAM BLOUNT, of Knoxville, TN and MOSES FISK, late Tutor in Dartmouth University (as referred to in prior instruments). Wit: ISAAC GREEN, HENRY MEIGS. Ack in State of New York before JAMES KENT(?), Chief Justice in state.

Page 70 Deed 9 May 1806 RALPH THURMAN and wife SARAH THURMAN, of New York, to SAMUEL THURMAN, $5.00 paid, 1 equal half or moiety of all estate right to property which is set out therein. Wit: HENRY MEIGS, DANL ALLIE. Ack before JAMES HUNT, Chief Jus of Supreme Ct, New York City.

Page 72 Deed 7 Dec 1804 DAVID GELSTON, of City of New York, merchant, to RALPH THURMAN of same city, 5 pounds paid, my rights to a tract of land contracted for me in Philadelphia between WILLIAM BLOUNT and MOSES FISK (as previously set out). Wit: JNO KEANEY, DAVID GELSTON. Ack before WM ROSE in New York State on 14 May 1805.

Page 75 Land Grant No 325 12 Dec 1796 NORTH CAROLINA to THOMAS WADE, 5000 acres in Middle Dist on Camp creek a branch of Caney fork of Cumberland. Executed at Raleigh. Surveyor's field notes attached - surveyed 16 June 1796.

Page 78 Land Grant No 321 Date and Parties in Grant above, 5000 acres on Caney fork. Surveyor's field note state land surv same date.

Page 80 Indenture 1 Oct 1806 JOHN WRIGHT, Junr, Anson Co, NC and STEPHEN COPELAND, Overton Co, TN, $1500 paid for tr in White Co, TN on Camp creek of the Falling waters of the Caney fork, 5000 acres patented 12 Dec 1796. Wit: THOMAS MATTHEWS, JAMES WINTON.

Page 82 Indenture 25 Sept 1806 JOHN WRIGHT, Junior, Anson Co, NC, and THOMAS MAY, Sen, White Co, TN, $640 paid, tr in White County on May's fork of Collins River and one of headwaters of Caney fork, near Hawkin's spring branch, and adj at one point ELIJAH CHISUM line, land conveyed including house & plantation whereon sd May, Senr now lives, being 640 acres, part of 5000 acre tr granted by NC to THOMAS WADE. Wit: MOSES GUEST, Jurat, REYNOLDS MAY, Jurat.

Page 85 Land Grant No 1191 23 Feb 1793 NORTH CAROLINA to LANDON CARTER, for 50 shillings for every 100 acres granted, tract of 200 acres in our Green County, joining on lower side of survey of sd Carter's No 1319. Signed by our governor, captain General & Commander in Chief at Newbern, RICHARD DOBBS SPAIGHT, and by Secty J GLASGOW. Surveyor's field notes attached, stating by virtue of a removed Warrant from the state AUTRY LAKER, No 925, located 1 Apr 1787. 200 acres. CC: JOHN RAY, JOHN SMITH.

Page 86 Land Grant No 1188 22 Feb 1793 Parties and consideration as in above Grant, 220 acres in Green County on waters of Elk river and joining Carter's 1156. Sur field notes attached.

Page 88 Land Grant No 1187 23 Feb 1793 Parties and consideration as above, tr of 300 acres in same county, including a walnut bottom about 30 poles from the tree where COL ROBERTSON left a letter for the Cherokee Chiefs. Located by THOS HICKMAN, Sur, on 1 Apr 1780.

Page 89 Land Grant No 1178 Date, Parties & consideration above, 50 acres in above mentioned Green County on a large creek supposed to be the waters of Duck, joining sur of sd Carter's on the West. Same surveyor as above.

Page 91 Land Grant No 1192 Date, Parties and consideration as in above Grant, 200 acres in Green County on waters of Elk river joining lower side sd Carter's No 1498. Field Notes attached, signed by THOS HICKMAN, D Surv, and CC being JOHN RAY and JOHN SMITH.

Page 93 Land Grant 1185 Date, Parties and consideration as above, 600 acres in Green County on waters of Duck, including improvement where COL JAMES ROBERSON and party lay on Thursday the 29th day Mar 1787. Field Notes attached.

Page 94 Land Grant No 1189 Date, Parties and consideration above, 200 acres in Green County, on large creek supposed to be branch of Elk river, including place where they ___ under command of COL JAMES ROBINSON ___ the same day they set up the letter directed to the Cherokee Chiefs. Field Notes attached.

Page 96 Land Grant 1181 Date, Parties and consideration above, 400 acres in Green County. Field Notes attached.

Page 97 Land Grant No 1179 Date, Parties & consideration above, 640 acres in above named county, beg a small distance below Lane leading from Nashville to Lookout mountain & running down the river. Field Notes attached.

Page 99 Land Grant No 1180 Date, Parties & consideration above, 150 acres. Field Notes attached.

Page 101 Land Grant No 1170 Date, Parties & consideration above, 200 acres in Green county on waters of Elk river joining on lower side of Sur No 925. Field Notes attached.

Page 102 Land Grant No 1247 12 July 1794 Parties & consideration above, 150 acres in above named county. Field Notes attached.

Page 104 Land Grant 1182 23 Feb 1793 NORTH CAROLINA to LANDON CARTER, 150 acres on waters of Elk river joining a sur of sd Carter's No 1882. Field Notes attached.

Page 106 Land Grant No 1183 Date, Parties & Consideration as above, 150 acres. Field notes.

Page 108 Land Grant 1186 Date, Parties & Consideration as above, 150 acres.

Page 110 Indenture 1 May 1797 STOKELY DONELSON, late of Hawkins County, by his Atty in fact HUGH DUNLAP of Knox Co, TN, and JOSIAH DANFORTH, Blount

Co, TN, $5000 paid, 11 tracts containing 20630 acres, being in Middle Dist on small creek which empties into a large one supposed to be waters of Cumberland river, Sur No 1. Wit: JOSEPH THURMAN, SAML PERRY. Thurman ack on 25 May 1807 in White Co, TN.

Page 112 Indenture 10 Sept 1806 JOHN WRIGHT, Junr, Anson Co, NC, and MOSES GUEST, $325 paid, tract in Wight Co, TN(?) on one of headwaters of Caney fork of Cumberland river called May's fork, 200 acres. Wit: THOMAS MAY, REYNOLD MAY.

Page 114 Indenture 1 Oct 1806 Grantor as above, to STEPHEN COPELAND, Overton Co, TN, $1,500 paid, tr on Camp creek a branch of the falling waters of Caney fork of Cumberland River, 5000 acres. Wit: THOS MATTHEWS, JAMES WINTON.

Page 116 Surveyor's Field Notes 16 June 1796 JOAB WORD, DS, surveyed by virtue of military land Warrant No 1315, dated 2 Nov 1785, for ELIZA WILLIAMS, 640 acres in Middle Dist in a Valley known as the Calf Killers Valley on waters of Cumberland river joining the Falling Spring Survey. L LEEPER, CB.

Page 116 Land Grant No 2784 20 Dec 1796 NORTH CAROLINA to ELIZA WILLIAMS, assee of JAMES CARBON, heir of JAMES CARBON, a private in Continental line of sd state, 640 acres in middle district in Valley known as Calf Killer, on waters of Cumberland River joining the Falling Spring Sur. Field Notes exec in Terr So of the Ohio or State of Tennessee, Mid Dist, attached and signed JONA WOOD(?), DS.

Page 118 Land Grant No 2785 Date and Grantor above to ELIZA WILLIAMS, assees of Heirs of ABRAHAM CLARK a private in Continental line sd state, 640 acres in Middle Dist on Cane creek, a branch of Caney fork of Cumberland River. Registered 26 May 1807. Field notes attached, surv 12 June 1796, by JONATHAN WOOD, DS, TO BLAIR, T LEEPER.

Page 119 Land Grant No 2786 20 Dec 1796 Grantor above to ELIZA WILLIAMS, assees of Heirs of NATHAN PERSON, private in Continental line of sd state, 640 acres on Caney fork on both sides of an Indian path that leads from the salt lick to Chicamaga.

Page 120 Land Grant No 2282 20 May 1793 NORTH CAROLINA by Act for relief of Officers & Soldiers in the Continental line & in consideration of signal bravery and persevering zeal of DANIEL GUINN, a private in sd line, granted JOSHUA DAVIS, assee of sd Guin 640 acres in Sumner County. Surveyor's Field Notes attached, having been by virtue of Military Warrant No 2358, located 19 Nov 1792, 640 acres on Caney fork for sd Davis. Signed by THOS HICKMAN, D Sur, SCC JOSIAH PAYNE, WILLIAM RUDE, MARTIN ARMSTRONG, Senr.

Page 122 Land Grant No 2252 Date, Grantor and consideration as above, pursuant to act for relief of Officers & Soldiers, etc, consideration of signal bravery and persevering zeal of ROBERT BLANSHOT(?) a private in sd Continental line grant unto JOSHUA DAVIS, assee of sd Blanshot's heirs, 640 acres in Sumner County on E side of Caney fork. Surveyed in Sumner Co, NC, by Military warrant No 2362, located 19 Nov 1792.

Page 124   Land Grant No 2250   Date & Grantor as above, 640 acres pursuant to Act for Relief of Off & Sold in Cont line, etc, to JOSHUA DAVIS, assee of AUGUSTINE HARRISON, tr of 640 acres in Sumner County, NC on Caney fork about 2 1/2 miles below WILLIAM REED.   Field notes located 19 Nov 1792.

Page 125   Land Grant No 1974   Date & Grantor as above, 640 acres granted pursuant as set out above, to WILLIS UPTON, a private in sd line, grant to JOSHUA DAVIS, assee of sd Upton, tract being in County of Sumner (NC) on Cainey fork.   Field Notes attached located on above date.

Page 127   Land Grant No 2260   20 May 1793   Grantor as above, 640 acres to JONATHAN ABBOTT, a private in Continental line of NC, JOSHUA DAVIS, assee of Abbott.   Field notes attached.

Page 129   Land Grant No 2020   Date, Grantor and consideration as above, 640 acres on Crabapple Creek supposed the waters of Doe Creek, to EDWARD SAGE, a private in Continental line of NC, and JOSHUA DAVIS, assee of Sage. Field Notes attached, located by virtue of Military Warrant from NC, No 2437, entry dated 29 Oct 1792.

Page 131   Surveyor's Field Notes of 15 June 1796, for ELIZA WILLIAMS, land including place named the Three Spring survey.

Page 131   Land Grant No 2787   STATE OF NORTH CAROLINA to ELIZA WILLIAMS, assee of JOHN HARRITT, heir of HOLLAND HARRITT, a private in Continental line, 640 acres to include Three Spring survey.

Page 132   Surveyor's Field Notes of 17 June 1796, signed by JONATHAN WOOD, DS, for 640 acres of land in middle district on E side of the Caney fork of Cumberland River, opposite the Falling spring.

Page 133   Land Grant No 2788   NORTH CAROLINA to ELIZA WILLIAMS, assee of heirs of JAMES PERRYMORE, land as above.   Dated 20 Dec 1796.

Page 134   Surveyor's Field Notes of 20 June 1796, tr sur for ELIZA WILLIAMS, assee of JAMES WILLIAMS, 640 acres on both sides of the Caney fork of Cumberland River.

Page 135   Land Grant No 2789   NORTH CAROLINA to ELIZA WILLIAMS, assee of WILLIAM DUGGIN, heir of JON HUGGINS(?), a private in Continental line of sd state, 640 acres on both sides Caney fork.

Page 136   Surveyor's Field Notes of 14 July 1796, by virtue of Military land Warranat No 1278, dated 21 Apr 1784, 640 acres on Caney fork, tr known as Little Walnut Valley.

Page 137   Land Grant No 2790   20 Dec 1796   ELIZA WILLIAMS, assee of PHILIP LOVE(?), a private in Continental line of NC, 640 acres as above.

Page 138   Land Grant No 342   NORTH CAROLINA to ROBERT KING, assee of JAMES WILLIAMS, 2500 acres including a spring known as Hopkins spring, also a sinking spring, the waters of Caney fork.   Dated 1 Mar 179_.   (Copy from the Records)

Page 138   Land Grant No 301   7 Mar 1796   Grantor as above to STOCKLEY

DONELSON & WILLIAM TYRRELL, 5000 acres on waters of Elk River joining their former sur of 5000 acres made to include Fendleton's spring. Copy WILL WHITE, Secty. Recorded 20 May 1807, JOS TERRY, DR.

Page 139 Surveyor's Field Notes Sur for JOHN GRAY & THOMAS BLOUNT 5000 acres on both sides of S fork of Duck River, on 28 Aug 1792, signed by JOHN DONELSON, DS.

Page 140 Land Grant No 229 NORTH CAROLINA, 10 pounds for every 100 acres hereby granted paid by JOHN GRAY & THOM BLOUNT, 5000 acres on both sides of S fork of Duck River.

Page 142 Registrar's certificate 22 May 1807 Executed in Rutherford County, TN, and stating that within grant was registered in his office in Book C, pages 27 & 28. JOHN DICKSON, Regr.

Page 142 Field Notes Surveyed 16 May 1788 by virtue of Military warrant from NC 3261 located 22 Mar 1788 for COL ELIJAH ROBERTSON, assee of JOHN HENRY, 640 acres on E fork of Stone River and adj one point land of RICHARD CATHEY. Signed by MAR C ARMSTRONG, Sur, JONATHAN DRAKE, SAMUEL WEAKLEY, SCC, D Sur R WEAKLEY.

Page 143 Land Grant No 810 21 Oct 1788, in 13th year of our Independence NORTH CAROLINA pursuant to act for soldiers of Continental line, signal bravery, etc of JOHN HENRY, Privet in sd line, have given to COL ELIJAH ROBERTSON, assee of sd Henry, 640 acres in Davidson County on E fork of Stone River, beg at line of WILLIAM CATHEY line, 20 chains N of RICHARD CATHEY NE cor. SAMUEL JOHNSTON, Esq, Governor, etc, J GLASGOW, Secty, JO TERRY, D Rec.

Page 144 Land Grant No 3061 7 Mar 1796 NORTH CAROLINA to JAMES GAINES, 1000 acres on both sides of a fork on Caney fork, beg about 1 mile from foot of Cumberland Mountain, including several Indian Camps. Field Notes attached, being sur for ELIZA WILLIAMS, assee of JAMES WILLIAMS 5000 acres on N of Cumberland Mountain on 24 May 1784.

Page 146 Land Grant No 326 20 Dec 1796 NORTH CAROLINA to ELIZA WILLIAMS, assee of JAMES WILLIAMS, 5000 acres in Middle Dist on North Cumberland Mountain, joining a sur known as Hopkins Spring Survey. Surveyor's field notes attached.

Page 147 Land Grant No 327 Date and parties as above, 2500 acres in Walnut Valley, beg near a large Buffalo path leading from the Great Salt lick to the Caney fork. Surveyor's field notes attached (18 June 1796), signed by Sur WILL WHITE, and CC DANL DAVISON & HENRY WOOD.

Page 148 Land Grant No 328 Date & parties as above, 2500 acres on N side Cumberland Mountain on waters of the Caney fork, lying in Walnut Valley. Surveyor's field notes attached (17 June 1796).

Page 149 Land Grant No 329 Date & parties as above, 2500 acres in Walnut Valley.

Page 150 Land Grant No 330 Date & parties as above, 1000 acres on Flat creek a branch of Muir's fork of the Caney fork. Surveyor's field notes attached.

Page 151   Land Grant No 2964   2 Mar 1797   NORTH CAROLINA, pursuant to act of Genl Assem for relief of officers & soldiers in Continental line, and for signal bravery, etc of GEORGE GALDERS, a private in sd line, JAMES COMAN, assee of Heirs of sd Galders, 640 acres on waters of Calf Killer's fork a branch of Caney fork. Surveyor's field notes attached, being by virtue military Warrant No 4596 dated 9 Feb 1797.

Page 153   Land Grant No 3034   10 Apr 1797   Grantor for reasons as in above grant, for services of JOHN SIMPSON a private in sd line of this state, grant to JAMES COWAN, assee of sd Simpson, 640 acres in our Davidson County on both sides of Meiers fork of the Caney fork of Cumberland.

Page 154   Indenture   17 Nov 1805   THOMAS DILLON, Davidson Co, and THOMAS N CLARKE, $1280 paid, 2 tracts of land in Tennessee, 1 being Miers fork of Caney fork, and other being 640 acres on S side of Caney fork. Wit: J EASTON, DAVID HOGG, STEPHEN HAYNES, JOHN ARMSTRONG.

Page 156   Indenture   22 Nov 1805   THOMAS DILLON, Davidson Co, TN and JOHN BRAHAN, Roane Co, TN, $640 paid, tr on waters of Calf Killers fork, a branch of Caney fork, as per Patent 2964 issued to JAMES COWAN for 640 acres. Wit: THOMAS N CLARK, DAVID HOGG. Surveyor's field notes attached, sur 15 July 1796 by STOCKLEY DONELSON, HENRY WOOD, JONATHAN WOOD, SCC.

Page 159   Land Grant No 2934   22 Feb 1797   NORTH CAROLINA to JAMES COWAN, assee of JACOB WHITE, a musician(?) in the Continental line of sd state, 1000 acres in Middle Dist on a fork of the Caney fork of Cumberland River known as the Mieirs fork. Surv on 17 June 1796 by JOAB WOOD, DS, FRANCIS LEEPER, HENRY WOOD, SCC.

Page 160   Land Grant No 2967   2 Mar 1797 Grantor as above for service of GEORGE C GATE, a private in Continental line of sd state, to JAMES COWAN, assee of Heirs of sd Gate, 640 acres on S side of Caney fork of Cumberland River & beg 2 miles S from junction on fork of Caney fork and Calf Killers fork.

Page 161   Indenture   23 Nov 1805   THOMAS N CLARKE, of 8th west point(?), and THOMAS DILLON, Davidson County (both of State of Tennessee), $640 paid, tracts on fork of Caney known as Mier's fork.

(Pages 163 and 164 omitted)

Page 165   Sheriff's Deed   15 July 1807   WILLIAM PHILLIPS, Esqr, Shff of White Co, TN, and ROBERT ALLEN, Shff having been ordered by court to get sum of ____ which JOSEPH MCGUFFIN and JAMES MCGUFFIN recovered against ROBERT KING, land affected being 2500 acres. Wit: THOS BOUNDS, ELY BENSON.

Page 169   Sheriff's Deed   16 July 1807 Grantor as above and THOMAS K HARRIS and JOHN GALE, goods of ROBERT KING being sold to pay $1612.50, a debt recovered by JOSEPH MCGUFFIN and JAMES MCGUFFIN, 2500 acres lying on Cane creek, a branch of Caney fork of Cumberland River, tr having been granted by NC to sd King, assee of JAMES WILLIAMS pr Grant No 341, dated 1 Mar 1797.

Page 171   Sheriff's Deed Date and Grantor and Grantees as above, and other names as above.

Page 174   Procession Certif JNO DOAK, DS, by W P ANDERSON, states on 9 July 1807 that he has processioned for THOMAS VINING 5000 acres on headwaters of the Caney fork grant of 12 Dec 1796, No 324, Warrant 1604, land adj that of ELIJAH CHISOM. SCC: JACK RUTLAND, DANIEL FORBECK. (Executed in 2nd District, Tennessee)

Page 176   Procession Certif 7 July 1807 JNO DOAK, DS, by W P ANDERSON, has processioned for THOMAS MATTHEWS 5000 acres in 2nd Dist on head waters of Caney fork, Grant dated 12 Dec 1796, Warrant 1721, Grant No 320, adj land of ELIJAH CHISUM.

Page 178   Indenture 21 July 1796 STOCKLEY DONELSON, by his Atty in Fact for HUGH DUNLAP, one part, and JOSIAH DANFORTH, Blount Co, TN, other part, $5000 paid, tr of 19000 acres in Knox Co, TN, tr beg at mouth of White's creek and abutting Cumberland mountain. Wit: JAMES BEARD, JOHN SHANTON(?).

Page 179   Indenture 28 Aug 1795 HUGH DUNLAP, Knox Co, and S of River Ohio, Merchant, Atty in Fact for STOCKLEY DONELSON, one part, and JOSIAH DANFORTH(?), Washington Co, VA, other part, $12,000 paid, tr surveyed for (very dim) and granted to Donelson by NC, being on waters of --____ creek of Tennessee River. Wit: JOHN THOMAS, (unreadable).

Page 182   Indenture 3 Dec 1793 STOCKLEY DONELSON, by his Atty in fact HUGH DUNLAP, of Knox County and Terr South of Ohio, one part, and DEVERIN(?) GILLIAM of sd county, $1000 paid for 2 parcels of land containing 1000 acres each. Wit: PETER MCNAME, JOHN CARTER, ABRAM JOHNSON. Ack before JOS LOWRY.

Page 184   Indenture 24 Mar 1796 STOCKLEY DONELSON of City of Raleigh, NC, by his Atty in Fact as above, to Grantee above, $750 paid, 1500 acres being his half or moiety of sur of 3000 acres granted to Donelson & WILLIAM TYRRELL by NC, Patent No 305, tr including a place known as Crab Orchard and being on both sides of the wagon road leading to Knoxville. Wit: JOHN HERAN, SAMUEL HUGHS.

Page 186   Indenture (Executed in Anson Co, NC) 10 Sept 1797 JOSHUA PROUT, Admr of will of THOMAS WADE, Decd, one part and JANE WADE, (relationship not stated), by her friend ISAAC JACKSON, Esqr, both of sd county, 11 pounds, tr being on Caney fork of Cumberland River. Wit: ANDREW WADE, DAVID POUNDS. Cert by TOD ROBINSON(?), Clk, Anson Co, NC, and by JAMES MARSHALL, Pres Jus.

Page 188   Indenture (Exec in Anson Co, NC) 10 July 1799 JANE WADE and JOSHUA PROUT, Esqr, for 100 pounds paid, tract being in NC when granted but now in state of Tennessee on Caney fork of Cumberland River, 5000 acres. Wit: ELIZABETH WADE, JARREL POUNDS. Certif at Wadesborough in Anson Co, NC by TOD ROBINSON, Clk.

Page 191   Indenture (Exec in Anson Co, NC) 10 Oct 1800   JOSHUA PROUT and ANDREW WADE, both of sd county, $500 paid, tr in NC when granted but now in TN on Caney fork of Cumberland river, being 5000 acres. Wit: ROBERT

CANNON(?). Certified by TODDY ROBINSON in Wadesborough on 21 Aug 1802, and by JAMES MARSHALL, PJ.

Page 192 Indenture 10 Mar 1796 STOCKLEY DONELSON and WILLIAM TYRELL, of White Co, NC, first part, and JAMES EASTON of Wake Co, NC, $2500 paid, 5000 acres on Elk River and being Grant No 301. Wit: JAMES C GORHAM, WM SHAW. Certif in TN by THOS EMERSON on oath of PETER CASSO who states on 28 May 1807 that Gorham is dead and Shaw is not an inhabitant of Tennessee.

Page 195 Land Grant No 198 22 Feb 1797 NORTH CAROLINA to DANIEL FRAZIER, assee of EBENEZER TITUS who served as a chain carrier for officers & soldiers in the Continental line, 400 acres of land being on waters of Cumberland River. JONATHAN WOOD, Sur, HENRY WOOD, D DAVIDSON, CC.

Page 197 Sheriff's Deed 13 Mar 1807 WILLIAM PHILLIPS, Shff White Co, Tn, and THOMAS WILSHIRE, writ having been executed in Hamilton Dist, against ROBERT KING as recovered by JAMES MAGAFFIN(?) and JOSEPH MAGAFFIN(?) (relationship not stated), 640 acres of land granted to King by NC on 29 Jan 1796, Grant 362, tr being on Caney fork of Cumberland River, beg near an old Indian path. Reg Oct tern 1807 by JOHN M CARRICK, Clk.

Page 200 Land Grant No 3085 12 Aug 1797 (22 yr of our Independence) NORTH CAROLINA to ROBERT KING, assee of heirs of JACOB MILES, a private in the Continental line, 640 acres on a branch of the Caney fork of Cumberland River beg 6 or 7 poles from head of Caplinger spring and near the Barrens. Field Notes by JOHN WOOD, DS, DANIEL DAVISON, HENRY WOOD on 14 June 1796.

Page 202 Indenture 22 Feb 1800 ROBERT KING, Knox Co, TN, and JOHN HENDERSON of Chatham Co, NC, $960 paid, 3 tracts of land. Wit: MERIWETHER SMITH, TOWNLEY DEAKINS, JAMES EASTON. (Note says deed was registered in Smith County.) Ack in Davidson Co, TN by Easton on 11 Jan 1803 before ANDREW JACKSON, Judge of Superior Court and reg in White Co on 16 Mar 1803.

Page 205 Indenture 10 Mar 1804 JOHN HENDERSON, as above, and JOHN MCAULEY, Orange Co, NC, $1920 paid, 640 acres on Caney fork of Cumberland River including the mouth of the Roring spring, being Grant No 3086 from NC; also 640 acres on N of Cumberland Mountain 1 mile from Hopkinses spring being Grant No 2951; also 640 acres on branch of Caney fork of Cumberland River and being 6 or 7 poles from head of a spring known as Hopkinses spring and near the Barrens, being Grant from NC No 3085. Wit: W STEDMAN, SAMUEL GUTHRIE, JAMES MCAULEY. Ack before JNO OVERTON.

Page 208 Affidavit 28 Jan 1808 (Exec at Raleigh, NC) BENJAMIN WILLIAMS, Gov, certif signature of WILLIAM WHITE, Esq, Secty for NC, who certifies Grant No 310 to JOHN RHEA and WILLIAM TYRRELL for 500 acres on a fork of Caney fork called by KING & COMPANY McClure River and on both sides of an Indian path that leads to Chimneys.

Page 210 Indenture 6 May 1808 THOMAS H HARRIS and STEPHEN AUSTIN, $100 paid, tr being on Cane creek a branch of Caney fork of Cumberland, a part of 2500 acres orig granted by NC to ROBERT KING, assee of JAMES WILLIAMS.

Page 211 Bill of Sale 1 Mar 1804 JOHN BOWEN, Jackson Co, TN, and JOHN BRYANT, $300 paid, 1 Negro girl CHANY about 25 yrs of age. Wit: ___ RAWLINGS, JR.

Page 212   Indenture   10 May 1808   THOMAS K HARRIS and THOMAS STONE, $100 paid, 2500 acres granted to ROBERT KING, assee of JAMES WILLIAMS, Grant No 341, being on Cane creek a branch of Caney fork of Cumberland River, after taking out of it 9 small tracts this day conv by deed to following persons, to-wit: STEPHEN AUSTIN, 309 acres, WILLIAM DYRE 207 acres, JOSEPH PARKER, 207 acres, PINK HUDSON, 170 acres, JOHN NELSON, 81 acres, RICHARD HILL, 170 acres, sd THOMAS STONE, 386 acres, WILLIAM RIDGE ____ acres, and BRYANT BREEDING ___ acres. 684 acres hereby deeded to THOMAS STONE.

Page 213   Indenture   Date and Grantor as in above deed, to JOHN NELSON, $100 paid, 81 acres as above stated.

Page 216   Quitclaim Deed   21 Aug 1807   THOMAS BLAGGE and wife SARAH BLAGGE, of Boston, Suffolk Co, MA, Merchant, to SAMUEL DENTON of City, County & State of New York, Merchant, $300 paid, any claim to undivided part of tr on Caney fork of Cumberland River in Sumner Co, TN, being 44,160 acres conv by deed of 2 July 1796 between WILLIAM BLOUNT, Knoxville, TN and THOMAS _____. Wit: BENJ BLAGGE, JOHN BLAGGE. Ack in Boston before JOS MAY, JP, and CHAS CUSHING, Clk CCP, WILLIAM WILMORE, CJ same court, EDWARD JONES, NP.

Page 219   Indenture   10 May 1808   THOMAS K HARRIS and RICHARD HILL, $100 paid, tr of 220 acres a part of 2500 acres orig granted to ROBERT KING.

Page 220   Indenture   Date and Grantor as above, to BRYANT BREEDING, $100 paid, 60 acres.

Page 221   Indenture   Date and Grantor as above, to WILLIAM DYER, $100 paid, 207 acres.

Page 222   Indenture   Date and Grantor as above, to JOSEPH PARKER, $100 paid, 207 acres.

Page 223   Indenture   Date and Grantor as above, to THOMAS STONE, $100 paid, 386 acres.

Page 224   Indenture   Date and Grantor as above, to PINK HUDSON, $100 paid, 176 3/4 acres.

Page 225   Indenture   Date and Grantor above, to WILLIAM RIDGE, $100 paid, 120 acres.

Page 226   Deed of Gift   21 Mar 1808   ELIZABETH POLLOCK, a widow, for love & affection I have for my daughter ELIZABETH POLLOCK of same state and county, goods now in my present dwelling house, also 1 roan mare. Wit: JOHN M CARRICK, MAJOR CARRICK(?).

Page 227   Deed of Gift   18 Apr 1807   HANNAH REAL for love, etc I have for my children EDWARD REAL, GEORGE REAL and ELIZABETH REAL, being goods & chattles in dwelling house. Wit: WE MCGUIRE(?), HENRY HORDIAN(?), SURANA TAYLER(?). Reg in White Co by JO TERRY, Clk.

Page 228   Sheriff's Deed   9 Feb 1808   WILLIAM PHILLIPS, Shff of White County by his dep JAS TAYLOR, Junr, writ directing property of GEORGE TAYLOR be sold to satisfy costs of a suit that JAMES COWAN(?) recovered, land on which sd George lives on road leading from Rock Island to Carthage about 2 miles from Rock Island.

Page 229   Surveyor's Field Notes of 1500 acres, sur 4 Mar 1787, tr given by state on 30 Apr 1784, Warrant No 1978, being sur for WILLIAM HILL, assee of CHARLES ALEXANDER, tr on W side of Richland creek of Elk River.   EDW HICKMAN, Sur, CHARLES ANDERSON and AMOS MOORE, CC.

Page 230   Land Grant 9 Dec 1797   NORTH CAROLINA to WILLIAM HILL, assee of CHARLES ALEXANDER (who paid 10 pounds for every 100 acres), 1500 acres (as in Field Notes above), adj sur of WILLIAM POLK.

Page 231   Deed 3 Mar 1808   WILLIAM HILL, York Dist, SC to JOHN GOWN(?), Greenville Dist, SC, $3000 paid, tr or plantation in Tennessee in Middle Dist on Richland creek of Elk River, 1500 acres. Wit: SOLOMON HILL, ALEXR L ROSS(?), JOHN CARRUTH, SAML CALDWELL, WILBY J BROWN. Ack by Brown before JOHN WHITTIER.

Page 233   Indenture 7 May 1808   JOHN GALE and THOMAS K HARRIS, $100 paid, 2 tracts being 2500 acres. Exec in Carthage. Wit: ARCHIBALD W OVERTON, NATHANIEL W WILLIAMS, WM P LAWRENCE, P W NUTT, ISAAC WALTON.

Page 236   Indenture 8 Mar 1808   THOMAS DILLIN, Davidson County, and ROBERT HOWARD and SAMUEL WEAVER, tr of 2500 acres (very difficult to read description). Wit: ISAAC TAYLOR, Junr, ELIJAH WEAVER, JOHN MCBRIDE, THOMAS STONE(?). Ack before DAVID CAMPBELL, Judge Superior Ct.

Page 238   Indenture 31 May 1808   THOMAS MCCORRY, Knoxville, TN, and DAVID MCDANIEL, $460 paid, tr vested in him by virtue of grant from NC to JOHN RHEA and WILLIAM TYREL, No 310, dated 7 Mar 1796, being 230 acres and beg in line of JOHN WHITE and adj DAVID NICHOLS. Wit: TURNER LANE, ANDREW BRYAN.

Page 241   Indenture Date and Grantor as above, to TURNER LANE, $110 paid, 55 acres from tract set out above, and adj WILLIAM BRIANT. Wit: WILLIAM M BRIANT, ANDREW BRIANT.

Page 243   Indenture Date and Grantor as above to ANDREW BRIAN, $198 paid, 99 acres in above referred to tract (Grant No 310), adj WILLIAM M BRYAN, ROBERT G ANDERSON. Wit: TURNER LANE, WILLIAM M BRYAN.

Page 245   Indenture 2 June 1808   THOMAS MCCORRY, of Knoxville, TN, and JAMES FULKERSON, $400 paid, 314 acres in sd Grant No 310. Wit: TURNER LANE, ROBERT G ANDERSON.   Reg by ELIJAH CHISUM, Dep.

Page 247   Indenture Grantor and date above to WILLIAM BRYAN, $300 paid, 150 acres in sd Grant No 310. Wit: TURNER LANE, JOSEPH ANDERSON.

Page 250   Indenture 1 June 1808 Grantor as above to JOHN WHITE, $700 paid, 519 acres beg in orig line of JACOB ANDERSON Sur and being part of Grant No 310. Wit: As on p 245.

Page 250a   Land Grant 1 Mar 1797   NORTH CAROLINA to ROBERT A KING, assee of JAMES WILLIAMS, 2,500 acres in Middle Dist on a branch of Caney Fork of Cumberland River known as Cane creek.

Page 254   Indenture   2 Oct 1804   ROBERT KING, Roane Co, TN and WILLIAM OWENS, Sullivan Co, TN, $300 paid, 300 ac part of undiv moiety of 600 acres on Cany fork of Cumberland River. Wit: WALTER EVANS, JOHN HACKETT. Ack in Hamilton Dist, TN by J RAMSEY, Clk of sd district.

Page 256   Indenture   10 Sept 1804   Grantor as above, to ROBERT YOUNG, Sullivan Co, TN, $400 paid, 300 acres being an undiv moiety of 600 acres as in above deed. Wit as above.

Page 258   Sheriff's Deed   17 Aug 1808   WALTER ALLY(?), Dep Shff, Hickman Co, TN, and ANTHONY STREET, Dist Ct having commanded that goods, etc of ROBERT A KING in sd county be sold to cover debt WILLIAM DODSON recovered against sd King. Land conveyed is 640 acres including the Post Oak springs. Wit: J H BOWAN, A R W OVERTON, H W WILLIAMS(?).

Pages 260 & 261 are blank.

Page 262   Land Grant No 2731   21 July 1796   NORTH CAROLINA to STOKELY DONELSON, assee of HENRY MCELWEE(?), a private in Continental line of sd state, 640 acres on both sides of the Chickemaga and on a large creek the waters of Caney fork called Lost creek and including an Indian encampment. Field Notes follow, having been sur 16 July 1795 by WILLIAM TYRELL, D.S. P JONES, WM CRELLEY, SCC.

Page 265   Land Grant No 2734   Date, Grantor & Grantee as above, Grantee in this case being of MOSES RICHARDSON, private in Continental line, 640 acres on waters of Caney fork of Cumberland River. Field Notes follow.

Page 268   Land Grant No 273_   21 July 1796   NORTH CAROLINA to Grantee as above, assee of JOHN PARRET, a private in Continental line, 640 acres in Sumner County on Cany fork adj Entry No 3173. Field Notes follow.

Page 271   Land Grant No 2736   Date, Grantor and Grantee as above, Grantee being assee of THOMAS PEADEN(?), a private in Continental line, 640 acres in Sumner Co. Field Notes follow. Copy of Warrant No 3178 for sd land follows (page 273).

Page 274   Indenture   __ Oct 1798   ROBERT KING for himself and also as Atty-in-fact for ETHELDRED WILLIAMS, Knox Co, TN and JAMES THOMPSON & THOMAS RAVENHILL, of Knoxville, $1400 paid, tr of 1400 acres in Sumner Co on Cany fork of Cumberland River 1/4 mile below the Roaring spring on a bluff, part of 2560 acre tr. Wit: SAMUEL LOVE, ROBT H MORROW. Ack on 18 Oct 1798 before ARCHABALD ROAN, Judge. THOMPSON & RAVENHILL (late agent for JAMES SHORT, late of York Borough, PA, Merchant & decd) convey premises to JOHN ODIE, Esqr, CONRAD LAUBAND(?) & WILLIAM DAVIDSON, Exrs of will of sd Short, Decd. Wit: JOSEPH T___, SAMUEL GRIFFITH. Ack before THOMAS MCKEAN, CJ, Supreme Ct in Pennsylvania.

Page 278   Indenture   1 Dec 1798   ROBERT KING for himself & as atty in fact for ETHELRED WILLIAMS, Knox Co, TN, and JAMES THOMPSON, Knoxville,TN, $1100 paid, 1160 acres on Cany fork of Cumberland River in Sumner Co, TN, part of 2560 acre tr in Patent No 2945 and dated 1 Mar 1797. Wit: THOMAS A CLARK, Junr, DAVID MAXWELL, JAMES BLARE. Certif in Sumner Co, TN by ROBERT BLITHE for JAMES DUGLAS.

Page 281   Land Grant No 3417(?)   8 June 1797   NORTH CAROLINA to STOCKLY DONELSON 1500 acres in middle district on waters of Cumberland River.

Page 282   Sheriff's Deed   31 July 1807   WILLIAM PHILIPS, Shff, by my Deputy THOMAS TAYLOR, Junr, $6.37 1/2 paid, to PETER SCALLION, 2 Negroes named ROSE and SALL in execution as the property of JOSEPH TERRY to satisfy a Judgment obtained by GEORGE HAVESHAW against Terry as security of JOHN ELSEY.   Wit: RENL RAGLAND.

Page 283   Power of Attorney   13 Aug 1808   THOS HOPKINS to DANCEL ALEXANDER, Esqr, to collect all debts due me.   Wit: ELIJAH CHISUM.

Page 283   Grant No 346   8 June 1797   NORTH CAROLINA to STOCKELY DONELSON, 5000 acres in middle dist on a large creek supposed to be the waters of Cumberland River.

Page 284   Grant No 349   Date & Grantor & Grantee as above, 1000 acres in area above.

Page 284   Grant No 348   Date & parties as in above grant, 2500 acres on Cumberland River.

Page 285   Grant No 350   Date & parties as above, 640 acres.

Page 285   Grant No 344   Date & parties as above, 1500 acres.

Page 286   Grant No 343   Date & parties as above, 1950 acres.

Page 286   Grant No 353   Date & parties as above, tract as set out above.

Page 287   Grant No 352   Date & parties as above, 200 acres.

Page 288   Deed   1 Jan 1793   (Exec in Anson Co, NC)   HOLDEN WADE, THOMAS WADE, JEAN WADE, Exrs & Extrx of Will of COL THOMAS WADE, Decd,   to WALTER LEAK, a tr in Western terr & being 30,000 acres entered in COLO JOHN ARMSTRONG office at Hillsborough and located on Duck River & Elk River. The 6 tracts entered to sd Thomas are transferred to sd Leak.   Wit: HENRY DRAKE WATSON, CHRISTOPHER GWIN(?).   Proved in Open Ct before WM JOHNSTON, Clk. Reg in White Co, TN by ELIJAH CHISUM, Reg.

Page 290   Will of THOMAS WADE of Anson Co, NC   2 June 1786   Leaves estate to his wife JANE WADE and to his 5 children: HOLDEN WADE, MARY VINING, THOMAS WADE, SARAH WADE and GEORGE WADE.   He appoints his wife as his Executrix and sons Holden and Thomas, together with his friends PATRICK BAGGAN and JAMES BAGGAN (no relationship stated) as Executors.   Wit: MARYIN BROWN, ELEBETH BROWN, GRISSEL BAYGIN.   Probate proceedings p 292, TODDY ROBERSON, Clk Anson Co, TN and JAMES MARSHAL, certifying.

Page 293   Will of THOMAS WADE of Anson Co, NC   18 June 1792   States that he is in perfect health but has taken small pox and is about to start to the Cherow hill to undergo the operation.   He is to be buried where his wife ELIZABETH WADE thinks proper.   He leaves his estate to be divided amongst his wife Elizabeth and his children, being THOMAS MCNAR WADE, WILLIAM HAMBLETON WADE, JUDITH LINK WADE, and any child born after his death.   If there is money for such, he wants his sons to be educated on the labour of their Negroes, on the interest of their money in as full and ample manner as the American seminaries of learning will admit. Appoints his wife as his Exrx and his friends WALTER LEAKE, THOMAS CHILDS (Junr), and JOHN PEMBERTON, Esq, as Exrs. Reg on 19 Dec 1808, on oaths re handwriting, by JAMES PUCKET, JOHN JENNINGS. Copy certif in Anson Co, NC by TOD ROBINSON, Clk.

Page 294   Letters of Administration   April Sess Ct, 1797   JOSHUA PROUT appt, 2000 pounds bond, ISAAC JACKSON, WILLIAM BERTON, Sureties. Copy certif by TOD ROBERSON, Clk, JAMES MARSHALL, Presid Jus.

Page 295   Indenture   10 July 1799   JANE WADE to JOSHUA PROUT, Esq, 100 pounds, tr lying in NC when granted but now in TN on Cany fork of Cumberland River, 5000 acres. Wit: JARED POUNDS, ELIZABETH WADE.

Page 296   Land Grant No 323   12 Dec 1796   NORTH CAROLINA to THOMAS WADE, 10 pounds for every 100 acres, 5000 acres on Caney fork of Cumberland River. Sur 16 June 1796 by STOCKLEY DONELSON, DS.

Page 298   Indenture   1 June 1808   THOMAS MCCARRY of Knoxville, TN, and ELIJAH LEWIS, of White Co, TN, $260 paid, tr granted by NC to JOHN RHEA & WILLIAM TYRRELL, No 310, on 7 Mar 1796, tr of 140 acres adj land of BENJAMIN LEWIS and WILLIAM BRYAN. Wit: TURNER LANE, ROBT G ANDERSON.

Page 300   Sheriff's Deed   13 Mar 1807   WILLIAM PHILLIPS, Shff, and THOMAS WILCHER, writ having been issued from court in Hamilton ordering lands of ROBERT KING be sold to satisfy debt JAMES MAGOFFIN and JOSEPH MAGOFFIN executed against King, land sold being 640 acres granted by NC to sd King on 29 Jan 1796, being located on Cany fork of Cumberland, and beg near an old Indian path near foot of a high hill, tract being sold for $16.00.

Page 302   Bill of Sale   15 Feb 1808   JOHN TURNER and RICHARD HILL, $135 paid, a Negro girl named EDE, 22 years of age. Wit: WILLIAM ROBISSON, WILLIAM GLENN.

Page 303   Land Grant No 565   1 Oct 1808   TENNESSEE to MORRISON WILLIAMS, assee of NEWTON STRIPLIN, by virtue of military service performed by sd Striplin to NC, Warrant No 3230 dated 23 Dec 1785 and entered on 1 Sept 1807 by No 282 as an Occupant claim. Tract conv is 130 acres, part sd warrant lying in White Co in first dist first range & eighth section, on waters of Caney fork. Signed by JOHN SEVEIR, R HOUSTON, Secty, D MCGAVOCK, Reg.

Page 304   Indenture   1 June 1808   THOMAS MCCORRY of Knoxville, TN, and BENJAMIN LEWIS, $396 paid, 198 acres beg in line of ELIJAH LEWIS, and tr also adj WILLIAM BRYAN cor. Wit: TURNER LANE, ELIJAH LEWIS.

Page 307   Indenture   2 June 1808   Grantor above and DAVID NICHOLAS, $300 paid, 200 acres adj land of JOHN WHITE. Wit: WOODSON P WHITE, TURNER LANE.

Page 310   Indenture   31 July 1806   JOHN RHEA, of Knox Co, TN, and THOS MCCORRY of same place, $200 paid, tr of 500 acres on fork of Caney fork called King & Co includes land on both sides of path that leads to Chickamaga and including the ford where path crosses same. Wit: R HARBIN,

JOSEPH NICHOL, JOHN WILLIAMS, H L WHITE.

Page 314   Indenture   30 July 1796   STOKELY DONALDSON, of Knoxville in Knox Co, TN, and PHILLIP WHITEHEAD JACKSON, Lunenburg Co, VA, $3200 paid, a tr of land in Sumner Co, TN on creek that JOS THOMAS was killed on about 7 miles below AARON LAMBERTS Entry No 1399 containing 640 acres granted by NC to SHERROD BARROW, assee of ARCHIBALD DAVIS by Patent No 2406, dated 20 Jan 1796, and by Barrow to Donaldson; also 1 other tr in Sumner Co on both sides of Chickamaga path and on large cr called Lost creek and including an Indian Encampment, 640 acres. Also other lands are described. Wit: JOHN ENRIGHT, WM MCQUISTEN, O BURTON(?), Reg in Orange Co, NC. Certif same co by JOHN TAYLOR, Esqr 28 Aug 1801.

Page 323   Sheriff's Deed   3 Oct 1808   WILLIAM PHILLIPS, Shff, to THOMAS DILLON, latter of Davidson County, due to court order that goods of STOCKLY DONALSON be sold to pay debt of $13,493.30 which Dillon obtained against him, $75.00 paid by highest bid (by Dillon), tr is conveyed to him, being described as lying on large creek (Cumberland River), being Grant No 351, to Donalson by NC. Wit: ADAM SWINEY, MICAJAH SOAMAS(?), ISAAC TAYLOR, Junr. Ack by Taylor before ANDREW EWING, DCC.

Page 325   Sheriff's Deed   1 Oct 1808   Parties as in above deed, several tracts conveyed thereby. Wit: ISAAC TAYLOR, Junr, JAS BLAKEMORE, JOS TAYLOR, Junr, WM L WATERSON.

Page 330   Indenture   11 Jan 1809   ISAAC ANDERSON and JOHN ANDERSON (relationship not stated), one part, and TURNER LANE, $80.00 paid, tr of 26 acres in Hickory Valley, it being part of Grant No 532 issued by TN on 26 Sept 1808.

Page 332   Land Grant No 557   30 Sept 1808   TENNESSEE to TURNER LANE, Certif No 63 having been obtained from Bd of Commiss for W TN by THOMAS DILLON on 7 Mar 1808, Lane being assee of Dillon, tr on waters of main fork of Caney fork in Hickory Valley, 80 acres.

Page 333   Indenture   6 Dec 1808   DAVID NICHOLAS and WILLIAM LEWIS, Senr, $220 paid, tr being 60 acres and beg at cor with BENJAMIN LEWIS and adj DAVID MCDONALD cor. Wit: TURNER LANE, JACOB A LANE.

Page 336   Indenture   28 Jan 1809   WILLIAM BRYAN and JOHN GOODPASTURE, latter of Overton Co, TN, $180 paid, tr adj TURNER LANE. Wit: JOHN BRYAN, JACOB BRYAN.

Page 339   Indenture   31 May 1808   THOMAS MCCORRY of Knoxville, TN, one part, and JACOB ANDERSON, other part, $330 paid, tr being 220 acres. Wit: TURNER LANE, ANDREW BRYAN.

Page 342   Land Grant No 528   26 Sept 1808   TENNESSEE by Certif 63 of 21 July 1807 from Commiss for West TN, is granted to THOMAS WILSON, assee of THOMAS DILLON, 100 acres in 3rd Dist in fork of Caney fork and adj ISAAC ANDERSON and JOHN ANDERSON.

Page 344   Land Grant No 2278   17 May 1793   NORTH CAROLINA to ROBERT HAYS, assee of WILLIAM BRIANT, a private in Continental line (for signal bravery, etc), 640 acres in Sumner County on Caney fork. Field Notes attached.

Page 347 Bill of Sale 26 Aug 1808   NATHANIEL DAVIS, Claiborne Co, TN, to
ABRAHAM BROYLE, $240 paid, a Negro boy named BENNET(?) about 9 yrs of age.
Wit: SAMUEL WEAVER, BENJAMIN WEAVER.

Page 348 Bill of Sale 14 Nov 1808   JOHN BRYAN to ELIAS WALLIS, $400
paid, 1 Negro girl named CHANY about 30 years of age. Wit: R BLACKBORN,
_AMES R BRYAN.

(Registered 20 Sept 1809 by JOHN M CARRICK, Deputy Registrar of White
County, Tennessee)

(Unnumbered page) Indenture 31 Jan 179_   STOCKLEY DONELSON, Hawkins Co
in Terr S of the Ohio by his Atty in fact HUGH DAMLOT(?), Knox Co in sd
Terr, $1000 paid, 5000 acres as set out (very difficult to read). Wit:
__TER MCNANCE, WILLIAM GILLIAM, JOHN LESLEY(?).

Volume B
Sept 1809 - Apr 1810

Page 1 Land Grant No 559 30 Sept 1808 TENNESSEE to DAVID ALEXANDER, assee of HENRY HARDISON who served in the military of NC, Warrant No 4175 (dated 8 Dec 1796), tr of 60 acres part of sd Warrant lying in Overton, White and Jackson Counties.

Page 3 Land Grant No 560 Date and parties as in above grant, 247 acres in above referred to counties.

Page 5 Deed 30 Sept 1808 JOSIAH KNAPP, of Boston, MA, assee of Bankrupt estates of JOHN MCLEAN, conveys to SAMUEL DENTON(?) one undiv tenth part of tr on Caney fork of Cumberland, 44,160 acres, $200 paid. Wit: SAMUEL BLAGGE, THOS W F BLAGGE. Ack in Suffolk Co, MA, by JNO TUCKER, Clk, WM WITMORE(?), CJ, and certif by WILLIAM STEPHENSON, NP.

Page 10 Indenture 14 Aug 1809 JOHN NELSON and ELIJAH WARD, $100 paid, tr on Cane creek a branch of Cany fork of Cumberland, part of tr of 2500 acres orig granted by NC to ROBERT KING, assee of JAMES WILLIAMS.

Page 13 Indenture 17 Apr 1809 SAMUEL WEAVER of one part and JACOB CATRON, latter of Grayson Co, VA, $1550 paid, tr of half of 2500 acre sur for Grant No 342 issued by NC to ROBERT KING, 1 Mar 1797. Wit: PINK HUDSON, GEORGE GRIFFITH.

Page 17 Indenture 17 Apr 1809 SAMUEL WEAVER and JOHN YOKUM, $100 paid, tr of 152 1/2 acres on S side of Cherry creek waters of Caney fork of Cumberland. Wit as above.

Page 21 Surveyor's Field Notes 25 May 1795 WILLIAM TYRRELL, DS, for STOCKLEY DONELSON and WILLIAM TYRRELL, assee of heirs of ZEDIKIAH BROCK, a private in continental line, 640 acres joining sd Donaldson & Tyrrell.

Page 22 Land Grant No 2560 7 Mar 1796 NORTH CAROLINA to above named Donelson & Tyrrell, assees of above named Brock, 640 acres (awarded for bravery, etc).

Page 24 Surveyor's Field Notes for Military Warr 3948 (Exec in Terr So of Ohio, Sumner County), WILLIAM TYRRELL, DS, has surv for STOCKLEY DONELSON & sd TYRRELL, assees of heirs of REUBIN MCCORMACK, a private in continental line of this state, 640 acres joining 640 acres joining sd Donelson & Tyrrell as assees of heirs of DAVID DAVIS.

Page 25 Land Grant No 2558 7 Mar 1709 NORTH CAROLINA to above named Donelson & Tyrrell, assees of above named MCCORMACK, 640 acres in Sumner County.

Page 27 Field Notes 25 May 1795 Land in Military Warr 3950 sur by above named Tyrrell for Donelson & Tyrrell, assees of heirs of MILES CLAYTON, private in Continental line, 640 acres joining tr they own as assees.

Page 28 Land Grant No 2559 7 Mar 1796 Above land is covered herein.

Page 31 Field Notes for Sur Mil Warr 2954 Above named surveyor and

Grantees named, being assees of heirs of JAMES CHISUM, a private in continental line, 640 acres.

Page 32   Land Grant No 2562   Covers tract above named, parties being assees of ISAIAH CHISUM (?).

Page 34   Sur Field Notes   25 May 1795 (Exec in Sumner Co, Terr So of River Ohio)   Sur for STOCKLEY DONELSON & WILLIAM TYRELL, assees of heirs of JOHN P STEPHENSON, a private in Continental line of this state, a tr of 640 acres joining land of sd Donelson & Tyrell as assees of McCormack.   Land Grant No 2551 follows on p 35, dated 7 Mar 1796.

Page 38   Sur Field Notes   Date and Parties above, assees of BAIRD DAVIS, a private in Continental line, 640 acres.   Land Grant No 2563 follows on p 39, date as above.

Page 42   Sur Field Notes   Date & Parties as above, assees of heirs of ARTHUR M RORY, a private as in deed above, 640 acres.   Land Grant No 2554 follows on p 43, date as above.

Page 46   Sur Field Notes   19 July 1795   Parties as above and also for ROBERT KING, assees of heirs of ZECHARIAH DURHAM, Sergeant in Continental line of NC, 1000 acres lying on waters of Caney fork.   Land Gr 2579 follows on p 47, dated at Raleigh 7 Mar 1896, 20th year of our Independence.

Page 50   Land Grant No 549   8 Oct 1807   TENNESSEE to THOMAS TAYLOR, Junr and ISAAC TAYLOR, assees of heirs of STEPHEN PERKINS, for Perkins mil serv to NC, Warrant 2977, dated 27 Dec 1803, 200 acres in White County in first dist first range & eight section at Taylor's creek, a fork of falling waters of Caney fork.   Sur 8 Oct 1807.

Page 52   Indenture   4 Jan 1809   THOMAS TAYLOR, Junr, one part, and ISAAC TAYLOR, Junr (relationship not stated), other part, $100 paid, undiv moiety of tr of 200 acres on Taylor's creek.   Wit: PEGGY TAYLOR, POLLY TAYLOR.

Page 55   Grant No 525   26 Sept 1808   TENNESSEE by virtue Certif 63 dated 21 July 1807 from Bd of Commiss for W TN by THOMAS DILLON on 28 Aug 1807 by No 168 as an occupant claim, there is granted to ISAAC BROWN, assee of sd Dillon, 100 acres in White Co in 3rd Dist on Cane creek, beg on bank sd creek the SW cor DOSIER T CRAIN & running W crossing the creek at foot of a mountain.   Sur 20 May 1808.

Page 58   Grant No 537   26 Sept 1808   TENNESSEE by virtue certif No 63 dated 21 July 1807 from Bd of Commiss for W TN by THOMAS DILLON & entered on date in prior grant, there is granted to HERCULES OGLE, assee of Dillon 100 acres adj WILLIAM BROWN.

Page 60   Grant No 529   Date & Grantee above by certif 63, to ISHAM BRADLEY, assee of Dillon, 50 acres beg on conditional line with JACOB MITCHELL and also JOSEPH HASTINGS.

Page 62   Grant No 530   Date & Grantor above to JACOB MITCHELL, assee above named DILLON, 50 acres.

Page 64   Grant No 550   20 Sept 1808   TENNESSEE by virtue Certif 63 dated

21 July 1807 from Bd Ld Commiss for W TN, obtained by THOMAS DILLON, entered 28 Aug 1807 by No 173, there is granted to JOSEPH HASTIN, assee of Dillon, 50 acres in White Co on 3rd Dist on the big spring branch adj ISHAM BRADLEY 50 acres.

Page 67   Grant No 683   8 Dec 1808   By certif No 237 dated 13 Aug 1807, entered from TENNESSEE to THOMAS DILLON, and entered on 13 May 1808 by No 1724, is hereby granted by Tennessee unto ALEXANDER IRWIN, assee of Dillon, tr of 50 acres in White County in 1st Dist on both sides of the waggon road leading from DANIEL ALEXANDER to Rock Island 1/2 mile from where the waggon rd crosses the S fork of Taylor's creek on S side sd fork.

Page 69   Indenture   15 Feb 1809   ISHAM BRADLEY and CHARLES MITCHELL, $400 paid, tr of 50 acres on big spring branch (Grant No 529 from TN to Bradley).   Wit: DAVID HASTIN, JOSEPH HASTIN (no relationship given), JACOB MITCHELL, JOHN MILES.   Ack in White Co before JACOB A LANE, DCWC.

Page 73   Sur Field Notes   17 June 1796   THOS KING, DSMD, by virtue of Warrant from TENNESSEE (JOHN ARMSTRONG office) and No 2252, dated 14 May 1784, King has surv for ROBERT KING (relationship not stated), assee of JAMES WILLIAMS, 2500 acres on mouth of a branch of Cane creek the waters of the falling water, a branch of Caney fork.   CC: JO BLAN, F LEEPER.

Page 74   Land Grant No 339   1 Mar 1797   NORTH CAROLINA for 10 pounds for every 100 acres hereby granted, to ROBERT KING, assee of JAMES WILLIAMS, 2500 acres in Mid Dist on mouth of branch of Cane lick the waters of falling water.

Page 76   Land Grant No 340   Date, Grantor, Grantee, consideration and acreage being same, being on Cain creek.

Page 78   Certificate   27 Sept 1809   DAVID STONE, Governor of NC certifies that WILL WHITE who has signed certificates annexed was and is Secretary of St for NC.   SIMON A BRYAN also signs certificate.

Page 79   Sur Field Notes   22 July 1795   WILLIAM TYRRELL, DS, & Certif by STOCKLEY DONELSON, says he sur for JAMES EASTON, Assee of heirs of JOSHUA PARNAL, private in Continen line, 640 acres on E side of a large fork of Caney fork, adj sur of assee of heirs of DAVID CANNADY.

Page 80   Land Grant No 2585   7 Mar 1796   NORTH CAROLINA to JAMES EASTON (as above), a private in Continental line sd state, 640 acres on E side large fork of Caney fork, br of Cumberland river, beg SE cor sd Easton's sur, as assee of heirs of DAVID KENNEDY.

Page 81   Surv Field Notes   22 July 1796   Terr So of River Ohio, Sumner Co, by Military Warr 3958, I have sur for JAMES EASTON, assee of heirs of JAMES ORAM, a private in line of this state, 640 acres on E side of large fork of Caney fork, beg NW cor Easton's sur as assee of heirs of JOHN CATRON.

Page 82   Land Grant No 2583   7 Mar 1796   NORTH CAROLINA to JAMES EASTON, assee of heirs of JAMES ORAN(?), a priv in Continen line of state 640 acres in Sumner Co on E side of Caney fork.

Page 83   Surveyor's Field Notes   Located 22 July 1795 & surv for Easton as above, assee of heirs of DAVID CANNADY, private in line of this state, 640 acres on E side large fork, etc.

Page 84   Land Grant No 2589   7 Mar 1796   NORTH CAROLINA has granted to JAMES EASTON, assee of heirs of DAVID CANNADY, a private in Continen line, 640 acres in Sumner County.

Page 85   Surv Field Notes   Located 22 July 1795 & surv for JAMES EASTON, assee of EDWARD ETHERIDGE, a private in Continen line, 640 acres on E side large fork of Caney.   Exec in Terr So of River Ohio, Sumner County.

Page 86   Land Grant No 2586   7 Mar 1796   NORTH CAROLINA grants to EASTON (as above), assee of heirs of ETHERIDGE, as above, sd tract.

Page 86   Surv Field Notes   Located 22 July 1795 (Terr So of River Ohio, Sumner Co) for EASTON (as above), assee of heirs of WILLIAM CARY, a private in Contin line, 640 acres on E side of large fork of Caney fork.

Page 87   Land Grant No 2504   7 Mar 1795   NORTH CAROLINA to EASTON (as above), assee of heirs of sd Cary, sd tract.

Page 88   Surv Field Notes   Located 22 July 1795 (Terr So of River Ohio, Sumner Co) for Easton, assee of heirs of JOHN CALVIN, private in Continen line, 640 acres on fork of Caney.

Page 90   Land Grant No 2582   Date and parties as on page 87, assees of sd Calvin.

Page 91   Surv Field Notes   Located date as on p 88, for Easton, assee Heirs of EDMOND BIBBY, a priv in Continen line, 640 acres on E side Caney fork, adj tr granted WILLIAM CANY.

Page 92   Land Grant No 2587   Date & parties as on p 91.

Page 93   Land Grant No 675   8 Dec 1808   TENNESSEE for Military serv by STEPHEN PERKINS to NC, Warrant 2977, dated 27 Dec 1803, grants to JONATHAN DILDINE, assee of heirs sd Perkins, 50 acres, part sd Warrant lying in White Co in 1st Dist on Taylor's creek of Cany fork.

Page 95   Indenture   29 Sept 1809   SAMUEL DENTON, New York City, merchant, first part, and THOMAS STORM of same place, Merchant, second part, by virtue deed executed to SAMUEL DENTON by JOSIAH KNAPP, of Boston, MA, assee of JOHN MCLEAN of same place.   Also SAMUEL BLAGGE of same place, and his wife SARAH BLAGGE executed deed giving title to undiv tenth part of tr lying on Caney fork in Sumner Co, TN, being 44,160 acres, $200.04 pd, interest is conveyed.   Wit: BENJ F BUBRICK(?), SAML D WALKER. Ack in city & co of New York before P C VAN WYCK, and certif there by T W ORFMAN.

Page 99   Indenture   2 Oct 1809   SAMUEL DENTON, New York City, Merchant, first part, and MOSES FISK, Esqr, second part, by virtue of deed as in above, 1 equal undiv third part of the 2/10 part of sd tr. Wit: As above.

Page 104 Indenture 12 Nov 1808   THOMAS DILLON and ROBERT HOWARD and SAMUEL WEAVER, $300 paid, tr of 2500 acres orig granted to ROBERT KING, assee of

JAMES WILLIAMS, Junr, Grant No 342. J TAYLOR, Junr, JNO LOTT, WM GLENN.

Page 107 Indenture 15 Feb 1809 JOSEPH HASTIN and DAVID HASTIN (relationship not stated), $200 paid, Joseph's interest in grant from TENNESSEE (No 550), 50 acres adj BRADLEY and JACOB MITCHELL. Wit: ISHAM BRADLY, CHARLES MITCHELL, JOHN MILLER.

Page 109 Indenture 15 Apr 1809 JOHN SCOGGAN and JAMES WILLIAMS, $123 paid, his int in Grant No 534 from St dated 26 Sept 1808, part of John Scoggon 144 acre tr in third dist on N side main Cany fork adj SPENCE MITCHELL 150 acre sur, sd tr beg at NE cor of JESSE SCOGGAN 64 acre tr, and also adj THOMAS MCCORRY 5000 ac tr. Wit: WOODSON P WHITE, JESSE SCOGGAN.

Page 113 Indenture 15 Apr 1809 Grantor above and JESSE SCOGGAN (relationship not stated), $123 paid, his right in Grant No 534 dated at Knoxville 26 Sept 1808, for 64 acres, part of sd John's 144 ac tr. Wit: WOODSON P WHITE, JAMES WILLIAMS.

Page 117 Indenture 14 Aug 1809 PINK HUDSON and ELIJAH WARD, $330 paid, grantor's int in tr on Cane creek, br of Caney fork of Cumberland river, part of 2500 ac orig granted by NC to ROBERT KING, assee of JAMES WILLIAMS, Grant No 341, dated 1 Mar 1797. Wit: As above.

Page 120 Land Grant No 351 8 June 1797 NORTH CAROLINA to STOCKLEY DONELSON, 640 acres in Middle Dist on waters supposed to be Cumberland River.

Page 121 Deed of Gift 5 June 1809 WILLIAM BOWERS and MARTHA JERUSHA PHILLIPS, wife of WILLIAM PHILLIPS, (no relationship stated between Bowers and Martha), for love & affection & for her better maintenance, 1 Negro man BAKER, one Negro woman CARESEY and her child HARRIET, a horse, cattle, household furnishings. Wit: JNO W CARRICK, BETSY CARRICK.

Page 123 Indenture 25 Dec 1809 JOHN MCIVER and WILLIAM P ANDERSON, one part, and WILLIAM P COLE and SOLOMON COX, other part, $1.00 paid, tr beg on N bdy of Sur connection orig granted by NC to JAMES EASTON and adj cor of Major ISHAM RUSSELL, 68 acres. Wit: THOS BOUNDS, THOMAS STONE, JOSEPH PACKER, JAMES COLE. Ack before JACOB A LANE, DCWC.

Page 126 Indenture 4 Feb 1810 WILLIAM DYER and JACOB ROBISON, $1000, parcel of land on Cane creek, part tr of 2500 (acres) orig granted by NC to ROBERT KING.

Page 128 Indenture 12 Feb 1810 JOHN FOX and THOMAS CRUTCHER, $80.00 paid, tr on Cane creek, part of 2500 acre tract as above. Wit: THOS MCBRIDE, BENJAMIN WEAVER.

Page 130 Bill of Sale 28 Oct 1809 ABRAHAM HENDRY, Carter Co, TN, for $300 paid by JOHN WALLING, convey to sd Walling a Negro woman PATT. Wit: JAMES SUTTON(?), ADAM HAYNES.

Page 131 Indenture 12 Feb 1810 THOMAS STONE and JACOB ROBINSSON, $150 paid, tr on Cane creek, part of 2500 acre tr as on p 128 (amount of land conv unreadable).

Page 133   Indenture   17 Oct 1808   BRYANT BREEDING and JOHN FOX, $80.00 paid, tr on Cane creek, part 2500 acres referred to above, 60 acres. Wit: THOMAS STONE, PINK HUDSON.

Page 135   Bill of Sale/Mtg   30 Dec 1809   JACOB HARTY to HALLETT PERCE, 1 wagon and several horses, a cow, furniture -to satisfy Judgment unless it is paid. Wit: SAM WEAR, J M BRIDE, TALB__ DALTEN.

Page 137   Indenture   20 Dec 1809   JOHN MCIVER, Alexandria, D C, and WILLIAM P ANDERSON, Rutherford Co, TN, one part, and JAMES COLE, $752 paid, 752 acres on falling water of Caney fork, part of tr granted by NC to JAMES EASTON. Wit: MOSES CARRICK, JOHN M CARRICK, JAMES CHISUM, ELIJAH CHISUM.

Page 141   Bill of Sale   2 Jan 1810   CHARLES MITCHELL and SAMUEL JOHNSTON, $400 paid, 1 Negro woman slave named MARY being 30 yrs, also 1 Negro child daughter of above named NANCY about 1 yr.Wit: J TAYLOR, Jnr, WM RIDGE.

Page 143   Indenture 16 Feb 1810   CALEB FRALEY and ROBERT PUCKET, $5.00 paid, tr vested by 2 deeds made by ROBERT BENTON and JOHN MCIVER, and also by ALEXANDER LOWREY to 114 acres, part of land on SE side of Calf Killers fork. Wit: JOHN PUCKET, TURNER LANE.

Page 146   Indenture   6 Jan 1810   JOSEPH FLEMING and JOSHUA BADGER, Junr, $400 paid, 100 acres in first dist, 9th sec of first range, abutting the Gum spring tr of 640 acres entered by THOMAS K HARRIS. Wit: TURNER LANE, JOSHUA BADGER, Senr.

Page 148   Land Grant No 796   20 Jan 1809   TENNESSEE by virtue of part of Certif 248 dated 15 Aug 1807 from Bd of Commiss for West Tennessee to LEWIS BEARD, there is granted to JOSEPH FLEMING, assee of sd Beard, tr of 100 acres in First Dist First Range & 9th Sec on Caney fork, adj THOMAS K HARRIS 640 acre tr. Signed by JOHN SEVEIR, Gov, and D MCGAVOCK, Reg W TN.

Page 150   Land Grant No 1399   21 July 1809   Grantor above for military serv by MICAJAH HENRY to NC, Warr 4755 dated 29 Feb 1797, & entered on 20 Sept 1808 by No 2444 that is granted by TN unto JOHN MILLER, Senr, assee of Henry, a tract of 160 acres part sd warrant.

Page 152   Land Grant No 1396   Date & Grantor above by virtue part of Certif No 57 dated 3 Aug 1808 obtained from Commiss of W TN by THOMAS DILLON and entered on 24 Aug 1808, tr being 200 acres in first dist, first range and ninth sec on Cany fork, beg on line of JOSEPH WALLING 100 acre survey.

Page 153   Land Grant No 1397   Date & Grantor above, and part of Certif No 57 as above, 100 acres, beg at JOHN MILLER 160 acre tr, and adj WILLIAM SHAW sur.

Page 155   Land Grant No 1270   1 July 1809   Grantor above for military serv by MATTHEW NAIL to NC, Warr 5170, dated 9 Dec 1797 and entered on 20 June 1808 by MCGAVAN occupant under act of 1807, there is granted by TN to PRETTYMAN JONES(?), assee of heirs of sd Nail, tr of 100 acres, part of tr of Caney fork.

Page 157   Land Grant No 2707   27 Mar 1786   NORTH CAROLINA grants to JAMES EASTON, assee of heirs of JOHN WINOAH, a priv in contin line of sd state,

640 acres in Sumner Co on Caney fork of Cumberland river sd Easton's sur as assee of heirs INGOLD MCCOY.

Page 160   Land Grant No 2704   27 Mar 1796   NORTH CAROLINA granted to JAMES EASTON, assee of heirs of WILLIAM GOODWIN, a private in Continental line of sd state, 640 acres in Sumner Co on Caney fork.

Page 161   Land Grant No 2705   Date & Grantor above to above named JAMES EASTON, assee of heirs of MATTIAS DUDLEY, a priv in Continen line, 640 acres in Sumner Co on Caney fork.

Page 162   Surveyor's Field Notes   Located 11 Mar 1795   I have surv for above named JAMES EASTON, assee of heirs of ____ a private in Continen line of NC, 640 acres in Sumner Co, joining sd Easton's sur as assee of heirs of JAMES M ADIE(?).

Volume C
July 1810 - Dec 1811

(Page 1 of instrument is missing)

Page 2 Tax Collector's Deed (Ack in Superior Ct in Winchester Dist before ARCHIBALD W OVERTON & registered on 5 July 1810 by JOHN M CARRICK, Dept Reg, White Co, TN) THOMAS MARTIN, Collector of 8 Collection Dist, to WILLIAM P ANDERSON and JOHN MCIVER for taxes, several tracts of land as described therein. Wit: ISAAC TAYLOR, Junr, JAMES CHISUM.

Page 9 Tax Collector's Deed 28 Aug 1809 Grantor as above to WILLIAM P ANDERSON. Several tracts as described therein. Wit: As above.

Page 16 Indenture 12 Mar 1810 JOSEPH FLEMING, Lincoln Co, TN, to HENRY KING, $300 paid, tr 100 ac in Hickory valley, being land convy to sd Fleming by ANDREW BRYAN. Wit: JOHN M CARRICK, JNO DAUGHERTY & ANDREW SMITH.

Page 17 Indenture __ Nov 1809 JAMES R BRYAN and JOSEPH FLEMING, $350 paid, 100 acres adj DAVID MCDANIEL cor and DAVID NICHOLS. Wit: ARTHUR MARKHAM, SAMUEL B SMITH.

Page 20 Indenture 8 May 1802 WILLIAM E PILLAR to HERRON KING & CO(?), $5.00 paid, his right to undiv third part of tr of 1000 acres held by deed of 1000 acres conv by JOHN MCIVER, assee of JOSIAH WATSON on Caney fork. Wit: JNO DOUGHERTY.

Page 22 Indenture 7 May 1810 WILLIAM E PILLAR and JAMES HERRON, surveying partner of HERRON KING & CO, $5.00 paid, tr at Hickory valley, and waters of Caney fork, 100 acres adj cor of DAVID MCDANIEL and DAVID NICHOLAS. Wit: JOHN M CARRICK, JOSEPH NEVILL.

Page 24 Indenture 27 Dec 1809 JOHN MCIVER of the town & county of Alexandria, Columbia Dist, assee of estate of JOSIAH WATSON, late of Alexandria, a Bankrupt, one part, and HERRON KING & CO, $544.44 Paid, convey 1 undiv third part of tract of 1000 acres in White (formerly part of Sumner) on waters of Caney fork including a lick and on both sides of a small creek called by King & Co little lick creek. Wit: JOHN M CARRICK, ELIJAH CHISUM, THOS CRUTCHER, BIRD SMITH.

Page 27 Indenture 1 June 1808 THOMAS MCCORRY, Kirksville, TN(?), one part, and ROBERT G ANDERSON, $500 paid, due to grant from NC to JOHN RHEA & WILLIAM TYRRELL No 310, dated 7 Mar 1796, 400 acres. Wit: TURNER LANE, WOODSON P WHITE.

Page 29 Field Notes 2 May 1788 In NC, Middle Dist, by virtue of Mil warr No 3447, surv for ROBERT KING, assee of HENRY BEAN, 640 acres in Calf Killer valley. SCB: Robert King, ALEXDR BLAIR. (There is note from J M Carrick that year may be 1788 or 1798)

Page 30 Land Grant No 2385 17 July 1794 NORTH CAROLINA to HENRY BEAN, a private in line of NC, grants to ROBERT KING, assee of sd Bean, 640 acres lying in Hawkins County in the Calf Killer valley.

Page 31   Indenture   13 Aug 1802   Commissioners of White County (THOMAS ROUNDS, AARON ENGLAND, BENJAMIN WEAVER, TURNER LANE, JAMES FULKERSON, ALEXANDER LOWRY and NICHOLAS GILLENTINE) to WASHINGTON LEDBETTER, $43.00 paid, 1 lot in town of Sparta, being Lot No 28.

Page 33   Indenture   Date and Grantors above, to JESSE M THOMAS, $50.00 paid, Lot 88 in Sparta.

Page 35   Indenture   Date & Grantors above, to WILLIAM BURDEN, $60.00 paid, Lot 45 in Sparta.

Page 36   Indenture   Date & Grantors as above, to Grantee above, $59.00 paid, Lot 46 in Sparta.

Page 39   Indenture   Date & Grantors as above, to HERON KING, $110 paid, Lot 7 in Sparta.

Page 41   Indenture   Date & Grantors as above, to Grantee above on behalf of HERON KING & CO, $80.00 paid, Lot 6 in Sparta.

Page 43   Indenture   Date & Grantors to Grantee above, $50.12 1/2 paid, Lot 25 in Sparta.

Page 45   Indenture   Date & Grantors as above, to EDMUND HARRISON, $50.00 paid, Lot 26 in Sparta.

Page 47   Indenture   Date, Grantors and Grantee as above, $50.00 paid, Lot 27 in Sparta.

Page 49   Indenture   Date, Grantors and Grantee as above, $151.12 1/2 paid, Lot 51 in Sparta.

Page 51   Indenture   Date and Grantors as above, $50.00 to WILLIAM GLENN, Lot 2 in Sparta.

Page 53   Indenture   Date, Grantors as above to Trustees of the PRIESTLY ACADEMY, $1.00 paid, Lot 87 in Sparta.

Page 55   Indenture   Date, Grantors & Grantee as above, $1.00 paid, Lot 86 in Sparta.

Page 57   Indenture   Date & Grantors as above, to ROBERT H DYER, $199, paid, Lot 10 in Sparta.

Page 59   Indenture   Date & Grantors as above, to THOMAS K HARRIS, $110.01 paid, Lot 9 in Sparta.

Page 61   Indenture   Date & Grantors as above, to JOHN GRIGSBY, $45.00 paid, Lot 83 in Sparta.

Page 63   Indenture   Date & Grantors above, to JOHN M CARRICK, $35.00 paid, Lot 1 in town of Sparta.

Page 65   Indenture   Date & Grantors above to WILLIAM ROBINSON, $97.00 paid, Lot 4 in town of Sparta.

Page 67 Indenture Date & Grantors above to JAMES TOWNSEND, $102 paid, Lot 20 in Sparta.

Page 68 Indenture Date & Grantors above to CALEB FRALEY, $100.12 1/2 paid, Lot 3 in town of Sparta.

Page 71 Indenture Date, Grantors & Grantee as above, $101.12 1/2, Lot 9 in town of Sparta.

Page 73 Sheriff's Deed 13 Aug 1810 WILLIAM PHILLIPS, Shff, and THOMAS STONE, by execution issued against ROBERT KING on 3 July 1800, tract on Cane creek a br of Caney fork, 228 acres being excepted from sale by virtue of redemption by WILLIAM P ANDERSON and JOHN MCIVER.

Page 75 Indenture 14 Aug 1810 Grantor as above and ISAAC TAYLOR, Junr and JOHN BRAHAW of Nashville,TN, by virtue of judgment at house of CALEB FRALY, being where court was held for White County, land in name of JAMES COWAN, 1000 acres formerly in White Co but now in Warren Co on W side Mures fork(?). Wit: JOHN CARRICK, WM E PILEAR.

Page 79 Indenture 14 Feb 1810 CALEB FRALY and ALEXANDER LOWRY, $5.00 paid, all right vested in Fraly by 2 deeds as described therein. Wit: TURNER LANE, WM E PILEAR.

Page 81 Land Grant No 1830 10 Jan 1810 TENNESSEE to WILLIAM ROBINSON and WILLIAM GASS, assees of heirs of STEPHEN MCDEWELL, tr of 200 acres, part of Warr 2937, in third Dist on Calf Killer fork and on W side of same.

Page 82 Sheriff's Deed 14 Aug 1810 WILLIAM PHILLIPS, Shff, to THOMAS ROUNDS, BIRD SMITH, THOMAS CRUTCHER, JAMES HERRON and ISAAC TAYLOR, Jnr, judgment having been entered against lands as described therein. Wit: JNO M CARRICK, WILLIAM E PILLAR.

Page 87 Land Grant No 1992 26 Feb 1810 TENNESSEE to THOMAS ROUNDS and THOMAS LOVELADY, assees of RICHARD PHILLIPS who performed Military serv for NC, Warr 1026, dated 26 May 1784 & entered 3 Dec 1808 by No 2789, 560 acres on waters of the Falling waters, including AARON PERRY, REUBEN RAGLAND, JAMES ROUNDS, JAMES DYER and THOMAS LOVELADY improvements. Sur 30 Mar 1809. Signed by WILLIE BLOUNT, Governor, R HOUSTON, Secty.

Page 88 Indenture 14 Aug 1810 CALEB FRALEY and THOMAS ROUNDS, ___ paid, 1 lot or piece of land being 81 perches, E of Sparta.

Page 90 Land Grant No 1627 11 Sept 1809 and of Independence of US the 34th TENNESSEE to ELIAS WALLACE, assee of heirs of STEPHEN MCDEWETT who received it for his mil serv for NC, Warr 2937, dated 30 Sept 1785, entered on 29 Aug 1807 by No 219, land being on waters of Calf Killer fork adj WILLIAM BURDEN 200 acre survey.

Page 92 Land Grant No 1858 18 Jan 1810 TENNESSEE by Certif 315 dated 21 Aug 1807 from Bd of Commiss for W TN to ELIJAH CHISUM tr of 450 acres in White Co in 3rd Dist & 22nd section, surv 6 Mar 1809 by JAMES CHISUM, DS.

Page 93 Land Grant No 1624 11 Sept 1809 TENNESEE Certif No 5 dated 9 July 1807 from Commiss of W TN to MARTIN ARMSTRONG, grants to ALEXANDER

THOMAS, assee of sd Armstrong, tr of 50 acres on Calf Killers fork, adj WILLIAM BURDIN, surv 9 May 1808.

Page 95   Land Grant No 1852   18 Jan 1810   TENNESSEE grants part of Certif 309 dated 20 Aug 1807, to JOHN CHISUM, assee of SAMPSON WILLIAMS, tr of 200 acres in 1st Dist, 1st Range & 9th Sec on Caney fork, 200 acres.

Page 96   Land Grant No 2183   21 Apr 1810   TENNESSEE grants for military serv by JULIAS SUMNER to NC, Warrant 4701, dated 14 Feb 1797, to JASBAR FITZGERALD, assee of heirs of sd Sumner, tr of 320 acres in 3rd Dist on Lost creek waters of Caney fork.   Surv 17 Aug 1808 by ISAAC TAYLOR, Junr, DS.

Page 98   Land Grant No 1831   10 Jan 1810   TENNESSEE grants for Military serv of STEPHEN MCDEWITT to NC (Warr 2937 dated 30 Sept 1785) to JOSEPH ROBERTSON, assee of heirs of sd Stephen, tr of 100 acres on W side of Calf Killer fork, beg in sink hole near Waggon rd leading from White courthouse to Rock island.

Page 99   Indenture   9 June 1810   CALEB FRALEY and JAMES HERON of Sparta, surviving partner of HERON KING & CO, $53.00 paid, 8 1/2 acres on SE side of Calf Killers fork & joining Sparta on West.

Page 102   Bill of Sale 9 Aug 1810   WILLIAM WILSON to my son WILLIAM WILSON, Washington Co, TN, $70.00 paid, 1 Negro boy named JACOB at this time, 2 yrs old.

Page 102   Indenture   10 July 1810   CALEB FRALEY and HERON KING & CO, $16.00 paid, tr of 5 acres north of Sparta. Wit: JACOB A LANE, JOHN A ANDERSON, SAML NELSON.

Page 104   Indenture   15 Aug 1810   Grantor above and BENJAMIN WEAVER, lot of 81 poles lying on E side of Sparta, beg at SE cor of THOMAS ROUNDS lot.

Page 106   Indenture __ ___ 1810   Grantor above and BIRD SMITH, lot of 1/2 acre on E side Sparta.

Page 108   Land Grant No 535   26 Sept 1808   TENNESSEE by part of Certif 63 dated 21 July 1807 obtained by THOMAS DILLARD, to DAVID HASTIN, assee of sd Dillard, tr of 150 acres in 3rd Dist on the big spring branch of Cane creek of main fork of Caney fork, adj JOSEPH HASTING and JACOB MITCHELL.

Page 110   Land Grant No 540   Date & Grantor above for Military service by WILLIAM NORTON to NC, Warr 41, dated 1 July 1801 & entered on 28 Aug 1807 by No 167 as an occupant claim, grants to DOSIER T CRAIN, assee of WINNEY NORTON, heiress of sd William, tr of 100 acres part sd Warr in 3rd Dist & 31st Sec, on Cane creek, adj WILLIAM BROWN.

Page 112   Division of property   13 Nov 1809   Commissioners of County Court (ISAAC TAYLOR, DAVID MITCHELL, ALEXANDER COOK, JOHN ROSE & DANIEL ALEXANDER) divide lands as submitted to court by MOSES FISK for himself & others, and grant land to THOMAS STORM (7360 acres), SAMUEL DENTON (13,984 acres), FISK (7360 acres), JAMES MANNING heirs (it is stated that sd James has lately deceased at part of premises comprehended in limits-2200 acres), WILLIAM ROBERTSON and SILVESTER ROBERTSON (2208 acres), JOHN NYDAM and

HENDRICK J WYCOFF (2208 acres), RALPH THURMAN, (2208 acres. Plat follows.

Page 119 Petition 14 Aug 1809 MOSES FISK, agent, in regard to above lands. (If interested, persons should send for copies of the case.)

Page 125 Sheriff's Deed 10 Nov 1810 WILLIAM PHILLIPS, Esq, Shff, and MOSES FISK, latter of Overton Co, TN, 4416 acres for $18.10 paid. Wit: ELIJAH CHISUM, JOHN CHISUM.

Page 129 Sheriff's Deed Date & parties as above, 2208 acres. Wit: As above.

Page 134 Indenture 2 Nov 1810 CALEB FRALEY and ISAAC WOODARD, $400 paid, tr of 76 acres, a part of 640 acre sur issued by NC to STOCKLEY DONNILSON and WILLIAM WYRRELL in 1796, beg in the Calf killer (fork) and adj GEORGE W GIBBS cor. Wit: JNO CARRICK, JACOB A LANE.

Page 136 Indenture 26 Dec 1809 WILLIAM P ANDERSON, Rutherford Co, TN, one part, and JOHN MCIVER of Alexandria, Dist of Columbia, other part, $485.75 paid, tr on Falling waters granted by NC unto JAMES EASTON on 27 Mar 1796, being 485 3/4 acres. Wit: THOS BOUNDS, ISAAC TAYLOR, Jnr.

Page 139 Indenture 9 Dec 1809 JAMES R BRYAN and JOHN GOODPASTURE, latter of Overton Co, TN, $105 paid, 1 tr of 30 acres in Hickory valley, part of sur of 200 acres on which sd Bryan now lives, tr also butted by tr of ISAAC ANDERSON. Wit: WILLM WILSON, TURNER LANE.

Page 142 Letter of Attorney 22 Jan 1810 WILLIAM P ANDERSON to MAJOR ISAAC TAYLOR, as Anderson and JOHN M MCIVER own several tracts occupied by WM DYER, WIDOW DYER, WILLIAM QUARLES, OBED GARDNER, WM HOWARD, JACOB ROBERTSON, CARTER MILLS, WILLIAM MILES, ALEXR MOORE, ALEXR FINDLEY, JOHN CRIS__, W FINNEY, JOHN HUTCHINGS, REUBEN FINNEY, JANE GOOLSBY, ___ POOT(?), JACOB YOUNG and others, giving Taylor the power to sell, etc, the lands. Wit: B SEARCY, JOHN FERGUSON, SAML LANE, WM DILLON, CHARLES CANADY(?), THOS CHILDRESS. Ack in Davidson Co, TN before ANDREW EWING, CCC.

Page 144 Land Grant No 1856 18 Jan 1810 TENNESSEE to JOSEPH CRABB, assee of JOHN SULLIVAN, tr of 62 acres, part of Warr 1052 dated 17 Dec 1802, adj FREDERICK MILLER 150 ac sur.

Page 145 Land Grant No 1857 Grantor & date above to FREDERICK MILLER, assee of WILLIAM FULTON, assee of JOHN SULLIVAN, tr of 150 ac.

Page 147 Indenture 14 Feb 1810 ALEXANDER LOWREY and CALEB FRALEY, $5.00 paid, by virtue of 2 deeds one by ROBERT BURTON and other by JOHN MCIVER (they being joint partners), part of 5 tracts of 931 acres on the SE side of Calf Killers fork, beg at EDWARD WHITE line. Wit: TURNER LANE, WM E PILLAR.

Page 149 Indenture 12 Nov 1810 JOSEPH ROBINSON and WILLIAM MAY, 100 acres beg near waggon road leading from White Court House to Rock Island.

Page 151 Indenture 10 Oct 1810 WILLIAM ROBINSON and WILLIAM GIST $5.00 paid, 77 acres on W side of Calf Killers fork, part of a 200 acre sur held by Grant 1830.

Page 154   Indenture   15 Oct 1810   Grantor above and JOSEPH ROBINSON (relationship not stated), tr of 99 acres 2 roods, part of 200 ac sur held by Grant 1830 issued by TN to sd William.

Page 157   Indenture   10 Oct 1810   WILLIAM GIST and WILLIAM ROBINSON, $5.00 paid, 122 acres.

Page 159   Indenture   8 Nov 1810   THOMAS M CORRY, of Knoxville, and JAMES HERRON of Sparta, $300 paid, 1800 acres, adj ELIJAH LEWIS & BENJAMIN LEWIS, JOHN WHITE, JOHN M CARRICK & JAMES FULKERSON.   Wit: TURNER LANE and 2 unreadable names.

Page 162   Indenture   13 Nov 1810   CALEB FRALEY and GEORGE W GIBBS, $5.00 paid, tr of 2 acres on SE side of Calf killer and N of Sparta, part of a 640 ac sur granted by NC to STOCKLEY DONNELSON and WILLIAM TYRRELL.

Page 164   Deed of Gift   18 Sept 1810   SAMUEL THOMAS for good will and affection I have for my son DANIEL THOMAS, a Negro man named EDWARD, about 23 years old.

Page 166   Bill of Sale   25 Sept 1810   ALEXANDER LOWREY to EDWARD HOGAN, latter of Jackson Co, TN, $400 paid, 1 Negro woman slave named MOLLY, about 29 yrs.   Wit: TURNER LANE, JACOB A LANE.

Page 167   Bill of Sale   Date and parties as above, $400 paid, 1 Negro woman slave named SALLY, about 22 yrs.

Page 168   Bill of Sale   Date, parties & consideration as above, 1 Negro man slave named ABRAHAM, about 22 yrs.

Page 169   Land Grant No 1623   TENNESSEE to JAMES R BRYAN, assee of MARTIN ARMSTRONG, 200 acres in 3rd Dist in the Hickory valley on main fork of Caney fork adj JOHN BRYAN 1150 ac survey.

Page 170   Land Grant No 532   26 Sept 1808   TENNESSEE to ISAAC ANDERSON & JOHN ANDERSON, assees of THOMAS DILLON (Certif No 63), 200 ac on waters of main Caney fork in Hickory valley.

Page 172   Land Grant 1048   13 Apr 1809   TENNESSEE to ISAAC ANDERSON, assee of THOMAS DILLON tr on main waters of Cany fork, adj above Isaac and also JOHN ANDERSON, and also JAMES R BRYAN and THOMAS M CORRY.

Page 173   Deed of Gift   7 Nov 1810   JACOB HELVY for love and affection I have for my son JACK HELVY, personal estate (land, horses, cattle, hogs, etc).

Page 174   Indenture   4 Oct 1810   THOMAS CRUTCHER and WILLIAM QUARLES, $428 paid, tr on waters of Cane Oak creek, a branch of Caney fork of Cumberland river, part of 640 ac tr granted by NC to JAMES EASTON.   Wit: ISAAC TAYLOR, Junr, SOLOMON COX.

Page 177   Power of Attorney   27 Dec 1809   JOHN MCIVER, Alexandria, Dist of Columbia, appoint WILLIAM P ANDERSON, Rutledge Co, TN, to act in conveying any part of several tracts 640 acres each.   Wit: ELIJAH CHISUM, ISHAM BRADLY, JOS L CONKLIN, E PRITCHETT.

Page 179 Commissioners Deed 20 July 1803 GEORGE GILPIN, JONAH THOMPSON and FRANCIS PEYTON, Commissioners, one part, (dividing property of JOSIAH WATSON, a Bankrupt), and JOHN MCIVER, Alexandria, Dist of Columbia, other part, tracts as set out in sd deed (persons interested should send for copy of this indenture - it goes through p 186). Wit: JOHN HARRISS. Certif copy by GEORGE DENEALE(?), Clk Cir Ct of Dist of Columbia, and by WILLIAM KELLY, Chief Judge CC.

Page 187 Indenture 1 June 1798 CHARLES HIGBEE of City of Richmond, VA, one part, and JOSIAH WATSON of town of Alexandria, Fairfax Co, VA and ROBERT BURTON, Granville Co, NC, other part, tr on head branches of Cane creek and the Sulphur fork, a branch of Red River in Sumner Co, TN, being sev tracts as described therein, and being 9960 acres. Wit: R J TAYLOR, ROBERT WATSON, THOS HERBERT. Ack in State of TN on 27 Sept 1800 by Watson before ANDREW JACKSON, Judge. Reg in Robertson Co, TN by B BROWN, Regr and on 28 Feb 1811 reg by ELIJAH CHISUM, Reg. Certif by THOS JOHNSTON, CRC.

Page 195 Indenture 25 Aug 1796 STOCKLY DONELSON and WILLIAM TYRRELL, Knox co, TN, one part, and CHARLES HIGBEE, City of Richmond, VA, other part, 5 shillings paid, sev tracts. ANDREW JACKSON also acknowledges. Rec in Reg Off in Greene Co, TN 3 Mar 1797 by JAMES STIMSON, Clk.

Page 205 Indenture 7 Aug 1810 JOSEPH NEVILL and JOHN GARNETT, latter of Barren Co, KY, 200 acres for $480 paid.

Page 206 Indenture 10 Nov 1810 CALEB FRALEY and JAMES BOWEN, $101.12 1/2 paid, Lot 8 in Sparta. Wit: JACOB A LANE, JAMES HERRON.

Page 208 Indenture 10 Nov 1810 WASHINGTON LEDBETTER and JAMES BOWEN, $100 paid, Lot 28 in Sparta. Wit: As above.

Page 210 Indenture 6 Feb 1811 WILLIAM ROBINSON and JAMES HERRON, latter of Sparta, $97 paid, Lot 4 in Sparta.

Page 212 Indenture 23 Mar 1810 THOMAS M CORRY, Knoxville, TN, and WILLIAM LEWIS, $350 paid, 214 acres as granted Corry by Grant 310 from NC on 7 Mar 1796. Wit: TURNER LANE, WILLIAM M BRYAN.

Page 214 Power of Atty (No date) JOHN MCIVER, Fairfax Co, VA, to MAJOR ISAAC TAYLOR, to convey my remaining int in tracts in White and Jackson counties orig granted by NC to JAMES PARTOW by patents dated 27 Mar 1796, 640 acres. Wit: CHARLES ROBERTSON, WM BURTINTON(?).

Page 219 Indenture 12 Feb 1811 THOMAS STONE and RICHARD HILL, $2.80 paid, 270 ac tr on Cane Break branch of Cumberland river.

Page 221 Land Grant No 2088 31 Mar 1810 & of Independence of US the 34th TENNESSEE to JOSEPH CUMMINGS, assee of DAVID ROSS, 50 acres in 3rd Dist & 31st Sec on main Caney fork, Warrant No 1679 to Ross dated 19 Feb 1787.

Page 222 Land Grant No 2086 Date, Grantor & Grantee as above, Cummings being assee of THOMAS DILLON who received it from TN by No 4564 as an occupant claim, 100 acres.

Page 224 Indenture 24 Dec 1810 JOHN M CARRICK and JOEL BRADSHAW, $300 paid, 184 acres conveyed to Carrick by deed dated 7 Nov 1810 by THOMAS M CORRY, tr beg at NW cor of Corry's large sur at 3 beach oaks, a post oak and poplar, & running th with orig line N 238 poles to JAMES FULKERSON cor a post oak; th with his line E passing his cor 220 poles to foot of the mountain; th with sd mtn & it meanders S 21 deg E 38 poles; th S 7 deg W 52 poles; th S 13 deg E 44 poles to orig line; th with sd line W 240 poles to beg. Wit: JOHN W SIMPSON & 1 unreadable signature).

Page 226   Indenture   12 Feb 1811   THOMAS STONE and JOSEPH PARKER, $0.80 paid, part of Cane creek, a branch of Caney fork of Cumberland river, beg at cor to RICHARD HILL on side of mountain containing 416 acres.

Page 228   Indenture   Date & Grantor as above, to ELIJAH WARD, $0.80   paid, 3 small pieces of land part of above desc 2500 acres.

Page 230   Land Grant 1051   13 Apr 1809   TENNESSEE to BENJAMIN BIRDEN, assee of THOMAS DILLON, tr of 50 acres in 3rd Dist on both sides of Calf Killer fork of Caney fork.

Page 231   Indenture   6 Feb 1811   JOHN GRIGSBY and JOHN JETT, $100 paid, Lot 24 in Sparta. Wit: FRANK PORTERFIELD, LAWSON NOURSE.

Page 233   Indenture   11 Feb 1811   ISAAC WOODARD and JAMES HERRON, $135 paid, tr of 10 acres being a part of 640 ac sur granted by NC to Stockley and Tyrrell. Wit: BIRD SMITH, DANIEL M NEIL.

Page 235   Indenture   14 Jan 1811   Grantor above and GEORGE W GIBBS, $366 & 2/3 dollar, tr of 66 acres, a part of a 640 ac sur as above. Wit: DANIEL MCNEIL, GILBERT BOWMAN(?). (Clerk of CC is in unreadable script - is perhaps _____ MEBANE).

Page 227a (Page numbers here are repeated but material is not same on the previous p 227, etc) Indenture   11 Feb 1811   ELIJAH CHISUM and JOHN ALLEN, $480 paid, tr of 125 acres on N side Caney fork & being part of Grants 2087 & 2089 issued by Tennessee. Pymt of State Tax certif by JACOB HORN(?), CCC.

Page 230a   Indenture   11 Feb 1811   THOMAS STONE and JOHN PICKRELL, for $0.50 paid, 49 acres part of 2500 acres on Cane creek a branch of Caney fork of Cumberland river. Note that Stone only conveys his title to the land, he having acted as Agent in purchasing land at auction, deed signed by WILLIAM PHILLIPS, late Shff of White County. Wit: THOMAS CRUTCHER, REUBEN RAGLAND.

Page 232a   Land Grant No 2182   21 Apr 1810   TENNESSEE to WILLIAM ROTTON, assee of JULIAS SUMNER, for his military serv to state of NC, Warrant 4701, dated 14 Feb 1797, 320 acres in 3rd Dist on Lost creek waters of Caney fork. Surv 17 Aug 1808 by ISAAC TAYLOR, Junr, DS.

Page 233a   Land Grant No 592   13 Oct 18__ & the 33rd of the Indepen of the US   Grantor above for military service by ABEL LITTON to NC, Warrant No 62 dated 13 Nov 1802, grants by sd Tennessee to JOHN WALLING, assee of sd Litton, 228 acres, part of Warr in 1st Dist 1st Range & 8th Sec.

Page 235a   Land Grant No 593   13 Oct 1808   TENNESSEE for military service performed by WILLIAM SCOTT to NC, Warr No 3347, dated 22 Dec 1798, grants to JOHN WALLING, assee of sd Scott, a tr of 100 acres part of sd warrant.

(Pages 236 - 237 are missing)

Page 239   Land Grant No 595   13 Oct 1808   Above Grantor for military serv by WILLIAM SCOTT to NC, Warrant No 4457, dated 22 Dec 1796, Tennessee grants to JOHN WALLING, assee of sd Scott, tr of 28 acres the residue of sd warrant lying in White Co in 2nd Dist 1st Range & 8th Sec on waters of Caney fork.

Page 240   Land Grant No 1584   4 Sept 1809   Above Grantor for military serv of MOSES NEWSOM to NC, Warr No 3716 dated 2 Jan 1790, Tennessee grants to MORGAN BRYAN, assee of sd Newsom, 100 acres part of sd warrant.

Page 242   Land Grant No 1585   4 Sept 1809   Above Grantor and Grantee, Warr No 62, dated 30 Nov 1802, Tennessee grants to above named Bryan, 100 acres.

Page 244   Land Grant No 1586   Date & Grantor above, to JOSEPH WALLING, assee of sd ABEL LITTON, tr of 100 acres in 1st Dist, 1st Range & 9th Sec on Caney fork.

Page 246   Indenture   6 Feb 1811   JOSEPH ROBINSON and WILLIAM ROBINSON (relationship not stated), $5.00 paid, tr of 29 acres & 2 roods, part of 200 ac sur held by Grant 1830 issued by TN to William Robinson and WILLIAM GIST, dated 10 Jan 1810.

Page 248   Bill of Sale   6 Feb 1811   WILLIAM ROBINSON to JOSEPH ROBINSON, $500 paid, one Negro man slave named SHADRACH, 39 yrs old. Wit: JACOB A LANE, WILLIAM GIST.

Page 250   Bill of Sale   16 Mar 1811   CALEB FRALEY to GEORGE W GIBBS, $465.00, a Negro woman named SCILLAR of age of 20 yrs, and Mulatto child named JANE, 2 months old.

Page 251   Bill of Sale   14 May 1811   WILLIAM NEVILL, Senr, to ISAAC TAYLOR, Junr, $500 paid, Negro man named ROLF, aged 21 yrs, and Negro woman named LUCY, aged 60. Wit: WILL GLENN.

Page 252   Indenture   22 June 1810   DAVID NICHOLDS and WILLIAM LEWIS, Senr, $100 paid, tr conv to Grantor by THOMAS MCCORRY on 2 June 1808, 29 acres. Wit: DAVID MCDANIELS, BENJAMIN LEWIS.

Page 253   Indenture   2 Apr 1811   JAMES BOWEN and JOSEPH RODGERS, $5.00 paid, Lot 28 in Sparta. Wit: CHARLES MCGUIRE, JACOB HANE.

Page 256   Indenture   12 Feb 1811   BENJAMIN BURDIN and JAMES BOWEN(?), $1000 paid, tr vested in Grantor by Grant from TN to him on 21 July 1807, 50 acres on N side Calf Killers fork of Caney fork. Wit: ALEX COOK, JOHN CHISUM.

Page 258   Indenture   13 May 1811   JAMES COLE and PETER BILLINGS, $300 paid, tr on Post Oak creek, being 109 acres. Wit: SAMUEL DYER, ZACHARIAS HANKS.

Page 260   Indenture   22 Oct 1810   JESSE N THOMAS, one part, and NEVILLE THOMAS, other part (relationship not stated), $5.00 paid, Lot 88 in Sparta. Wit: JACOB A LANE, ALEXANDER THOMAS.

Page 262   Indenture   13 May 1810   ALEXANDER THOMAS and HARDY JONES, tr on Calf Killers fork adj WILLIAM BURDEN 200 ac sur, being 50 acres.

Page 263   Bill of Sale   4 Mar 1811   HALLET PIERCE(?) to ROBERT STEWART, wagon, horses, etc.   Wit: ROBT ARMSTRONG, THOMAS MASSY, JESSE NETTLES.

Page 265   Indenture   __ May 1811   JOHN MCBRIDE and RICHARD COLE, $800 paid, tr on waters of Cherry creek adj THOMAS MCBRIDE, being where sd John now lives.   Wit: ROBT ARMSTRONG, THOMAS RIDGE.

Page 267   Indenture   1 Sept 1810   Grantor above to THOMAS MCBRIDE (relationship not stated), $155 paid, 50 acre tr on NE side of Cherry creek.   Wit: JO MCBRIDE, RILEY MCBRIDE. (Relationships not stated)

Page 270   Comm of Bankruptcy   15 Apr 1803   United States of America to GEORGE GILPIN, FRANCIS PEYTON and JOSIAH THOMPSON   Whereas JOSIAH WATSON of Alexandria, Dist of Col doing trace as a merchant & about 13 day present month became a bankrupt, all persons shall proceed in collecting debts according to laws.   Signed by W KITTY, Judge, and certif by GEORGE DENCALE, Clk USCC, Columbia Dist.   Certif in Kentucky by ACHILLES SNEED, CCA, and in Harrison Co, KY by W MOORE, CHC.

Page 273   Land Grant No 536   26 Sept 1808   TENNESSEE by part of Certif 63 dated 21 July 1807 obtained by THOMAS DILLON, grants to SAMUEL GILMORE, assee of Dillon, tr of 100 acres on Rush spring creek.

Page 274   Land Grant No 1036   10 Apr 1809   TENNESSEE for mili service of JOHN COWAN for NC, Warr 5094 dated 6 Dec 1797, grants to COWAN 100 acres, part sd warr lying on N side Calf killer fork.

Page 276   Indenture   28 May 1811   GEORGE RUSSELL, one part, and THOMAS SHIRLEY and WILLIAM MEDCALF, other part, $500 paid, tr of 100 acres in 3rd Dist on head water of Calf killer fork including where he now lives.   Wit: WILLIAM WELCH, THOMAS HORNE, S__ DEARING.

Page 278   Indenture   19 Sept 1810   THOMAS CRUTCHER and SAMUEL DYER, $200 paid, tr on Cane creek, a branch of Caney fork of Cumberland River, it being part of 640 acres orig granted by NC to JAMES CAR_STON by Grant No 2698, and being 98 1/2 acres.   Wit: HOWARD CASH, ISHAM RUSSELL.

Page 280   Indenture   13 Aug 1811   JAMES HERRON, one part, and MATTHIAS ANDERSON and WILLIAM ANDERSON, Smith Co, TN, other part, $200 paid, 10 acres part of 640 acre sur granted by NC to STOCKLEY DONELSON & WILLIAM TYRRELL.

Page 283   Indenture   7 Nov 1810   THOMAS MCCORRY of Knoxville, TN, one part, and JOHN M CARRICK, other part, $200 paid, his interest in Grant from NC to JOHN RHEA and WILLIAM TYRRELL, 184 acres beg at SW cor sd grant and abutting land of JAMES FULKERSON.   Wit: JACOB A LANE, TURNER LANE.

Page 285   Indenture   25 Sept 1810   SAMUEL GILMORE, Pulaski Co, KY, one part, and STEPHEN WALTER, $400 paid, 100 acres being granted to sd Gilmore by TN, No 536, dated 7 Mar 1808. Wit: JOHN BRYAN, WILLIAM M BRYAN.

Page 287 Indenture __ ___ 1811 WILLIAM P ANDERSON, Jefferson Co, TN, and JOHN MCIVER, _____ Co, VA, to THOMAS CRUTCHER, a 640 ac tr lying on waters of the Falling water granted by NC to JAMES EASTON on 27 Mar 1796. Is provision that if an earlier title is proved, grantors herein are not liable to Grantor. Wit: JNO DIRGAN, ISAAC TAYLOR, Jnr.

Page 290 Land Grant No 2809 5 Jan 1811 TENNESSEE, by Certif 165 dated 7 Feb 1809 obtained from Commiss for W TN by JOHN GRAY BLOUNT and entered by No 1232 as an Occupant claim, grant to HENRY LYDIA assee of sd Blount, 120 acres on S side Calf Killers fork of Caney fork.

Page 292 Indenture 7 June 1811 WILLIAM QUARLES and JOHN PICKRELL, $200 paid, parcel of land a part of 640 acres granted by NC to JAMES EASTON, Grant No 2698. Wit: THOMAS CRUTCHER, THOMAS BOUNDS.

Page 294 Indenture 29 May 1811 JOHN ANDERSON and TURNER LANE, $3.50 paid, tr of 119 acres in Hickory valley, part of 200 acres granted by TN to ISAAC ANDERSON and JOHN ANDERSON. Wit: ALEXANDER LOWRY, ROBERT PUCKET.

Page 297 Indenture 13 Nov 1810 JAMES R BRYAN, one part, and WILLIAM BRYAN, Senr, latter of Overton Co, TN, other part, $1500 paid, 2 tracts being 200 acres. Wit: JOHN BRYAN, JOHN MCGILVRAY.

Page 300 Indenture 12 Aug 1811 CALEB FRALEY, late of White Co, TN, one part, and ALEXANDER LOWREY, 112 pounds current money paid, 140 acres on SE side of Calf Killers fork, part of Grant No 2562 issued by NC, and conv to Fraley by ROBERT BURTON, JOHN MCIVER and sd Lowrey. Wit: ISAAC TAYLOR, Jnr, TURNER LANE.

Page 303 Sheriff's Deed 15 July 1807 WILLIAM PHILLIPS, Shff, one part, and JOHN C HAMILTON & GEO MATLOCK, other part, due to writ issued by Super Ct of Hamilton Dist, dated 16 Oct 1806, directing Shff that goods of ROBERT KING be assessed for debts due, including 2500 acres hereby conveyed. Wit: ISAAC TAYLOR, DANL ALEXANDER, ROBERT ARMSTRONG.

Page 306 Deed 7 Nov 1809 ROBERT ALLEN, Smith Co, TN, $200 paid by GEORGE GORDON, Greene Co, TN, $200 paid, transfer all my claim in 2500 acres conv to me by Shff of White County by deed dated 15 July 1807, which sd tr was sold to Allen by Shff by writ dated 16 Oct 1806 at instance of JOSEPH MAGAFFIN and JAMES MAGAFFIN against ROBERT KING. Wit: WM PHILLIPS, JNO JETT.

Page 309 Indenture 6 Nov 1809 GEORGE MATLOCK, Smith Co, TN, and GEORGE GORDON, Greene Co, TN, $1.00 paid, all his claim to 2500 acres as described above. Wit: ISAAC TAYLOR, Jr, WM PHILLIPS.

Page 311 Indenture 1 Oct 1811 MOSES FISK, Overton Co, TN, and SAMUEL DENTON, Esq, $10.00 paid, tr in Township of Fisk, land sold to Fisk by WILLIAM PHILLIPS, then Shff of White County, land sold for taxes due by JONATHAN RUSSELL and NICHOLAS COOK, this tr being part of same as reserved for heirs of sd Russell and Cook. Wit: R WOTHERSPOON. Ack New York City 1 Oct 1811 by Fisk before JNO FERGUSON, JP, and subscribed in same place by

JOHN SIDELL, Clk.

Page 313 (Incomplete) Indenture 1 Oct 1811 MOSES FISK, Overton Co, TN, and THOMAS STORM, Esq, of New York (City, Co, State) that in consideration ....

(Unnumbered page) JOHN SIDELL, Clk certifies he has subscribed his hand, etc Oct __ ____. Regis & exam 4 Dec 1811 by ELIJAH CHISUM, Reg.

Volume D
Dec 1811 - June 1812

Page 1   Land Grant No 1159   28 June 1809   TENNESSEE by virtue of part of Certif No 245 dated 14 Aug 1807, to JOHN BEAN, there is granted by TN to sd Bean a tr of 330 acres in 1st Dist, beg on W bank of Caney fork river.

Page 2   Land Grant No 1160   Date & parties as in above Grant, 210 acres in 1st Dist & also on W bank of Caney fork.

Page 4   Land Grant No 1161   Date & parties as in above Grants, 100 acres in 1st Dist on E side sd fork.

Page 5   Land Grant No 1304   3 July 1809   TENNESSEE, for military service by PATRICK CARNEY to State of NC, Warr 5191, dated 9 Dec 1797, grants to WILLIAM MORRISON, assee of sd Carney, 20 acres, part of sd Warr on W side of Morrison's Mountain (on Caney fork).

Page 7   Land Grant No 526   26 Sept 1808   TENNESSEE, by virtue of Certif 63 dated 21 July 1807, to THOMAS DILLON, entered 28 Aug 1807 by No 169 as an Occupant claim, there is granted by TN to WILLIAM BROWN, assee of Dillon, a tr of 100 acres on 3rd Dist of Cane creek, the waters of Caney fork.

Page 8   Land Grant No 539   26 Sept 1808   TENNESSEE in consideration of military service performed by WILLIAM NORTON to NC, Warr 41, dated 1 July 1801, there is granted by TN to WILLIAM BROWN, assee of WINNIE NORTON, heiress of sd William, 20 acres, part sd warrant.

Page 10   Land Grant No 2566   29 Sept 1810   TENNESSEE by virtue of Certif No 46 dated 26 Feb 1810, issued to THOMAS GIST, there is granted tr of 200 acres in 1st Dist on waters of Calf killer's fork in 9th Sec & 1st Range, beg in W bdy of JOHN MILLER sur on side of a spur of Town mountain 10 poles below a rocky spring.

Page 12   Land Grant No 2672   17 Nov 1810   TENNESSEE for military service of JOHN SULLIVAN to St of NC, Warr No 1052, dated 17 Dec 1802, entered by No 899, (TN) grants to SOLOMON JORDON, assee of WILLIAM TUTOW(?), assee of sd Sullivan, tr of 187 acres, part of sd warrant, in 3rd Dist on Cherry creek.

Page 13   Land Grant No 2959   14 Mar 1811   TENNESSEE by virtue part of Certif No 64, dated 21 July 1807 by THOMAS DILLON, grants to JOHN MEDLEY, assee of Dillon tr of 100 acres in 1st Dist, 1st Range & 10th Sec on N side Caney fork, adj GEORGE W SAUNDERS.

Page 15   Bill of Sale 4 Sept 1811   WILLIAM WINTER to ELISHA WALLING, $1000 paid, slaves RACHEL and VINY, JAMES, ALFRED and CHARLES. Wit: JACOB MILLER, JAMES M KINNEY.

Page 16   Indenture 5 Nov 1811   ELISHA WALLING and WILLIAM WINTER, $1000 paid, 200 acres of land on waters of Calf Killer fork, joining JOHN MILLER land.

Page 18   Indenture 25 Nov 1809   WILLIAM BROWN and JOHN TERRY, $500 paid, 100 acres on Cane creek. Wit: RICHARD CLEMENTS, JESSE BROCK, NICHOLAS

GILLENTINE.

Page 20   Indenture Date and parties as above, $100 paid, tr of 20 acres, part of Warrant on Cane creek adj Brown's 100 ac sur on his W bdy. Wit: As above deed.

Page 22   Land Grant No 680 8 Dec 1808   TENNESSEE by part of Certif No 237 dated 13 Aug 1809 obtained by THOMAS DILLON, TN grants to WILLIAM SHAW, assee of sd Dillon, tract of 100 acres on waters of Caney fork.

Page 24   Indenture 8 Nov 1811   SOLOMON JORDAN, one part, and GEORGE GRIFFITH and WILLIAM GRIFFITH, other part, $700 paid, tr in 3rd Dist on Cherry creek, a branch of Calf Killers fork, being 157 acres taken from Grant No 2672 of 187 acres granted by TN to Jordan on 17 Nov 1810, Warr 1052, abutting tr of ROBERT HOWARD and SAMUEL WEAVER. Wit: ELIJAH CHISUM, Senr, W RIDGE, JAMES HOWARD.

Page 26   Bill of Sale 24 Oct 1811 HOWEL G HARRIS to THOMAS K HARRIS (relationship not stated but are probably brothers), $84.27 1/2 paid, a Negro girl named SYNTHIA and a boy named JOE. This is result of Davidson Co Cot direction to divide estate of my Decd father HOWEL HARRIS between myself & my brothers and sisters.

Page 27   Indenture 18 Mar 1811   EDMUND HARRISON of Sparta, and DAVID SMITH, 5 shillings paid, Lot 27 in Sparta. Wit: JACOB A LANE, JNO JETT.

Page 29   Indenture 8 June 1811   Parties as in above deed, Lot 26 in Sparta. Consideration $5.00. Wit: JACOB A LANE, JAMES HERRON.

Page 31   Indenture 12 Nov 1810   Commissioners of Sparta (THOMAS BOUNDS, AARON ENGLAND, BENJAMIN WEAVER, TURNER LANE, JAMES FULHERRON, ALEXANDER LOWREY and NICHOLAS GILLENTINE), $65.00 paid, Lot 85 in Sparta. Wit: JOHN BRYAN, DAVID M DANIELS.

Page 33   Indenture 2 June 1810   CALEB FRALEY and JAMES HERON for HERON KING & CO of Sparta, $1380 paid, 138 acres on SE side of Calf Killers fork, it being part of same land Fraley holds by 3 deeds (as set out). Wit: BIRD SMITH, TURNER LANE, ALEXANDER LOWRY).

Page 34   Indenture 19 Sept 1810 THOMAS CRUTCHER and HOWARD CASH, $438 paid, tr on Post Oak creek, a branch of Caney fork, it being part of 640 acres orig granted by NC to JAMES EASTON, Grant No 2698. Wit: SAMUEL DYER, ISHAM RUSSELL.

Page 38   Indenture __ Nov 1811   JAMES COLE and THOMAS CRUTCHER, $300 paid, tr on Post Oak creek, part of tr conv to Cole by William P Anderson & John McIver, orig granted by NC to JAMES EASTON. Wit: WILLIAM HOWARD, CHARLES ISHAM.

Page 41   Indenture 16 Jan 1811   JAMES COLE and CHARLES ISHAM, $110 paid, tr on Post Oak creek, part of tr conv as in above deed, being 102 1/2 acres. Wit: THOMAS CRUTCHER, JOHN WOMACK, WM HOWARD.

Page 43   Indenture 31 May 1811   THOMAS CRUTCHER and WILLIAM HOWARD, 41 pounds 4 shillings paid, 103 acres on Post Oak creek. Wit: JAMES COLE,

JAMES HAWES.

Page 45   Indenture 4 Sept 1811   CALEB FRALEY and WILLIAM ROBERTSON, $2000 paid, 400 acres beg in E bdy line of town of Sparta at the Turnpike street, cor with JAMES HERON, and tr adj ROBERT PUCKET and JAMES BOWEN.

Page 49   Indenture 20 Jan 1810   PROTIMAN JONES, Jackson Co, TN, and ZACHARIAH JONES (relationship not stated), $400 paid, tr of 100 acres in 1st Dist on Caney fork beg near Zachariah's dwelling house. Wit: EBENEZER JONES, JOHN CLEMENS, JAMES RUSSELL, JOHN WINDLW.

Page 50   Indenture 18 Aug 1810   JABAN FITZGERALD, Franklin Co, TN, one part, and JOHN GREEN, $100 paid, tr on Lost creek, 320 acres.

Page 53   Indenture 1 Oct 1811   ISHAM RUSSELL, Lincoln Co, TN, one part, and THOMAS CRUTCHER, $1200 paid, tr on waters of the Falling water, granted by NC to JAMES EASTON on 27 Mar 1796, and adj lands of WILLIAM R COLE and SOLOMON COX, 485 3/4 acres. Wit: JNO JETT, WILL GLENN.

Page 55   Sheriff's Deed 14 Aug 1810   WILLIAM PHILLIPS, Shff & Collector of White County, one part, and WILLIAM IRWIN and ALEXANDER IRWIN, other part, court in 1809 having ordered (at place of holding court being house of CALEB FRALEY) tr sold for taxes (being part of lands owned by JOHN RHEA and WILLIAM TYRRELL), 225 acres (sold for $17.17), being part of Grant No 309 from NC to sd Rhea & Tyrrell. Wit: JNO M CARRICK, WM E PILLAR, THOS BOUNDS.

Page 61   Deed of Gift 12 Aug 1811   WILLIAM BROWN for natural love for my 2 younger sons WILLIAM BROWN and JOHN BROWN, all my estate in White County, granting an equal right to each. Wit: TURNER LANE, ALEXANDER THOMAS. Inventory included, 150 acres, live stock, and also a Negro woman slave named FRANCES, 17 yrs, now in Hawkins County.

Page 63   Power of Attorney 1 Nov 1810   NATHANIEL TAYLOR being very sick and unable to do my business, in consideration of services my son JAS P TAYLOR has bound himself to do settling of my business in West Tennessee, giving me $1000 bond, convey to sd James all my entries of land in W TN not heretofore sold. Wit: AND TAYLOR, WM BOYD, EDWD HARRISON, JAMES HERON and JACOB STIGAL.

Page 65   Land Grant No 2569 29 Sept 1810 & of Indepen of US the 35th TENNESSEE by virtue of part of Certif 135 dated 25 Nov 1808 from TN to THOMAS TAYLOR, TN, now grants to JOHN KNOWLES, assee of sd Taylor, tr of 129 1/4 acres on waters of Caney fork.

Page 67   Land Grant No 3494   Date & Grantor as above, for military serv by EPHRAIM DANIEL to NC, Warr 2976, dated 27 Dec 1803, to ABEL HUDSON, assee of heirs of sd Ephraim, 20 acres part of sd Warr on Caney fork.

Page 68   Land Grant No 3501 23 Oct 1811   TENNESSEE by Certifs to NATHANIEL TAYLOR and RAWLEY RALLS, and entered on 22 Oct 1811 as Occupant claim, grants to Ralls 300 acres on Caney fork near Hickorycrest Mountain.

Page 69   Land Grant No 2676 20 Nov 1810   TENNESSEE by virtue part of Certif No 32, dated 18 Aug 1807, issued to heirs of GEORGE RUSSELL as entered on 11 day of Aug 1808 by No 2162, grants to FREDERICK MILLER, assee sd heirs of Russell, 28 1/2 acres on Calf Killer fork.

Page 71 Land Grant No 531 26 Sept 1808 TENNESSEE by virtue part of Certif 63 dated 21 July 1807 obtained by THOMAS DILLON and entered on 28 Aug 1807 by No 180 as Occupant claim, there is granted to JOHN BRYAN, assee of sd Dillon 150 acres on main fork of Caney fork and in Hickory valley.

Page 72 Bill of Sale 1 July 1809 ELIJAH HITCHCOFF to THOMAS K HARRIS, $350 paid, a Negro girl named MARY, about 14 or 15 yrs old. Wit: ELIJAH BARNETT, JOHN CLARY.

Page 73 Bill of Sale 24 Dec 1811 EDWARD GLEESON(?) to Grantee as above, $400 paid, a Negro boy named GEORGE, 13 or 14 yrs old. Wit: BIRD SMITH, TURNER LANE.

Page 75 Bill of Sale 28 Dec 1811 EDWIN L HARRIS to Grantee above, $1300 paid, 5 Negroes to wit: ANTHONY, 25 yrs, JENNY, a yellow Negro woman, 19 yrs, and Jenny's 3 children LOUISA, HANNAH, and an infant boy child. Wit: HOWEL G HARRIS, JOHN B LONG.

Page 76 Power of Attorney 6 Feb 1812 WILLIAM ROBINSON appoints friend THOMAS HERBERT to defend a suit now pending in White County wherein myself and NATHANIEL HERBERT are defendants and JOHN TATE, plaintiff. Wit: ZACHARIAH ANDERSON, SARAH ROBINSON.

Page 77 Indenture 23 Jan 1812 BENJAMIN WEAVER and WILLIAM HAYS, $600 paid, land beg on NE side Cherry creek, 80 or 90 acres. Wit: ELIJAH CHISUM, Senr, BENJAMIN ROSE.

Page 79 Indenture 25 Jan 1812 THOMAS K HARRIS of Sparta, one part, and ELISHA WALLING, other part, $1200 paid, 343 acres in 1st Dist on E side Caney fork and being part of Harris Grant No 640 for 640 acres.

Page 81 Indenture Date and Grantor as above, to THOMAS ROBINSON, $1000 paid, 297 acres in above named Harris Grant 640.

Page 83 Indenture 23 Dec 1811 Grantor as above, to EDWARD GLENN, $1200 paid, 400 acres on Caney fork. Wit: BIRD SMITH, TURNER LANE.

Page 85 Indenture 12 Aug 1811 DAVID M DANIEL and JOHN DALE, $1350 paid, tr of 230 acres in Hickory valley, it being part Grant 310 issued by NC and beg in W line of JOHN WHITE and adj DAVID NICHOLDS line. Wit: TURNER LANE, JOSEPH SMITH.

Page 88 Indenture 11 Nov 1811 THOMAS SHIRLY and WILLIAM MEDCALF, one part, and LEWIS ROBINSON, other part, $500 paid, 100 acres on head waters of Calf Killer fork, being same where GEORGE RUSSELL now lives. Wit: WOODSON P WHITE , JACOB A LANE.

Page 89 Land Grant No 3257 24 July 1811 TENNESSEE for military service by DAVID GRANT to NC, Warr No 3761, dated 6 Sept 1792, entered on 28 Aug 1807, No 185, TN grants to NATHANIEL TAYLOR, assee of sd Grant, 99 acres, part of sd Warr, being in 3rd Dist on Falling waters of Caney fork joining his entry of 90 acres on S side.

Page 91   Land Grant No 3255   24 July 1811   TENNESSEE for military service by GRANT (as above), 90 acres to above Grantee as assignee.

Page 92   Land Grant No 640   8 Nov 1808   TENNESSEE by part of Certif No 248 dated 15 Aug 1807 from W TN by LEWIS BEARD, grants to THOMAS K HARRIS, assee of sd Beard, 640 acres on E side of Caney fork.

Page 94   Indenture   4 Apr 1811   JOHN MCBRIDE and ROLAND LEE, $600 paid, tr of 145 acres on NE side Cherry creek, a branch of Calf Killer fork.   Wit: OLLIVER BADGER, JAMES MCBRIDE.

Page 96   Indenture   14 Feb 1812   MORGAN BRYAN and JOSEPH WALLING, $50.00 paid, 50 acres.   Wit: A MCBRIDE and unreadable name.

Page 98   Indenture   1 Feb 1812   RAWLEIGH RALLS, late of White Co, TN, by his Atty in fact JOHN KNOWLES, one part, and JOHN KNOWLES (relationship not stated), other part, $400 paid, 300 acres on Caney fork granted by TN to sd Ralls by Patent No 3501, beg near Hickory Nut mountain and E of road leading from Alexandria to Rock Island.   Grantor states he would not be liable if prior claim was found legal.

Page 100   Indenture   6 Jan 1812   EDMUND HARRISON of Sparta, and EDWARD FOSTER, also of sd town, $500 paid, Lot 51 in the town.   Wit: JACOB A LANE, JAMES HERON.

Page 102   Indenture   26 Nov 1811   WILLIAM ROBERTSON, Claibourne Co, TN, and THOMAS HARBERT, $2500 paid, tr lying E of Calf Killers fork, and being 400 acres.   Wit: As above.

Page 105   Indenture   12 May 1812   White Co Commissioners (THOMAS ROUNDS, AARON ENGLAND, BENJAMIN WEAVER, TURNER LANE, JAMES FULKINSON, ALEXANDER LOWREY and NICHOLAS GILLENTINE) one part, and PETER ALEXANDER of Sparta, second part, for $10.31 1/4 paid, Lot 35 in Sparta.

Page 107   Indenture   16 May 1812   PETER ALEXANDER, one part, WINEFRED THOMAS, other part, $20.00 paid, Lot 35 in Sparta.

Page 108   Indenture   17 Dec 1811   White Co Commiss (as on p 105), and LAWSON NOURSE, $17.00 paid, Lot 73 in Sparta.

Page 111   Indenture   24 Jan 1812   White Co Commiss (as on p 105), and Grantee as above, $10.00 paid, Lot 74 in Sparta.

Page 113   Indenture   28 Mar 1812   JOHN W SIMPSON and WILLIAM GLENN, latter of Sparta, $19.00 paid, Lot 13 in Sparta.   Wit: JNO JETT, JOHN GLENN.

Page 115   Indenture   Date and Grantor above, to WILLIAM GLENN, of Sparta, $100 paid, Lot 12 in Sparta.   Wit: As above.

Page 117   Indenture   24 Jan 1812   Commiss of White County and DRURY PUCKET, $30.62 1/2 paid, Lot 27 in Sparta.

Page 119   Indenture   23 Jan 1812   Parties as in above deed, $25.00 paid, Lot 31 in Sparta.

Page 121   Indenture   12 Nov 1810   Commiss of White Co (as in above deeds), to ANDREW SMITH, $77.00 paid, Lot 5 in Sparta.

Page 123   Indenture   18 Dec 1811   Commiss of White Co (as in above deeds), to THOMAS TAYLOR, $20.25 paid, Lot 48 in Sparta.

Page 125   Indenture   18 Dec 1811   Commiss of White Co (as above), to Grantee above, $20.12 1/2 paid, Lot 49 in Sparta.

Page 127   Indenture   24 Jan 1812   Commiss of White Co (as above), to ISAAC TAYLOR, $15.25 paid, Lot 77 in Sparta.

Page 129   Indenture   22 Jan 1812   Commiss of White Co, TN to ISAAC TAYLOR, Junr, $20.00 paid, Lot 34 in Sparta.

Page 131   Indenture   Date and parties as above, $18.50 paid, Lot 56 in Sparta.

Page 133   Indenture   16 Dec 1811   Commiss of White Co, TN (as listed above) to JACOB A LANE, Lot 30 in Sparta.

Page 135   Indenture   Date and parties as in above deed, Lot 32 in Sparta.

Page 137   Indenture   Date and Grantors as above, to ALEXANDER LOWREY, $19.50 paid, Lot 54 in Sparta.

Page 139   Indenture   12 Nov 1810   Grantors as above, to JOHN W SIMPSON, $202.00 paid, Lot 12 in Sparta.

Page 140   Indenture   19 Dec 1811   Grantors and Grantee as above, $30.00 paid, Lot 13 in Sparta.

Page 142   Indenture   20 Jan 1812   Grantors as above, to GEORGE W GIBBS, $29.00 paid, Lot 33 in Sparta.

Page 144   Indenture   23 Jan 1812   Grantors & Grantees as above, $11.00 paid, Lot 55 in Sparta.

Page 146   Indenture   17 Dec 1811   Grantors as above to EDWARD HARRISON, $25.12 1/2 paid, Lot 53 in Sparta.

Page 149   Indenture   Date and parties as above, $30.00 paid, Lot 50 in Sparta.

Page 151   Land Grant No 3028   17 Apr 1811   TENNESSEE by virtue Certif 2, 10 Jan 1810, issued to ISAAC TAYLOR, entered on 29 May 1810 by No 1019, TN grants to DREWRIE MAINSARD, assee of sd Taylor, tr of 88 acres in 3rd Dist on S side main Caney fork.

Page 152   Land Grant No 3029   Date & Grantor above, part of sd Certif is issued to JOHN GRIGGS, assee sd Taylor, 12 acres in same area.

Page 153   Indenture   11 Feb 1812   EDMOND HARRISON and EDWARD FOSTER, $100 paid, Lot 50 in Sparta.   Wit: JACOB A LANE, JAMES HERON.

Page 155   Indenture   20 Oct 1811   JAMES HERON and BENJAMIN BURDIN, $550 paid, Lot 11 in Sparta.   Wit: JOHN E CONN, ELIJAH CHISUM.

Page 157   Indenture   28 Jan 1812   BENJAMIN BURDIN and WILLIAM BURDIN (relationship not given), $1000 paid, Lot 11 in Sparta.   Wit: WILL GAIRY, ELISABETH BURDIN.

Page 159   Indenture   15 Jan 1812   NATHAN WOODS and MARGARET BOYED(?), $200 paid, tr of 100 acres of Grant No 3496.   Wit: WOODSON P WHITE, DAVID HASTON, WILLIAM GLENN.

Page 161   Indenture   9 May 1812   WILLIAM BROWER and ISAIAH SHOCKLEY, $400 paid, tr of 100 acres out of grant from state for 267 acres.   Wit: NICHOLAS GILLENTINE, NATHAN WOODS, THOMAS GEORGE(?).

Page 163   Bill of Sale   24 Dec 1810   SAMUEL ENGLISH to ISAAC TAYLOR, Junr, $300 paid, 1 yellow boy slave named JERRY, 9 or 10 yrs old.   Wit: REUBEN RAGLAND, THOMAS ROUNDS.

Page 164   Bill of Sale   3 Feb 1812   EDWARD GLEASON to Grantor as above, $500 paid, a Negro woman slave named JENNY, aged 26 yrs and her sucking child named STEPHEN, about 5 months old.   Wit: JOHN GLEASON, JAMES GLEASON.

Page 165   Indenture   25 Jan 1812   THOMAS K HARRIS and THOMAS ROBINSON, $84.00 paid, 28 acres in 1st Dist on Caney fork (part of same land sd Harris holds by Grant No 3579) for 500 acres.

Page 167   Indenture   14 May 1812   WILLIAM B USSERY and BENJAMIN GRIFFITH, $200 paid, 66 acres on Calf Killers fork, being Grant No 3502.   Wit: CALEB FRALEY, THOMAS USSERY, ROBERT PERRIN.

Page 170   Land Grant No 341(?)   1 Mar 1797   NORTH CAROLINA to ROBERT KING, assee of JAMES WILLIAMS, 2500 acres in middle Dist on Cane creek, a branch of Caney fork.

Volume E
June 1812 - Feb 1817

Page 1 Land Grant No 2568   29 Sept 1810   TENNESSEE by virtue part of Certif 303, dated 19 Aug 1809, entered by No 4478, grants to MORGAN BRYAN, assee of THOMAS DILLON, 39 acres on Calf Killers fork.

Page 2 Land Grant No 2756 22 Dec 1810   Grantor above for military serv by EDWARD CARTER of NC, Warr No 58, dated 24 Nov 1802, entered on 8 May 1809 by No 3390, grants to AQUILA GREER, assee of heirs of sd Carter, tr of 640 acres, part of sd Warr in 1st Dist, 1st Range & 8th sec on Caney fork, adj line of JOHN WALLING.

Page 3 Deed of Gift 4 May 1812   THOMAS STONE for love he has for his son, IREBY W B STONE, tr on Cane creek, a branch of Caney fork and being part of 2500 ac tr orig granted by NC to ROBERT KING, assee of JAMES WILLIAMS, Jr, all household goods, horses, cattle, and 1 Negro girl about 3 yrs old named MINTA.

Page 4 Indenture 3 Aug 1811   WILLIAM BRYAN, Senr, Overton County, and JAMES R BRYAN, one part, and TURNER LANE, other part, $900 paid, 170 acres in Hickory valley on main fork of Caney fork adj 150 acre sur of JOHN BRYAN. Wit: JOHN BRYAN, ALEXANDER LOWRY.

Page 5 Bill of Sale 22 Aug 1810   WILLIAM BROWN and SAMUEL WHITE, to ISAAC MIDKIFF, $500 paid, 1 Negro woman slave named MILLEY, about 30 yrs old, and also 1 Negro child slave named VINEY, about 1 month. Wit: JOSEPH SMITH, MARY SMITH.

Page 5 Sheriff's Deed _ __ 1812   ISAAC TAYLOR, Shff, and GEORGE W GIBBS, by writ ordering sale 38 acres where JAMES HERON now lives, 2 town lots in Sparta (6 and 25), Heron being surv partner of HERON KING & CO. $360 paid.

Page 7 Sheriff's Deed 7 Nov 1810 WILLIAM PHILLIPS, Shff, one part, and THOMAS WITCHER, Warren Co, TN, THOMAS TAYLOR, Jr, and JESSE MURPHREY, other part, by direction of Ct at their May session 1809, gave judg to Shff to sell tr in name of CAMPBELL & PHILLIPS, 640 acres of ROBERT KING, including McClure's Battleground, land of NATHAN GOODWIN, 640 ac of WILLIAM HOGG in a remarkable bend of the Caney fork. Wit: BRITAIN BAILEY.

Page 9 Sheriff's Deed 6 May 1812   ISAAC TAYLOR, Junr, Shff in behalf of WILLIAM PHILLIPS, former Shff, one part, and JOSEPH PARKER, by direction of Court conveys 1000 acres on Caney fork on creek known as Cherry creek, or enough to pay taxes, land of JOHN WILLIAMS to whom it was granted by NC - $10.50 paid.

Page 11 Land Grant No 3500 23 Oct 1811   TENNESSEE by virtue Certif 85 dated 10 Sept 1808 to ROBERT BARNET(?), entered 23 Feb 1811 by No 1330, grants HERETUS OGLE, assee of Barnet, 50 acres in 3rd District.

Page 11 Indenture (No date)   STOCKLEY DONNELSON and BURR POWELL, latter of Virginia, 2 tracts on waters of Caney fork, each 640 acres. Wit: JAMES WATSON, NATHAN B MARKLAND, SAMUEL A LOVE. Ack by Markland in Knox Co, TN on 14 Aug 1812 before FRANCIS A RAMSEY, Clk CCKC, by his deputy JOHN N GAMBLE. Map dated 9 Feb 1797, with certif from Donnelson stating lots sold to JOHN B ARMISTEAD. Wit: GEO T TOD. Sale by Armistead to Powell dated 29 Aug 1800. Wit: HUGH MINOR.

Page 14 Indenture 31 July 1812 THOMAS BOUNDS and THOMAS LOVELADY, 50 cents pd, tr on Caney fork & being 109 acres, part of tr granted by TN to Bounds and Lovelady dated 26 Feb 1810. Wit: REUBIN RAGLAND.

Page 15 Indenture 1 Aug 1812 Above Bounds and Lovelady, one part, and JOHN CROOK, Senr, other part, tr on falling water of Caney fork being 20 acres beg on Lovelady's cor on S bdy of 560 acre sur, and being part of tr granted by Tennessee to sd Bounds and Lovelady. Wit: REUBIN RAGLAND, AAROW PERROW.

Page 16 Indenture 16 Jan 1811 JAMES COLES and JOHN WOMACK, $209 paid, tr on Post Oak creek, a branch of Caney fork, 209 acres. Wit: THOMAS CRUTCHER, CHARLES ISHAM.

Page 18 Indenture ____ 1812 THOMAS BOUNDS and THOMAS LOVELADY, one part, and JAMES BOUNDS, other part, (relationships not stated) 60 cents paid, tr on Falling waters of Caney fork, 240 acres being part of tr granted Grantors herein by Tennessee. Wit: REUBEN RAGLAND, AARON PERROW.

Page 19 Indenture ____ 1812 Grantors above to JOHN CROOK, Senr, 42 cents paid, tr on Falling waters of Caney fork, 84 acres. Wit: RICHARD RAGLAND, AARON PERREN(?).

Page 20 Indenture Date and Grantors as above, to REUBEN RAGLAND, other part, 55 cents pd, 110 acres. Wit: JOHN CROOK, AARON PERREN.

Page 22 Indenture 15 Jan 1812 WILLIAM R COLE and SOLOMON COX, one part, and JOHN CROOK, Senr, other part, $200 pd, tr on Falling waters of Caney fork and being 50 acres. Wit: THOMAS CRUTCHER, JOHN CRELEY GOOLSBY, RICHARD HILL.

Page 23 Indenture 11 Nov 1811 THOMAS CRUTCHER and WILLIAM DYER, $340 paid, tr part of 640 acres granted by NC to JAMES EASTON the 27 Mar 1796 and beg on S bdy of tract, cor of JACOB ROBINSON, being 140 acres. Wit: JAMES COLE, WILLIAM HOWARD.

Page 24 Indenture ____ 1812 THOMAS ROUNDS and THOMAS LOVELADY, one part, and AARON PERRIN, other part, 50 cents paid, tr on falling waters of Caney fork, 85 acres beg in line of Military Reservation line where line between Jackson County and White County crosses, sd Mil line being part of a 560 acre sur of Rounds & Lovelady. Wit: REUBIN RAGLAND, JOHN CROOK.

Page 25 Indenture 15 July 1812 Commissioners of White County (THOMAS ROUNDS, AARON ENGLAND, BENJAMIN WEAVER, TURNER LANE, ALEXANDER LOWREY, JAMES FULKERSON and NICHOLAS GILLENLEND) and BIRD SMITH, $26.50 paid, Lot 91 in Sparta.

Page 26 Indenture 18 July 1812 Grantors as above and BIRD SMITH, $18.00 paid, Lot 90 in Sparta.

Page 27 Indenture Date, Grantors and Grantee as above, $20.00 paid, Lot 64 in Sparta.

Page 28   Indenture   20 July 1812   Grantors and Grantee as above, $30.00 paid, Lot 76 in Sparta.

Page 29   Indenture   15 July 1812   Grantors & Grantee as above, $15.62 1/2 paid, Lot 89 in Sparta.

Page 31   Indenture   18 July 1812   Parties as in above deed, $19.00 paid, Lot 43 in Sparta.

Page 32   Indenture   Date & Parties as above, $20.00 paid, Lot 42 in Sparta.

Page 33   Indenture   20 July 1812   Parties as in above deed, Lot 78 in Sparta.

Page 34   Land Grant No 678   8 Dec 1808   TENNESSEE by virtue part of Certif 237, dated 13 Aug 1807, to THOMAS DILLON, 50 acres to WILLIAM IRWIN, assee, tr being in 1st Dist, 1st Range & 8th Sec on N fork of Taylors creek of Caney fork.

Page 35   Land Grant No 3027   17 Apr 1811 Grantor above for military serv by PATRICK CARNEY to NC, Warr No 5191, dated 9 Dec 1797, 50 acres to WILLIAM IRWIN, assee, part of sd warr being in 1st Dist on waters of Caney fork.

Page 35   Land Grant No 2022   16 Mar 1802(?)   Grantor above by Warr No 228 dated 14 May 1803 to SAMUEL JACKSON, entered 31 Aug 1807 by No 498, is granted to RICHARD PORTERFIELD, assee of sd Jackson, 50 acres in 1st Dist, 2nd Range & 7th Sec.

Page 36   Land Grant No 2024   16 Mar 1810   TENNESSEE for Military service by SAMUEL PRICE to NC, Warr 4051 on 1 Dec 1796, entered on 20 Apr 1808 by No 1, as an Occupant claim under Law of 1807, is granted to Grantee as above, 260 acres, part of sd Warr in 1st Dist on head of S fork of falling waters.

Page 37   Indenture   9 Mar 1811   CHARLES MCCLUNG, Knox Co, TN, one part, and ROBERT D PIERCE, Campbell Co, TN, $200 paid, tr of 100 acres in 3rd Dist in the Hickory valley on waters of main fork of Caney fork adj THOMAS M CORRES(?).   Wit: ROBERT MILLER, HUGH MCCLUNG.   Ack before JOHN N GAMBLE, KCT.

Page 39   Land Grant No 3254   24 July 1811   TENNESSEE for Military serv by DAVID GRANT to NC, Warr No 3761, 6 Sept 1792, entered 15 Aug 1807 by No 53, grants to NATHANIEL TAYLOR, assee, 35 acres, part sd Warr lying in 3rd Dist on Falling waters Caney fork & in 16th Sec adj HENRY BOHANNON Entry No 52 on W, tr crossing line of Jackson County.

Page 40   Land Grant No 1837   10 Jan 1810   Grantor above by part of Certif 63, 21 July 1807 obtained by THOMAS DILLON on 7 Aug 1808 by No 537, grants to STEPHEN CRANE, assee Dillon, 100 acres in 3rd Dist on Cane creek of main fork Caney fork, adj ISAAC BROWN 100 acres.

Page 41   Bill of Sale   4 Aug 1812   WILLIAM CHISUM, of Warren Co, TN, to JOHN CHISUM (relationship not stated), $1000 paid, horses, cattle and hogs. Wit: GEO C WITT, ISAAC TAYLOR, Jnr.

Page 41   Indenture   20 July 1812   White County Commissioners (as listed in previous deeds) and ROBERT HOWARD, $20.00 paid, Lot 65 in Sparta.

Page 43   Indenture   5 Aug 1812   Grantors as above, to NATHAN HAGGARD, Jackson County, $8.50 paid, Lot 83 in Sparta.

Page 44   Indenture   22 Aug 1812   JOSEPH CUMMINGS and DAVID CUMMINGS (relationship not stated), $120 paid, 30 acres on S side of Caney fork being part Grant 2086.

Page 45   Indenture   20 Nov 1811   JOSHUA BADGER, Junr, Jackson Co, TN, and JOHN H BADGER, $550 pd, 100 acres in 1st Dist in 9th Sec of 1st Range. Wit: HENRY BROOKS, NATHAN SMITH. Ack JOHN ROWEN, Clk JCT.

Page 46   Indenture   27 Jan 1812   WILLIAM P ANDERSON, Davidson Co, TN, and JOHN MCIVER, Fairfax Co, VA, by their Atty in fact ISAAC TAYLOR of the one part and CURTIS MILLS of White Co, TN, $400 paid, 540 acres on Caney fork, orig granted by NC to JAMES EASTON, assee of heirs of JAMES MCADOE(?). Wit: J MCBRIDE, ELIJAH CHISUM, Sur.

Page 47   Indenture   1 Aug 1812   JOHN OGEE, one part, and HERCULES OGEE, Senr, other part, (relationship not stated), $76.00 paid, tr on Cane creek, part of tr granted by W TN to Ogee, 73 acres. Wit: ROBERT WATSON(?), LEVI DAN_, JEREMIAH WINKLER.

Page 49   Indenture   30 July 1812   Parties as in above Indenture, $275 paid, tr of 108 acres & 32 poles, tr being on Cane creek, a part of tr granted by W TN to sd John Ogee No 63. Wit: As above.

Page 50   Indenture   16 Jan 1812   CHARLES MITCHELL and DAVID HASTON, $610 paid, interest vested in Grantor by Grant No 529 issued to ISHAM BRADLEY on 26 Sept 1808, tr of 50 acres in 3rd Dist on Big spring branch.

Page 51   Indenture   28 Apr 1812   JOHN MILLER, Senr, one part, and JACOB MILLER, other part, for natural love & affec John has for his son Jacob, and for better maintenance of sd Jacob, 160 acres in 1st Dist, 1st Range & 9th Sec on waters of Caney fork. Wit: WILLIAM WINTER, JAMES ANDERSON.

Page 53   Indenture   23 Mar 1812   JOHN ALLEN and JOSEPH ANDERSON, $450 paid, 125 acres on N side Caney fork, being part of 2 grants (2087 & 2089) issued to ELIJAH CHISUM. Wit: BENJAMIN WEAVER, WILLIAM HAYES. Reg 7 Nov 1812 before sd Chisum, Reg, White County.

Page 54   Indenture   27 July 1812   JOHN WOMACK, Jackson Co, TN, one part, and WILLIAM PARKISON, $500 paid, tr on Post Oak creek, a branch of Caney fork of Cumberland, being 209 3/4 acres. Wit: THOMAS BOUNDS, AARON ENGLAND.

Page 55   Land Grant No 1833   10 Jan 1810   TENNESSEE by virtue of part of Certif No 5, 9 July 1807, to MARTIN ARMSTRONG and entered on 27 Aug 1807 by No 158, there is granted by TN to DAVID MITCHELL, assee of sd Armstrong, a tr of 70 acres in 3rd Dist on Calf Killer fork of Caney fork adj WILLIAM CLARY 101 acre sur on his S bdy.

Page 56   Land Grant No 1834   Same date and parties as above, 100 acres.

Page 57   Land Grant No 1835   20 Apr 1811   TENNESSEE to JOHN SMALLWOOD(?), assee of ROBERT GAMMELL(?) for sd Gammell's military service to NC, Warr 5173, dated 9 Dec 1797, 50 acres in 1st Dist, 1st Range & 10th Sec on S side of Caney fork in Buck Cove.

Page 58   Land Grant No 2634   23 Oct 1810   TENNESSEE to JOSEPH FRANKS, assee of THOMAS DILLON, 50 acres in 1st Dist, 2nd Range & 10th Sec on N side Caney fork.

Page 59   Land Grant No 3110   12 June 1811   TENNESSEE to ALIJAH CRANE, assee of ROBERT BARNETT, by Certif 85, dated 10 Sept 1808, entered as an occupant claim under Act of 1800, 50 acres in 3rd Dist on Cane creek, adj WILLIAM BROWN 100 acres.

Page 60   Indenture   7 Aug 1812   JOHN WILLIAMS and JONATHAN EAVES, $20.50 paid, Lot 26 in town of Sparta. Wit: DAVID PHELPS, LUCY PHELPS.

Page 61   Indenture   29 Oct 1812   WILLIAM ROWLAND, Knox Co, TN, and JESSE MANARD, $500 paid, tr on Cane creek of main Caney fork, being 60 acres. Wit: J A LANE, WILL GLENN.

Page 63   Land Grant No 4172   21 Sept 1812 & of US Indepen the 37th TENNESSEE by virtue part Certif 176 dated 25 Dec 1810 issued to JOHN MCIVER, tr of 60 acres in 3rd Dist on Cane creek of main Caney fork.

Page 64   Indenture   14 Nov 1812   DAVID PHELPS and JOSEPH CAPLIN, $100 paid, Lot 88 in Sparta.

Page 66   Indenture   7 Sept 1812   JOHN GARNETT(?), Barren Co, KY, one part, and JOHN JETT, $100 paid, Lot 31 in Sparta. Wit: GEORGE C WITT, J A LANE.

Page 67   Indenture   17 Dec 1811   JAMES FULKERSON and ISAAC PLUMBLEY, $220 paid, part of a 314 acre tr (part Grant 310) issued by NC to JOHN RHEA and WILLIAM TYRRELL, 110 acres. Wit: DAVID MITCHELL, SPENCE MITCHELL.

Page 68   Land Grant No 1739   24 Nov 1809   TENNESSEE by virtue of part of Warr 1686, dated 19 Feb 1787 issued to DAVID ROSS by JOHN ARMSTRONG entry officer of claims for NC, grants to DANIEL ALEXANDER, assee of sd Ross, 50 acres in Overton County, 3rd Dist, 13th & 16th Sec.

Page 69   Land Grant No 3910   18 May 1812   TENNESSEE in consideration of military serv by HARDY HARDISON to NC, Warr No 4175, dated 8 Dec 1796 and entered 13 Aug 1807 by No 46, there is granted by TN to DANIEL ALEXANDER, assee of heirs of sd Hardison, tr of 122 1/2 acres, part sd Warrant and lying in 3rd Dist & 16th Sec. Tr adj WILLIAM PRYOR tr. Sur 31 May 1811 by JAMES CHISUM, DS.

Page 70   Land Grant No 3911   18 May 1812   TENNESSEE for military service by NICHOLAS RODIN(?) to NC, Warr 5090, dated 6 Dec 1797, entered 23 Feb 1809 by No 739, there is granted by TN to DANIEL ALEXANDER, assee of heirs of sd Rodin, 54 acres part of sd Warr, in 3rd Dist in the Dry valley.

Page 71   Indenture   4 May 1811   RICHARD BRASEL, by his Agent SAMUEL USSERY, one part, and WILLIAM B USSERY, other part, (relationship not stated), $400 paid, 100 acres on N side of Calf Killer fork of Caney fork.

Wit: JAMES COOPER, _____ TABOR, HENRY PEARROW(?).

Page 72   Indenture   9 Nov 1812   ROBERT G ANDERSON and JOHN SCOGGON, $300 paid, 117 acres in Hickory valley, a part of a 400 acre sur Grantor hold by deed from THOMAS M CORRY.

Page 73   Indenture   5 Nov 1812   JOHN SMALLWOOD and NICHOLAS GILLINTINE, $200 paid, 50 acres in 1st Dist, 1st Range & 10th Sec on S side of Caney fork in Beech cove.   Wit: JOSEPH CUMMINGS, DAVID HASTON, NATHAN WOODS.

Page 74   Indenture   5 Nov 1812   JOSEPH FRANK and JOSEPH CLARK, $200 paid, tr in 1st Dist, 2nd Range & 9th Sec on N side Caney fork, 50 acres.   Wit: WILLIAM FISHER, JAMES NAYLOR, Senr.

Page 75   Bill of Sale   4 Sept 1812   WILLIAM ROBERTSON to PHILLIP HUGGINS, 1 Negro girl named HANNAH, $150.00 paid.   Wit: WILLIAM MAY, ELIJAH CHISUM.

Page 75   Receipt   12 Nov 1809   THOMAS B SAMPLE received as an heir of ROBERT ENGLISH, Decd, of Buck County, in full of my part of aforesd decd estate.   Wit: REUBIN RAGLAND.

Page 76   Indenture   2 Jan 1813   ROBERT D PEARCE, Campbell Co, TN, and ISAAC BRASELTON, Anderson Co, TN, $400 paid, tr of 100 acres in 3rd Dist in Hickory valley on main fork of Caney fork adj THOMAS M CORRY 500 acre sur on his N bdy, and also adj W bdy line of JOHN BRYAN 150 acre sur.   Wit: J DEHART, JOHN DUNNAM.   Ack by sd Dunnam (or DENNISON) in Anderson County by HUGH BARTON, Clk, by his Dep JAMES MORTON.

Page 77   Land Grant No 4311   9 Oct 1812   TENNESSEE by virtue part of Certif No 64 dated 21 July 1807, from West TN, obtained by THOMAS DILLON & entered on 29 Sept 1807 by No 897, there is granted to LEWIS POWELL, assee of sd Dillon, tr of 50 acres in 1st Dist, 1st Range & 9th Sec.   Sur 20 Feb 1812 by JAMES TOWNSEND, DS.

Page 78   Land Grant No 3454   24 Sept 1811   TENNESSEE by part Certif 235 dated 13 Apr 1809 obtained by above named Dillon, grants JOHN TEMPLETON, assee, 80 acres.

Page 79   Land Grant No 4312   9 Oct 1812   Grantor as above for military serv by LEWIS GUTHERIDGE(?) to NC, Warr No 4378, dated 20 Dec 1796, entered 8 Jan 1812 by 7407, TN grants to JOHN TEMPLETON, assee of heirs of sd Gutheridge, 40 acres, part pf sd warr on 1st Dist, adj line of RAWLEY RAWLIN 300 acre Occupant claim.

Page 80   Land Grant No 3453   24 Sept 1811   Grantor as above by virtue part Certif 235, dated 13 Apr 1809, to JOHN TEMPLETON, assee of THOMAS DILLON, tr of 20 acres in 1st Dist on Caney fork.

Page 82   Sheriff's Deed   13 May 1812   ISAAC TAYLOR, Junr, Shff, one part, and WILLIAM TRIGG, surviving Executor of WILLIAM KING, Decd, of Washington Co, VA, other part, by Court order that lands, etc, of JAMES HERON, surviving partner of HERON KING & CO in White County, be sold, Lots 6, 7 & 25 in Town of Sparta are conveyed.

Page 83   Sheriff's Deed   12 May 1812   Parties as above, Lots 3 & 4 in

Sparta, and several tracts of land.

Page 85   Land Grant No 4450   TENNESSEE, for military serv by HARDY HARDESON to NC, Warr No 4175, dated 8 Dec 1796, grants to DANIEL ALEXANDER, assee of heirs of sd Hardison, 37 1/2 acres beg at foot of a mountain S of NW cor entry of THOMAS COLDWELL, No 44, 200 acres.

Page 86   Power of Attorney   17 Nov 1808   VINSON TURNER to JOHN TURNER to act for him in Madison Co, KY or elsewhere in sd state.

Page 87   Indenture   28 Jan 1813   JOHN W SIMPSON and WILLIAM GLENN, $100 paid, a part of Lot 12 in Sparta.   Wit: ROBERT PUCKET, ALEXANDER LOWREY.

Page 89   Indenture   Date & Parties as above, $19.00 paid, Lot 13 in Sparta. Wit: As above.

Page 90   Indenture   26 Feb 1813   WILLIAM GIST and JOHN JETT, $113.50 paid, 19 1/4 acres, part of 200 acres in name of WILLIAM ROBERSON and sd Gist. Wit: WILLIAM GLENN, ALEXANDER LOWREY.

Page 91   Indenture   26 Nov 1812   JOSEPH ROBERSON and JOHN JETT, $700 paid, tr on Calf Killer fork of Caney fork, being 99 acres & 2 roods, part of 200 acre sur held by Grant No 1830.   Wit: EDWARD FOSTER, LAWSON NOURSE.

Page 92   Indenture   9 Feb 1813   MORGAN BRIANT and ANDREW COPE, $30.00 paid, tr of 40 acres in 1st Dist on N side Caney fork, adj ELISHA WALLING sur.

Page 93   Indenture   19 Dec 1812   JOHN WILLIAMSON and ISHAM GOAD, $400 paid, 3 tracts as set out therein (adj Rutledges Mill creek).   Wit: DANIEL NEWMAN, THOMAS K HARRIS, ADMISTON RODGERS.

Page 94   Land Grant No 2969   29 Mar 1811   TENNESSEE by virtue Warr No 8, dated 31 July 1807, issued to WILLIAM MITCHELL, Esq, Surveyor of 3rd Dist & entered on 3 Oct 1807 by No 438, there is granted to WILLIAM PRIOR, assee of Mitchell, 180 acres in 3rd Dist including where he lives in the dry valley, beg at NE cor DANIEL ALEXANDER.

Page 95   Land Grant No 2970   Same date and grantor as above, grants to WILLIAM PRIOR, assee of WILLIAM TATOM, assee of JOHN SULLIVAN, 50 acres.

Page 96   Indenture   4 Mar 1813   THOMAS K HARRIS and ELISHA WALLING, $200 paid, tr on waters of Caney fork, being 58 acres.

Page 97   Indenture   Same date and Grantor as in above Indenture, and THOMAS WALLING, $300 paid, tr on Caney fork and being 89 1/4 acres on Caney fork.

Page 98   Indenture   10 Sept 1812   Commissioners of Town of Petersburg (ROBERT GREEN, JOHN WALLING, EDMUND HARRISON and JOHN WILLIAMSON), one part, and JAMES NAILOR, other part, $25.00 paid, 1/2 acre and being Lot 4.

Page 99   Indenture   4 Nov 1812   Grantors and Grantee as above, $20.00 paid, Lot 7 in Petersburg.

Page 100   Indenture   5 Nov 1812   Commiss of Petersburg (ROBERT GLENN, JOHN

WALLING, EDMUND HARRISON, & JOHN WILLIAMSON, Senr) and CASON SWINDLE, $10.25 paid, Lot 22 in town of Petersburg.

Page 101 Indenture 6 Nov 1812 WILLIAM ROBERTSON and JOSEPH ROBERTSON (relationship not stated), $500 paid, 99 acres & 2 roods, part of 200 acre sur held by Grant 1830 issued by TN to sd Robertson and WILLIAM GIST on 10 Jan 1810. Wit: EDWIN L HARRIS, URIAH MURPHRESS.

Page 102 Land Grant No 2626 15 Oct 1810 TENNESSEE by Certif 322 of this same date, No 5312, as an Occupant claim under Act of 1807, grants to EZEKIEL RAY, assee of JOHN NICHOLAS, tr of 200 acres in 1st Dist, beg in E bdy line of WILLIAM KING.

Page 103 Indenture 4 Mar 1813 ELISHA WALLING and THOMAS WALLING (relationship not stated), $1000 paid, 125 acres beg on SE cor LEVI RODIN sur. Wit: JOHN SMITH.

Page 104 Land Grant No 542 26 Sept 1808 TENNESSEE for military serv by STEPHEN PERKINS to NC, Warr 2977, dated 27 Dec 1803, entered 2 Sept 1807 by No 591, grants to THOMAS TAYLOR, Senr, assee of heirs sd Perkins, tr of 50 acres part sd Warr being in 1st Dist on Taylors creek.

Page 105 Land Grant No 543 26 Sept 1808 TENNESSEE for military service by STEPHEN PERKINS as above described, grants Taylor as above, 200 acres.

Page 106 Land Grant No 3499 23 Oct 1811 TENNESSEE by virtue part Warr No 1642 dated 30 Nov 1784, issued to CHARLES ROBISON by JOHN C ARMSTRONG, entry officer of claims for NC Western lands & entered 22 June 1811 by No 1432, grants to WILLIAM ROGERS, assee sd Robison, tr of 100 acres lying in 3rd Dist on waters of Calf Killers fork of Caney fork.

Page 107 Indenture 13 Jan 1813 EDMUND BEAN and ANDREW S PUCKET, $30.00 paid, Lot 75 in Sparta. Wit: JACOB A LANE, GEORGE FOX.

Page 108 Land Grant No 3539 14 Nov 1811 TENNESSEE by part Certif 235, dated 13 Apr 1809, to THOMAS DILLON, entered 29 Sept 1809 by No 3954 as an Occupant claim, grants to JACOB DRAKE, assee sd Dillon, 102 acres in 1st Dist, 10th Sec in 1st Range, including improvement of THOMAS LAXRON, on S side Caney fork.

Page 109 Land Grant No 3540 Date & Grantor as above, for military serv by ROBERT GAMBLE to NC, Warr 5772, dated 9 Dec 1797, entered 21 July 1808 by No 2051, grants to JACOB DRAKE, assee Gamble, 100 acres, part sd Warr in same area as above grant.

Page 110 Land Grant No 1268 1 July 1809 Grantor as above, for military serv of DANIEL MCCLOUD to NC, Warr No 3398, dated 22 Dec 1796, entered 3 Apr 1809, No 3267, as Occupant claim, grants to BENJAMIN HAWKINS, assee McCloud, 211 acres, part sd Warr in 1st Dist on Caney fork on Rutledge's creek.

Page 111 Land Grant No 4119 8 Sept 1812 Above Grantor, by virtue part Warr 2618, dated 30 Nov 1784, issued to GRAY BYNUM in office of claims for NC Western lands, entered 30 Aug 1808 by No 561, TN grants tr of 150 acres in 3rd Dist on headwaters of Calf Killers fork of Caney fork.

Page 112 Indenture 26 Feb 1813 JACOB DRAKE, Warren Co, TN, one part and ABRAHAM DENTON and ABSALOM DENTON (relationship not stated), other part, $600 paid, tr of 100 acres in 1st Dist in 10th Sec of 1st Range on S side Caney fork, beg near present dwelling house of THOMAS LAXRON, adj JAMES HOLMES. Wit: ALEXANDER COOK, ROBERT ARMSTRONG.

Page 113 Indenture 26 Feb 1813 Grantor as above to SAMUEL DENTON, $600 paid, 102 acres in same area as above. Wit: ALEXANDER COOK, ROBT ARMSTRONG.

Page 114 Land Grant No 3789 3 Mar 1812 & of Indepen of US the 36th TENNESSEE by virtue part Certif 303, 19 Aug 1809, entered 28 Sept 1810 by No 5202, grants to MORGAN BRYAN, assee THOMAS DILLON, 40 acres in 1st Dist on N side Caney fork.

Page 115 Indenture 24 Feb 1813 ALEXANDER COOK and ROBERT BATES, $300 paid, 100 acres in 1st Dist on N side Caney fork. Wit: JOHN SHROPSHIRE, ELIJAH CHISUM.

Page 116 Indenture 20 Feb 1813 Grantor above and ELIJAH BATES, $300 paid, 100 acres in 1st Dist in 10th Sec & 1st Range. Wit: WILLIAM IRWIN, ELIJAH CHISUM.

Page 117 Indenture 7 July 1812 JOHN BEAN, Davidson Co, TN, and JESSE ALLEN, Smith Co, TN, $600 paid, tr of 100 acres. Wit: JAMES TABB, JAMES B MEREDITH, ___ ROBINSON, CONROD LAMBERSON, CHRISTOPHER ROBINSON, WM E PILLAR.

Page 118 Indenture Same date, Grantor and Grantee as above, $600 paid, 210 acres. Witnesses as above.

Page 119 Indenture 10 Feb 1812 DAVID THOMPSON and SAMUEL THOMAS, $100 paid, tr Thompson had by Grant No 3497, dated 23 Oct 1811, 83 acres. Wit: WILLIAM NEVILL, RICHARD LUNDY.

Page 120 Indenture 18 July 1812 THOMAS STONE and JESSE WILSON, $1.00 paid, a part of 2500 acre tr on Cane creek. Wit: IREBY W B STONE, JAMES CASH.

Page 121 Deed of Gift 4 Sept 1812 GREEN WOODS in consideration of natural love, etc, for eldest son WILLIAM C WOODS, and likewise my youngest son ALFRED H WOODS, 1 Negro man slave named DAVID, about 24 yrs, and for same natural love, etc, I have for second son MICHAEL L WOODS, 1 Negro woman slave named REBEKAH, about 14 yrs. Certif by GEO M GIBBS, Clk.

Page 121 Power of Attorney 20 Apr 1812 ARMISTEAD STUBBLEFIELD appoints GREEN WOODS as his atty for purpose of doing necessary things for Iron works. Wit: THOMAS HARBUT, JOHN MCELHANIE and HENRY COOK.

Page 122 Land Grant No 4174 21 Sept 1812 TENNESSEE by virtue part Certif 100 dated 29 Oct 1810 issued to THOMAS M CORRY and entered 23 Oct 1811 by No 1561, grants to THOMAS GEORGE, assee of Corry.

Page 123 Land Grant No 4178 Date & Grantor as in above Grant, to JOHN MCBRIDE, assee of JAMES P TAYLOR, 25 acres on S side Caney fork.

Page 124   Land Grant No 4179 .Date & Grantor as in above, to RICHARD WALLIS, assee of Taylor, as above, 15 acres in 3rd Dist on Cane creek.

Page 125   Land Grant No 3344   24 Aug 1811 TENNESSEE for military serv by JETHRO SUMNER to NC, Warr No 4338, dated 16 Dec 1796, & entered on 5 Apr 1809 by No 790, grants JOHN GRIGGS, assee of heirs of Sumner, 45 acres part of sd Warr and being on S side main Caney fork.

Page 126   Land Grant No 4176   21 Sept 1812 TENNESSEE by virtue Certif 284 dated 13 May 1811, issued on 8 Oct 1811 by No 1539, grants to JOHN ROBISON, assee of JAMES P TAYLOR, 60 acres.

Page 127   Land Grant No 4022   11 July 1812   Grantor as above by virtue part Certif 49, dated 30 May 1809, entered 12 Oct 1810 by No 1175, grants to GEORGE SUGG, assee heirs of JOHN ISH(?), 267 acres in a cove of a mountain on S side of main Caney fork adj DANIEL HORTON 150 acre sur.

Page 128   Land Grant No 4023 Date & Grantor as above, by part of Certif No 49 dated 30 May 1809 obtained by heirs of JOHN ISH on 12 Oct 1810 by No 1174, grants to HAREL SUGG, assee of sd heirs, 121 acres onmain or dry fork of Caney fork adj RILAND BURKS, occupant on E bdy.

Page 129   Land Grant No 4169   21 Sept 1812   TENNESSEE by virtue part Certif 322, dated 17 Sept 1811 issued to NATHANIEL TAYLOR, entered on 10 Feb 1812 by No 1665, grants to THOMAS FRANK, assee sd Taylor, tr of 30 acres on main Caney fork.

Page 130   Land Grant No 4094   26 Aug 1812   Grantor as above by part of Certif 42, dated 17 July 1807, entered on 19 July 1808 by No 524, grants to WILLIAM HAYS, assee JAMES MABANE, tr of 110 acres on Cherry creek, a tr of Calf Killer fork of Caney fork, tr adj ELIJAH CHISUM sur line and BENJAMIN WEAVER line.

Page 131   Land Grant No 4168   21 Sept 1812 Grantor as above, part of Certif No 322 dated 17 Sept 1871 and entered on 28 Mar 1812 by No 1739, grants to ALEXANDER FRASER, assee of NATHANIEL TAYLOR, 30 acres on main Caney fork & E of THOMAS FRASER.

Page 132   Indenture 3 Sept 1812   SAMUEL THOMAS and SAMUEL USSERY, $200 paid, interest of Thomas in Grant No 3497 dated 23 Oct 1811, tr of 83 acres. Wit: WILLIAM B USSERY, ROBERT BRASEL.

Page 133   Indenture 26 Jan 1813   SAMUEL THOMAS and ABRAHAM BRILES, $800 paid, 228 acres in 3rd Dist on Calf killer creek, beg near N bdy SHARP WHITLEY 115 acres. Wit: ABNER ROSE, REUBEN BRILES.

Page 134   Land Grant No 4180   21 Sept 1812   TENNESSEE by virtue part Certif No 104, dated 23 Mar 1810, issued to WILLIAM HENRY and entered 23 July 1811 by No 1454, grants to ISAAC PREWIT, assee sd Henry, 150 acres on waters of main Caney fork, adj 100 acre sur of JOSEPH SMITH and S bdy of THOMAS MEEK(?), sur 24 Apr 1812 by WOODSON P WHITE, DS.

Page 135   Indenture 6 Aug 1812   DAVID PHILPS and THOMAS WALTERS, latter of Sparta, $10.00 paid, Lot 75 in sd town. Wit: CHARLES ROBERSON and ALEXANDER THOMAS.

Page 136   Indenture   22 Jan 1812   THOMAS BOUNDS, JAMES ENGLAND, BENJAMIN WEAVER, TURNER LANE, JAMES FULKERSON, ALEXANDER LOWREY & NICHOLAS GILLENTINE, Commissioners in trust for County of White, one part, and DAVIDSON WILLIS, other part, $12.00 paid, Lot 15 in town of Sparta.

Page 137   Indenture   Same date and parties as in above deed, $36.00 paid, Lot 16 in sd town.

Page 138   Indenture   29 Dec 1812   DAVID SMYTH and ROBERT W ROBERTS, latter of Smith Co, TN, $30.00 paid, Lot 22 in Sparta. Wit: JACOB A LANE, GREEN WOODS.

Page 139   Indenture   3 Mar 1812   BENJAMIN BURDIN and WALTON LEDBETTER, latter of Lincoln County, $300 paid, Lot 8 in Sparta. Wit: JOHN C WILLIAMSON, HOWEL G HARRIS.

Page 140   Indenture   27 Feb 1813   JOHN OGLE and WILLIAM BARTON, $200 paid, tract in 3rd Dist on Cane creek of Caney fork adj THOMAS DILLON 200 acre survey.

Page 141   Indenture   25 Feb 1813   DAVID MITCHELL, Esq, one part, and JAMES BOWEN, other part, $100 paid, tr on Calf killer, being 15 acres. Wit: ARTHUR LEDBETTER, JOHN MITCHELL.

Page 142   Indenture   2 Mar 1813   JAMES SCARBROUGH and JAMES ROBINSON, $140 paid, 70 acres on Calf killers fork, it being part of Grant No 3120 issued to sd Scarbrough, beg in W line of THOMAS HARRIS Entry Location No 18, and adj a mountain. Wit: JACOB A LANE & ANDREW BURK.

Page 143   Indenture   16 Feb 1813   WILLIAM ROGERS, Barren Co, KY, one part, and JONAS TURNER, other part, $465 paid, 100 acres on waters of Calf killers fork which land was granted by TN to sd Rogers, Grant No 3499, which tr begins on W bdy of SAMUEL THOMAS 220 acre survey. Wit: J A LANE, DAVID SMYTH, RICHARD M ROTTON.

Page 144   Indenture   15 Dec 1812   JACOB BROWN, Washington Co, TN, and ANDREW TOWNSEND, $350 paid, 333 1/3 acres, being an undiv moiety of 1000 acres patented to STOCKLEY DONNELSON, WM TYRRELL & ROBERT KING, lying on Caney fork river including a lick, & on both sides of Taylor's creek. Wit: JOHN TOWNSEND, THOMAS J BROWN, WILLIAM BROWN.

Page 146   Indenture   1 Mar 1813   JOSEPH PARKER and CORDER STONE, $600 paid, 212 acres on Cherry creek a branch of Calf killers fork of Caney fork, being part of 1000 acres from NC to JOHN WILLIAMS, Patent No 312 & conv to sd Parker by Shff of White County on 6 May 1812.

Page 147   Indenture   12 Feb 1813   THOMAS WILCHER, Warren Co, TN, one part, and JACOB CATRON, other part, $640 paid, a tr of 640 acres on Caney fork, orig granted by NC to ROBERT KING by Patent 362 & conv to Wilcher by WILLIAM PHILLIPS, former Shff of White Co, on 13 Mar 1807, tr beg near an Indian old path near the foot of a steep hill. Wit: ISAAC TAYLOR, Junr, JACOB A LANE, HOWEL G HARRIS.

Page 149   Land Grant No 2651   29 Oct 1810   TENNESSEE for military service by JETHRO SUMNER to NC, Warr No 4338, 16 Dec 1796, entered on 9 Dec 1808,

No 541, grants to THOMAS WILSON, assee of Sumner, 39 1/2 acres, part sd Warr in 3rd Dist in Hickory valley adj sd Wilson forever, 100 acres on his N & E boundaries.

Page 150   Indenture 1 Mar 1813   WILLIAM P ANDERSON, Davidson Co, TN, and JOHN MCIVER of Fairfax Co, VA, by their Attorney in fact ISAAC TAYLOR, of one part, and JOHN HUTCHINGS, of other part, $310 paid, 640 acres on Caney fork orig granted by NC to JAMES EASTON, assee of heirs of WATRON REID by Patent No 2702.

Page 151   Indenture 1 Feb 1812   Parties as in above deed, $320 paid, 640 acres on Caney fork, tr orig granated by NC to above Easton, assee of heirs of JOHN DAVISS MOORE, by Patent No 2703. Wit: J M BILDO, ELIJAH CHISUM, Senr.

Page 152   Land Grant No 3100   11 June 1811   TENNESSEE for military serv of JETHRO SUMNER to NC, Warr No 4338, dated 16 Dec 1796, entered on 18 Nov 1808 by No 622, grants to ISAAC ANDERSON, assee of heirs of sd Sumner tr of 50 acres, part sd Warr in 3rd Dist & in the hickory valley.

Page 153   Land Grant No 4170   21 Sept 1812   TENNESSEE by virtue part of Certif 322 dated 17 Sept 1811, issued by E TN to NATHANIEL TAYLOR, entered 16 Mar 1812 by No 1712, grants to JESSE MAINSARD, assee of sd Taylor, tr of 20 acres in 3rd Dist on Cane creek, tr beg in S line of WILLIAM BOWMAN 61 acre survey.

Page 154   Land Grant No 2284   14 June 1810   TENNESSEE for military serv by STEPHEN MCDOWELL(?) to NC, Warr No 2937, dated 30 Sept 1785, entered on 1 Aug 1808 by No 533, grants to JOHN CHISUM, assee of heirs of sd McDowell, 50 acres part sd Warr in 3rd Dist on Calf killer fork of Caney fork, adj FREDERICK MELLER 150 acre sur, on his S bdy.   Tr sur on 19 Jan 1809 by ISAAC TAYLOR, Junr,DS.

Page 155   Indenture 15 May 1813   ISAAC ANDERSON and THOMAS WILSON, for $115 paid on 29 Feb 1812, tr of 50 acres in Hickory valley. Wit: JOHN BRYAN, WILLIAM WILSON.

Page 156   Indenture 7 June 1813   BLUFORD WARREN and JOHN DALE, $160 paid, tr conv to Grantor by JAMES R BRYAN for 130 acres and butting on Hickory valley, beg at NE cor of DAVID MCDANIELS survey.

Page 158   Bill of Sale 5 Jan 1813   REBEKAH HILL, JAMES HILL and WILLIAM HILL (relationships not stated) to MARGET CHISUM, 1 Negro girl ANNEY, about 14 yrs, $2.00 paid.

Page 158   Bill of Sale Same date, Seller & Buyer as in above Bill of Sale, $2.00 paid for one Negro girl EADY, about 26 or 27 yrs of age. Wit: THOS MCBRIDE, JAMES ANDERSON.

Page 159   Indenture 3 Feb 1813   LEWIS POWEL by his Atty in fact BENJAMIN HAWKINS, of one part, and JOHN TEMPLETON, other part, $500 paid for 50 acres in 1st Dist, 1st Range & 9th Sec, it being same land granted to Powel by TN by Grant No 4311, dated 9 Oct 1812. Wit: DANIEL NEWMAN, ALEXANDER GLENN.

Page 160 Indenture 8 June 1813 DANIEL ALEXANDER, Smith Co, TN, one part, and JOHN ROBERSON, other part, $700 paid for tr in 3rd Dist in the dry valley included in 3 grants (as set out therein). Wit: WM QUARLES, ROBERT READ.

Page 161 Indenture 12 June 1813 ANDREW SMITH and WILLIAM SIMPSON, $100 paid, Lot 5 in town of Sparta.

Page 162 Indenture 27 Aug 1812 RICHARD COLE, CALVIN HOWEL & JOHN HOWEL (relationship not stated), one part, and SAMUEL JOHNSTON, Esqr, other part, $400 paid, 1 tr on Cherry creek, beg on conditional line between THOMAS MCBRIDE and where Richard now lives, tr being 150 or 160 acres. Wit: MARSHAL DUNCAN, PETER PROW.

Page 163 Indenture 1 Mar 1813 JOHN TEMPLETON and JOHN KNOWLES, Senr, $20.00 paid, 5 acres & being part of 129 1/4 acres, and being in 1st Dist, and beg at SE cor JOHN KNOWLES. Wit: ELLISON RUTLEDGE, JAMES KNOWLES, JOSIAH HUNTER.

Page 164 Indenture 1 Mar 1813 JOHN KNOWLES and JOHN TEMPLETON, $20.00 paid, tr of 5 acres, a part of 20 acre sur granted to Templeton by TN, being in 1st Dist. Wit: ELLISON RUTLEDGE, JAMES KNOWLES, ISAIAH HUTRON.

Page 165 Indenture 5 Jan 1813 JAMES HILL and MARGARET CHISUM, of one part, and WILLIAM HILL and REBEKAH HILL, other part, $2.00 paid, sold to Rebekah & William all right we ever had as heirs of RICHARD HILL, Decd, to land near head of Cherry creek & being where William & Rebekah Hill now live, being 270 acres. Relationships are not stated. Wit: THOMAS MCBRIDE, ELIJAH WARD.

Page 166 Indenture 29 Mar 1813 THOMAS STONE, one part, and JOSEPH PARKER, RICHARD HILL, ELIJAH WARD, CHRISTOPHER CATRON & WILLIAM DYRE, other part, $5.00 paid, all Thomas's right to tract on Cane creek, a branch of Caney fork of Cumberland river, part of 2500 acres. Wit: SAMUEL DYER, WM HILL.

Page 167 Deed of Gift 14 Jan 1812 ELIJAH BATES for love & affection I have to my daughter POLLY MAY and her husband JOHN MAY, tract from a certain cross fence that divides my plantation & his, as far as my claim extends on that side. Wit: J SHROPSHIRE, WM HILL.

Page 167 Indenture 6 Sept 1813 THOMAS CRUTCHER and JACOB ROBERTSON, $182 paid, tr on Post oak creek it being a part of 640 acres granted by NC to JAMES EASTLAND, being 60 3/4 acres.

Page 168 Indenture 8 June 1812 THOMAS CRUTCHER, Bedford Co, TN, one part, and JESSE INGLAND, other part, $1200 paid, tr of 135 acres. Wit: WILLIAM R COLE, WILLIAM DANIEL.

Page 170 Indenture 13 June 1813 PHILIP USSERY and ANDREW BURK, $700 paid, my right to tr of 100 acres orig granted to RICHARD BRASIL, tr being on both sides of Calf killers fork. Wit: WILLIAM SIMPSON, JACOB A LANE.

Page 171 Indenture 27 Feb 1813 WILLIAM BALSH and HARRISON HOLLAND, $100 paid, 200 acres in 1st Dist on Caney fork. Wit: ABEL HUTRON, JULIANNA

HATRON(?).

Page 172   Deed of Gift   Ack on 8 Sept 1813   WILLIAM PRYOR to JOSEPH PRIER, my son, 50 acres in 3rd Dist in the dry valley, tr surv 23 Feb 1809 by JAMES CHISUM, DS.

Page 172   Indenture   17 Hab 1713   WILLIAM NEVILL and RICHARD LUNDY, $1000 paid, 150 acres, it being part of Grant No 2873 granted by TN to Grantor herein for 300 acres. Wit: JAS TOWNSEND, DAVID THORNTON.

Page 173   Indenture   1 Oct 1811 & 36th year of Am Independence   JOHN TERRY and SPENCER A KEY, $100 paid, tract of land it being part of land sd Terry now lives on. Wit: ABIJAH CRANE, JESSE KITCHEN.

Page 174   Indenture   14 June 1813   SAMUEL DENTON of New York City, Merchant, and MARY (DENTON), his wife, of first part, and WILLIAM LITTLE, at present of the same place, Merchant, second part, $896 paid, all 1 undivided half of parcel, beg in W bdy of township of Manningvale in NW cor tr lately allotted to THOMAS STORIN, Esqr, cor Grant No 2612, crossing river and being SW cor township of Fiskland, adj Cumberland mountain, tr being 13,984 acres; also undivi part tr of 280 acres. Ack in New York City, NY by SAML D MONFORD on 15 June 1813, before JOHN T BAINBRIDGE, Clk, and Certif by ROSWELL W LEWIS, Presid Judge.

Page 177   Surveyor's Field Notes   Sur by virtue of Military land Warr No 2695, located 1 June 1795, for EDWARD HARRIS, assee of heirs of THOMAS TOTTON, a private in Continental line of this state, 640 acres on S side Cumberland River & on a large fork of Caney fork. Sur by WILLIAM TYRRELL, DS. Wit: JNO MAN, WILLIAM LYTLE, SCC, ROBT KING, Marker.

Page 178   Land Grant No 2612   4 June 1796   NORTH CAROLINA pursuant to Act for relief of officers and soldiers in Continental line, and for bravery, etc of THOMAS TATTON, a private in sd line, grants to EDWARD HARRIS, assee of Tatton's heirs, tr of 640 acres in Sumner County ON S side Cumberland River. Surveyor's Field Notes attached, being of Warr No 3856 located 1 June 1795.

Page 179   Land Grant No 2613   Date & Grantor above, JOHN DUNBAR, a private in Continental line, grants Grantee above, assee of sd Dunbar. Surveyor's plat & field notes attached of Military land Warr of No 2740, located 1 June 1795.

Page 180   Land Grant No 2614   Date & Grantor above, for zeal of HANNON JOHNSTON, a private in Continental line, grants to Grantee above, 640 acres lying in Sumner County. Surv plat attached of Mil land Warr No 2747 located 1 June 1795.

Page 181   Land Grant No 2615   Date & Grantor above, for bravery of TIBIAS MARCH, a private in Continental line, grants to Grantee above, 640 acres in Sumner County, as assee of heirs of HARMON JOHNSTON. Surv plat attached of Military land Warr No 2662.

Page 182   Land Grant No 2616   4 June 1796   NORTH CAROLINA for relief of officers & soldiers in Continental line and for bravery, etc of JOEL HADSON, a private in sd line, grants to EDWARD HARRIS, assee sd Hadson heirs, 640 acres in Sumner County, joining Harris Sur. Plat and Survey attached of Warr No 2498. CC: WILLIAM LYTLE, ROBT KING. Marker: JNO MARR. DS WILLIAM TYRRELL.

Page 182 Land Grant No 2617 Date and Grantor above for Continental line soldier NATHANIEL WOODS, private in sd line, grants to Grantee above, as assee of heirs of sd Woods, being 640 acres in Sumner County & joining Harris Sur.

Page 183 Land Grant No 2618 Date & Grantor as above due to services of PETER POWELL in Continental line, grants to Grantee above, as assee heirs of NATHANIEL WOOD, 640 acres in Sumner County. Plat attached, Warr No 2470.

Page 184 Land Grant No 2619 Date & Grantor as above, for services in Continental line by PATRICK VENNS, a Private in sd line, grants EDWARD HARRIS, his assee, 640 acres in Sumner County, Military Warr No 2780. Plat and survey attached.

Page 185 Land Grant No 2620 Date & Grantor as above, for services of GREEN WALKER in Continental line, a private, grants above named Harris, assee of Walker's heirs, 640 acres in Sumner County. Military Warr No 3698.

Page 185 Land Grant No 2621 Date & Grantor as above, for services in Continental line of ISAAC ROBERTSON, grants above named Harris, 640 acres in Sumner County. Military Warr No 2759.

Page 186 Land Grant No 2022 Date & Grantor above, for services of DAVID NEVER(?) in Continental line, grants above Harris, 640 acres in Sumner County. Military Warr 2677.

Page 187 Land Grant No 2623 Date & Grantor above for services in Continental line by ALEXANDER PARTON, grants Harris 640 acres in Sumner County. Military Warr 2757.

Page 187 Land Grant 2624 As above, services by HENRY GRIFFITH, private, to Grantee above, 640 acres in Sumner Co. Mil Warr 2455.

Page 188 Land Grant 2625 As above, services by ELISHA IVEY, private in Continental line, to above Grantee, 640 acres in above county. Mil Warr 2462.

Page 189 Land Grant 2626 As above, services by ANTHONY HOBBERT(?), private in Continen line, to above Grantee, 640 acres in Sumner County. Mil Warr No 2723.

Page 190 Land Grant No 2027 Services by JOHN DUGGIN, private sd line, 640 acres to above Grantee. Mil Warr 2799.

Page 191 Land Grant No 2628 Services by HARDY SKIPPER, private sd line, 640 acres. Mil Warr No 2795.

Page 191 Land Grant No 2629 Services by MORRIS MCPHEY, private sd line, 640 acre in Sumner County to above Grantee. Mil Warr 2751.

Page 192   Land Grant No 2630   4 June 1796   NORTH CAROLINA for services by MEREDY SKETCHING(?), private in Continental line, 640 acres to above Grantee.   Mil Warr 2770.

Page 193   Land Grant 2631   Above Date & Grantor, for services by WILLIS HAMMONDS, private in Continen line, 640 acres to above Grantee, Sumner County.   Military Warr No 3006, located 1 June 1795.   Plat and description attached.

Page 194   Land Grant No 2632   Above date & Grantor, for services by JOHN MCNEILL, a private in Continental line, assee of Thomas as in above several grants, 640 acres in Sumner Co to above Grantee, Mil Warr 2614.

Page 195   Land Grant No 2633   Date & Grantor as above, for services in Continen line by TITUS PETERS, a private in Continen line as above, 640 acres to above named Harris, Mil Warr 2461.

Page 196   Land Grant No 2634   Date & Grantor as above, for serv in Continen line by PHILIP EVANS, a private, 640 acres to Harris, Mil Warr 3001.

Page 196   Land Grant No 2635   Date & Grantor above, service in Continen line by JOSEPH CHESNUT, a priv in Continen line, 640 acres to Harris, Mil Warr 2996.

Page 197   Land Grant No 2636   Date & Grantor above, service in Continen line by SAMUEL GREEN, a private in Continen line, 640 acres in Sumner co to Harris, Military Warr 2720.

Page 198   Land Grant No 2637   Date & Grantor as above, grants ARTHUR TINER, a private in Continental line, etc, 640 acres to EDWARD HARRIS, assee sd Tiner, Military Warr 1802, located 1 June 1795.

Page 199   Land Grant No 2038   Date & Grantor above, to JEREMIAH FRASIER, a private in Continen line, 640 acres in Sumner County, to Grantee above, Mili Warr 2040.

Page 200   Land Grant No 2630   Date & Grantor above, to ISAAC BAGLEY, a private in Continen line, 640 acres in above co to Harris, Military Warr 1807.

Page 201   Land Grant No 2040   Date & Grantor above, to ABSALOM ROGERS, a private in Continen line, 640 acres in Sumner Co to Harris, Mili Warr 2224.

Page 202   Land Grant No 2041   Date & Grantor above, to JOHN FLETCHER, a private in Continen line, 640 acres in Sumner Co to Harris, Mili Warr 1992.

Page 203   Land Grant No 2042   Date & Grantor above, to ELLICK SNEED, a private in Continen line, 640 acres in Sumner Co to Harris, Mili Warr 2704.

Page 204   Land Grant No 2043   Date & Grantor above, to THOMAS LOVETT(?), private in Continen line, 640 acres to sd Harris, in above named county, Mili Warr 2670.

Page 205   Land Grant No 2044   Date & Grantor above to ROBERT POWERS, priv in Continen line, 640 acres in above co to Harris, Mili Warr 2471 (?).

Page 206 Land Grant No 2645 Date & Grantor above to THOMAS GEORGE, a priv in Continen line, 640 acres in above co to Harris, Mili Warr 2452.

Page 207 Land Grant No 2646 Date & Grantor above to SAMPSON ROBERTS, priv Continen line, 640 acres in Sumner Co to Harris, Mili Warr 2476.

Page 208 Land Grant No 2647 Date & Grantor above to DAVID LEWIS, a private in Continen line, 640 acres Sumner co to Harris, Military Land Warr 2672.

Page 209 Land Grant No 2046 Date & Grantor above to JAMES HOWARD, a private in Continen line, 640 acres Sumner Co to Harris, Mili Warr No 2459.

Page 210 Land Grant No 2649 Date & Grantor above to RICHARD MORGAN, a priv in Continental line, 640 acres Sumner Co to Harris, Mili Warr 1400.

Page 211 Land Grant No 2650 Date & Grantor above to ANDREW HINDS, a priv in Continen line, 640 acres Sumner Co, Mili Warr No 2458.

Page 212 Land Grant No 2651 Date & Grantor above to THOMAS HINES, a priv in Continen line, 640 acres Sumner Co to Harris, Mili Warr No 1889.

Page 213 Land Grant No 2652 Date & Grantor above to BRYAN BUSBY, a priv in Continen line, 640 acres Sumner Co to Harris, Mili Warr 1340.

Page 214 Land Grant No 2653 Date & Grantor above to HARDY GUM, a priv in Continen line, 640 acres Sumner Co to Harris, Mili Warr 2718.

Page 215 Land Grant No 2654 Date & Grantor above to JOSHUA PROCTOR, a priv in Continen line, 640 acres Sumner Co to Harris, Mili Warr 2619.

Page 216 Land Grant No 2655 4 June 1796 NORTH CAROLINA to MICHAEL DELANEY, priv in Continen line, 640 acres in Sumner Co to Harris. Military Warr No 3838.

Page 217 Land Grant No 2656 Date & Grantor above to DUGALD KELLEY, a private in Continen line, 640 acres in Sumner Co to Harris. Mili Warr No 832.

Page 218 Land Grant No 2657 Date & Grantor above to SAMUEL CARTER, a priv in Continen line, 640 acres in above co to Harris. Mili Warr 3845.

Page 219 Land Grant No 2658 Date & Grantor above to STEPHEN EMMERY, a priv in Continen line, 640 acres in above county to Harris. Mili Warr 1414.

Page 220 Land Grant No 2659 Date & Grantor above to DILLARD COLLINS, a priv in Continen line, 640 acres in above county to Harris. Mili Warr 1135.

Page 221 Land Grant No 2660 Date & Grantor above to BURRELL COLLINS, a priv in Continen line, 640 acres in above county to Harris. Mili Warr No 1134.

Page 222 Land Grant No 2661 Date & Grantor above to SAMUEL JEWELL, a priv in Continen line, 640 acres in above county to Harris. Mili Warr No 3756.

Page 223 Land Grant No 2662 Date & Grantor above to ROBERT WHITE, a private in Continental line, 640 acres in above county to Harris. Military Warr No 3357.

Page 224 Land Grant No 2663 Date & Grantor above to GILBERT GRANT, a private in Continen line, 640 acres above county to Harris. Mili Warr No 2803.

Page 225 Land Grant No 2664 Date & Grantor above to ABRAHAM THURRELL, a priv in Continen line, 640 acres above county to Harris. Mili Warr No 3840.

Page 226 Land Grant No 2665 Date & Grantor above to ANDREW KING, priv in Continental line, 640 acres in above county to Harris. Mili Warr No 2463.

Page 227 Land Grant No 2666 As above to RICHARD WARREN, private, etc. Mili Warr 3888. (See previous Grants)

Page 228 Land Grant No 2667 As above to JOHN STEPHENS, private etc. (See previous Grants). Mili Warr 3830.

Page 229 Land Grant 2668 As above to RICHARD EVANS, private etc. Mili Warr 3881.

Page 230 Land Grant No 2669 As above to HARPER JOHNSTON, private etc. Mili Warr 2734.

Page 231 Land Grant No 2670 As above to JOSEPH JORDAN, a private, etc. Mili Warr 2735.

Page 232 Land Grant No 2671 As above to DUNCEY ROE, a private etc. Mili Warr 2434.

Page 233 Land Grant No 2672 As above to JOHN WORSLEY, a priv, etc. Mili Warr 1888.

Page 234 Land Grant No 2673 As above to THOMAS JERENING(?), a private, etc. Mili Warr 2425.

Page 235 Land Grant No 2674 4 June 1896 NORTH CAROLINA for service in Continental line of CHARLES SMITH, a private, etc, grants EDWARD HARRIS, assee sd Smith's heirs, 640 acres in Sumner County. Military Land Warr No 2436.

Page 236 Land Grant No 2675 Date & Grantor as above, HANCOCK STANLEY, a private etc, 640 acres. Mili Warr 2772.

Page 237 Land Grant No 2676 Date & Grantor as above, JOHN STEADMAN, a private etc. Mili Warr 3023.

Page 238 Land Grant No 2677 Date & Grantor as above, ZEBULEN WILLS, a private etc. Mili Warr 3032.

Page 239 Land Grant No 2676 Date & Grantor as above, TIMOTHY COVENER, a private etc. Mili Warr 2993.

Page 240 Land Grant No 2679   Date & Grantor as above, GEORGE WOODWARD, a private etc. Mili Warr 3028.

Page 241 Land Grant No 2080   Date & Grantor as above, SETH GARRIS, a private etc. Mili Warr 952.

Page 242 Indenture 2 July 1796   WILLIAM BLOUNT, Esq, of Knoxville Co, TN, one part, and THOMAS STORM, Esq, New York City, other part, $22,080 paid, tract on Caney fork of Cumberland River in Sumner Co, TN, being 44,160 acres granted by North Carolina to EDWARD HARRIS in 69 different grants of 640 acres each, being Grant Numbers 2612 to 2680, inclusive, in Trust for sd Storm and for JOHN F SNYDAM, SAMUEL DENTON, HENDRICK J WYCKOFF and JOHN SNYDAM, all of sd city, 1 equal undivided tenth part same for TIMOTHY GREEN of sd city, 1 undiv 20th part for WILLIAM ROBERTSON and SYLVESTER ROBERTSON of sd city, 1/20th part for NICHOLAS COOK, STEPHEN TILLINGHAST and LIBBENS LOOMIS all of sd city, undiv 1/10 for JONATHAN RUSSELL, 1/10 for DAVID GELSTON, of sd city, 1/10th for JOHN M LEAN of Boston, MA, 10th for SAMUEL BLAGG, also of Boston, MA, and for MOSES FISK, late a Tutor in Dartmouth College in New Hampshire. Wit: JAMES KENT and ANNUL BEEBEE(?). Certified 2 July 1796 by JAMES KENT of Chancery in New York and ack before HOWEL TATUM, Esq, JJC.

Page 244 Land Grant 5035 27 Sept 1813 STATE OF TENNESSEE by virtue part Certif 409, dated 15 Mar 1810, issued by Commiss of W TN to THOS SIMPSON and entered by No 4689, grants BENJAMIN HAWKINS, assee of sd Simpson, tr of 50 acres in White county on headwaters N fork Rutledge Mill creek, part of 200 acre sur of EDWARD HOOPER.

Page 245 Land Grant 5036 Date & Grantor as above, for military serv performed by DANIEL MCDANIEL to NC, Warr 3086 dated 5 Dec 1785, grants BENJAMIN HAWKINS, assee of heirs of McDaniel, 50 acre tr in White County.

Page 246 Land Grant 4647   9 Apr 1813   Grantor as above for military serv by HENRY HICKS, private, to NC, Warr No 1073, dated 1 June 1784, entered as No 7040 on 15 Oct 1811, grants to BENJAMIN HAWKINS, assee of ANDREW HADDOCK, heir of sd Hicks, 150 acres in White Co on Caney fork.

Page 247 Land Grant 3790   3 Mar 1812 Grantor as above, part Certif 303, dated 19 Aug 1809, obtained by THOMAS DILLON, entered on 12 Oct 1809 by No 4310, grants JOSEPH WALLING, assee of Dillon, 93 acres in White County, 1st Dist, 1st range & 9th Sec on Calf killer fork.

Page 248 Land Grant No 4740   25 May 1813   Grantor as above by virtue part of Certif No 389, dated 7 Mar 1812, entered 19 Dec 1812 by No 2171, grants to JESSE BABB, assee of PETER BENNETT, tr of 5 acres in White County in 3rd Dist on main Caney fork.

Page 249 Land Grant No 4173 21 Sept 1812   Grantor above by part Certif 152, dated 30 Oct 1810, issued to ANDREW M LUSK, grants to JOHN DUDLEY, his assee, tr on S side main Caney fork, beg on SW cor GEORGE W SAUNDERS.

Page 250 Land Grant No 2725 13 Dec 1810 Grantor above by part of Warr No 2618, dated 30 Nov 1784 issued to GRAY BYRUM(?), grants to BURRELL HUDSON, assee sd Gray, tr of 190 acres in White County.

Page 251   Power of Attorney   20 Sept 1809   RICHARD BRASIL being about to remove to Mississippi Territory appoints his friend SAMUEL USSERY, his attorney, able to transfer right to 100 acres known by my occupant claim to WILLIAM B USSERY (relationship not stated), having transferred claim to him. Wit: RORIA ROSE & STEPHEN PATTISON.

Page 252   Indenture   17 Sept 1813   THOMAS HORNE and WILLIAM STAMPS, $100 paid, tr of 14 3/4 acres. Wit: JAMES NETHERTON, W H HARGIS.

Page 253   Indenture   9 Dec 1813   ALEXANDER LOWREY, one part, and JAMES GRACEY and JOHN GRACEY (relationship not stated), other part, $600 paid, 160 acres on SE side Calf killers fork, part Grant 2562 issued by NC and which sd Alexander holds by deed from CALEB FRALEY. Wit: WILLIAM GLENN, WILLIAM IRWIN.

Page 255   Indenture   4 Sept 1813   WILLIAM B USSERY and JOHN MCBRIDE, $510 paid, 100 acres in 3rd Dist on N side Calf killers fork of Caney fork. Wit: WM BROWN, ELIPHABIT JARVIS(?).

Page 256   Indenture   18 Dec 1811   SPENCER ACUFF and JESSE BROCK, $100 paid, tr being part of land Acuff bought of TERRY. Wit: JOHN BROCK, ISAACK BROWN.

Page 257   Indenture   7 Jan 1814   DAVID NICHOLDS and THOMAS LUSK, $50.00 paid, tr vested in Nicholds by deed executed by THOMAS MCCORRY, 8 1/2 acres. Wit: URIAH MURPHREE, ABNER MOORE.

Page 258   Indenture 1 Feb 1813   JAMES HERON and ELIJAH BATES, $200 paid, Lot 85 in Sparta. Wit: JAS TOWNSEND, WILLIAM GRACY.

Page 259   Indenture   27 Mar 1812   NATHANIEL TAYLOR, Carter Co, TN, and JACOB HYDE, $360 paid, 180 acres on waters of Caney fork in 3rd Dist & in 16th Section. Tract includes place where Jacob now lives. Wit: WM QUARLES, JACOB WORK, LOYD ROCKHOLD, JAS P TAYLOR.

Page 260   Indenture   7 Dec 1813   JOSEPH WALLING and JAMES RANDAL, $80.00 paid, tr of 80 acres on Calf Killers fork in 1st Dist, 1st Range & 9th Sec, tr adj JOEL FOSTER, and being part of Grant No 379 for 93 acres. Wit: TURNER LANE, ROBERT B GLENN.

Page 261   Indenture   18 Jan 1814   ABNER HILL and JOSEPH UPCHURCH, $80.00 paid, tr of 40 acres on N side Caney fork, entered by No 6571 on Certif No 290. Wit: MATTHEW BABB, DAVID BUTCHER.

Page 262   Indenture   Date and parties as in above Indenture, $60.00 paid, tr in 3rd Dist on main Caney fork entered 26 Dec 1809, location No 9594 on Warr 1724. Witnesses as above.

Page 263   Indenture   5 Oct 1813   JAMES BOWEN and JESSE BABB, $200 paid, tr on Caney fork, 100 acres. Wit: WOODSON P WHITE, DAVID MITCHELL.

Page 264   Indenture   6 Dec 1813 & 38th year of Independence of the US BENJAMIN HAWKINS and EDWARD HOOPER, $200 paid, 2 tracts of 50 acres each. Wit: JOSEPH KERR, WILLIAM HAWKINS, DANIEL NEWMAN.

Page 265 Indenture 4 Jan 1814 ZACHARIAH JONES and JOHN CLARA, $400 paid, tr on waters of the Falling water, tr including improvement where DAVID ROBERTSON formerly lived & a spring, being tr of 100 acres. Wit: ROBERT ARMSTRONG, JOHN CLARA.

Page 266 Indenture 11 Dec 1813 JOSEPH SMITH, one part, and WILLIAM ANDERSON and MATTHIAS ANDERSON (no relationship stated), other part, $16.00 paid, Lot 63 in Town of Sparta. Wit: GASPER BARGER, WESLEY W KEAS.

Page 267 Indenture 30 Mar 1813 THOMAS STONE, JOSEPH PARKER, ELIJAH WARD, WILLIAM DYER and CHRISTOPHER CATRON, one part, and JACOB ROBERTSON, other part, $1.50 paid, tract of 264 acres. Wit: SAMUEL DYER and WILLIAM HILL.

Page 268 Indenture 12 Dec 1810 WILLIAM HAYS and SAMUEL THOMAS, $300 paid, tr of 228 acres in 3rd Dist on Calf Killer fork of Caney fork. Wit: WILLIAM B USSERY, JOHN GRIGSBY.

Page 269 Indenture 21 Apr 1814 JACOB A LANE and WESLEY W KEAS & CO, $750 paid, Lot 30 in Sparta. Excepted from deed is house now occupied by JOHN D CLIFFORD, Merchant.

Page 270 Land Grant No 3965 12 June 1812 TENNESSEE by virtue of 21 July 1807, obtained from Bd of Commissioners for West TN by THOMAS DILLON, and entered on 18 Nov 1808 by No 624, grants to ISAAC ANDERSON, assee of Dillon, 9 acres in 3rd Dist & in Hickory Valley, beg at SW cor his 50 acre sur & being in N bdy of JAMES R BRYAN 200 acre survey.

Page 271 Land Grant No 5021 25 Sept 1813 TENNESSEE for military serv by JETHRO SUMNER to NC, Warr No 4338, stated 16 Dec 1796 & entered on 5 June 1810 by No 1021, grants to HARDY JONES, assee of heirs of sd Sumner, 40 acres, part sd Warr on Calf Killers fork of Caney forks.

Page 272 Land Grant No 4880 15 July 1813 TENNESSEE as part of Certif 674, dated 25 Dec 1710, issued to JOHN MCIVER, entered on 16 Feb 1811 by 1319, grants to ELIJAH CHISUM, Senr, assee of sd McIver, tr of 30 acres in 3rd Dist on both sides Calf Killer fork of Caney fork, adj 100 acre tr in name of GEORGE RUSSELL.

Page 273 Land Grant No 4888 15 July 1813 TENNESSEE by virtue Certif 361 dated 5 Nov 1811 issued to above named McIver, entered 17 Apr 1812 by No 1767, grants above named CHISUM, assee sd MCIVER, 25 acres in 3rd Dist on both sides Calf Killers fork of Caney fork adj his other entry of 30 acres above.

Page 274 Indenture 9 Feb 1814 ISAAC ANDERSON and THOMAS WILSON, $20.00 paid, 9 acres in 3rd Dist in Hickory Valley, beg in N bdy line of JAMES R BRYAN 200 acre sur. Wit: JOHN MCGILVRAY, WILLM WILSON.

Page 275 Indenture 19 Mar 1814 EDWARD FOSTER, one part, and WILLIAM & GEORGE MORGAN & CO, second part, $1100 paid, Lots 50 & 51 in Sparta. Wit: GEO W GIBBS.

Page 276 Indenture 12 Apr 1814 ELIJAH CHISUM, Senr, and SHERROD KORN, $75.00 paid, 25 acres being on both sides of Calf Killers fork of Caney fork, adj 30 acres granted to Chisum by Grant No 4809 above. Wit: JAMES CHISUM.

Page 277 Indenture Date & Parties as in above deed, $75.00 paid, 30 acres, as per Grant No 4889.

Page 278 Indenture 7 Jan 1814 JOHN WHITE, Senr, one part, and WOODSON P WHITE, other part, (relationship not stated), $280 paid, all his interest in deed from THOMAS MCCORRY to sd John on 1 June 1808 to 152 acres. Wit: WILLIAM H WHITE, ROBERT HOWARD.

Page 279 Indenture 2 Mar 1813 JAMES STINSON & WILLIAM STINSON (relationship not stated), one part, and JOHN DOLLAR, latter of Jackson Co, TN, $106 paid, 106 acres, part of a 640 acre acre tr purchased by Grantors from WILLIAM P ANDERSON and JOHN MCIVER, on Caney fork. Wit: EDW HARRISON, JOSEPH C MCBRIDE.

Page 280 Indenture 16 Apr 1814 JOHN KEITHLEY and WILLIS KEITHLEY, (relationship not stated), $100 paid, tract on N side Caney fork, beg at SE cor ELIJAH CHISUM, Junr, tr including spring where sd parties now live, being 50 acres.

Page 281 Indenture 5 Mar 1814 IREBY W STONE and THOMAS STONE, my father, $300 paid, 386 acres on Cane creek, a branch of Caney fork of Cumberland River, being a part of 2500 acres orig granted by North Carolina to ROBERT KING, assee of JAMES WILLIAMS, by Grant No 341, dated 1 Mar 1797, sd Thomas to be able to make anyone his heir that he pleases. Ireby also delivers to sd Thomas the remainder of my personal estate that he had granted to me by Deed of Gift - household equipment, and also one Negro girl named MINTA, about 5 years old. Said goods is to be for the proper use of sd Thomas Stone and at his disposal forever. Wit: JOHN DOLLAR, CORDER C STONE, Junior.

Page 282 Land Grant No 2087 31 Mar 1810 TENNESSEE by Certif No 235, dated 13 Apr 1809, obtained by THOMAS DILLON and entered 30 Mar 1810 by No 4665 as an Occupant claim under law of 1807, grants ELIJAH CHISUM, his assee, tract of 255 1/2 acres in 1st Dist & including improvements of sd Chisum on N side Caney fork, 1st Range & 9th Sec, adj lines of WILLIAM FITZGERALD & ABNER HILL.

Page 283 Land Grant No 2089 Date & Grantor as above, for Military service performed by MOSES NEWSOM to NC, Warrant No 3716, dated 2 Jan 1790, entered on 29 Aug 1807, by No 467, grants ELIJAH CHISUM, assee of sd Newsom, a certain tr of 100 acres, part of sd Warrant.

Page 284 Land Grant No 1677 18 Oct 1809 TENNESSEE grants for military service by DAVID MCCLOUD to NC, Warr 4498, dated 22 Dec 1796 and entered on 21 Apr 1809 by No 4363, grants BENJAMIN HAWKINS, assee of sd McCloud, tr of 10 acres, part sd Warr in 2st Dist, on N side Caney fork.

Page 284 Indenture 15 Jan 1814 JOSEPH CRABB and BERRYMAN HAMLETT, $200 paid, 100 acres in first Dist on Caney fork, beg W bdy line JOSEPH WALLING 100 acre survey. Wit: JOSEPH UPCHURCH, STEPHEN CRABB.

Page 285 Bill of Sale 21 Jan 1814   JESSE DAY, Brunswick Co, VA, to JACOB

A LANE, $350 paid, 1 Negro woman slave about 13 or 14 yrs old, named FANNY. Wit: TURNER LANE, JOHN WILLIAMSON.

Page 286 Bill of Sale 25 Jan 1813 JOHN CLARY (signed JOHN CLAY) to ZACHARIAH JONES, $750 paid, 3 Negroes to wit: 1 woman named DINAH, supposed to be 28 yrs of age, and 1 girl named MILLY upwards of 4 yrs of age, and 1 boy child upwards of 2 yrs old. Wit: ROBT ARMSTRONG.

Page 287 Indenture 18 Jan 1814 DAVID SMYTH, one part, and ALEXANDER S SIMPSON, CHRISTIAN MAY and THOMAS HARBERT, of other part, $1000 paid, Lots 26 & 27 in town of Sparta. Wit: ANDREW BURK, WILLIAM RIDGE.

Page 288 Land Grant No 3340 22 Aug 1811 TENNESSEE by virtue of Warr 865 dated 23 Mar 1811, issued to JOHN JONES by Commiss of E TN, founded on an entry made by EVAN SHELBY, entered on 28 July 1811 by No 1453 as an Occupant claim, grants unto WILLIAM BROWN, assee sd Jones, 267 acres lying in 3rd Dist in the cove of a mountain on waters of main fork of Caney fork, adj DANIEL HASTINGS 150 acre sur on his S bdy. Wit: WILLIAM KILLION, JOEL BURDIN.

Page 290 Bill of Sale 2 Mar 1814 MARY LYDA to WILLIAM MORRISON, $150 paid, 1 Negro boy named BENJAMIN about 4 yrs of age. Wit: HENRY LYDA, BOON STILL.

Page 291 Bill of Sale 20 June 1814 JAMES SIMPSON to Grantee above, $400 paid, 1 Negro girl CHERRY, 18 yrs. Wit: ELI SIMS, HENRY LYDA.

Page 292 Land Grant No 5721 15 June 1814 TENNESSEE by Warr 743, dated 1 May 1805, issued to GEORGE D BLACKAMON, entered on 31 Aug 1807 by No 539, grants THOMAS K HARRIS, assee of sd Blackamon, tr of 50 acres in 1st Dist, 1st Range & 9th Sec, being 50 acres.

Page 293 Land Grant No 2881 6 Feb 1811 TENNESSEE by virtue part Certif 409, dated 15 Mar 1810, obtained by THOMAS SIMPSON & entered on 28 Sept 1810 by No 5204, grants to WILLIAM GLENN, assee of sd Simpson, 50 acres on N side Caney fork & W of Morrison mountain, beg near a cabin orig built by ALEXANDER GLENN and now occupied by sd Glenn.

Page 294 Indenture 9 Dec 1813 WILLIAM BROWN and WILLIAM DENNY, $700 paid, 132 acres (very dim microfilm). Wit: WILLIAM GLENN, NICHOLAS GILLENTINE(?), JOHN TAYLOR.

Page 295 Indenture 18 July 1814 JAMES DAVIS and JOHN HEATH, $300 paid, tr on Caney fork river. Wit: GREEN WOODS, ISAAC TAYLOR, Jr.

Page 296 Bill of Sale 6 May 1814 GEORGE W GIBBS and TEMPLE POSTON, $250 paid, by ISAAC TAYLOR. Junr, 1 Negro girl slave ERLEN(?), about 9 yrs old. Wit: WILLIAM GLENN, ELISHA SWIFT.

Page 296 Bill of Sale 2 Apr 1814 ALEXANDER GLENN and WILLIAM GLENN, $90.00 paid, 1 Negro girl named LET, about 2 yrs old. Wit: JESSE RAGSDALE.

Page 297 Sheriff's Deed 6 Nov 1810 WILLIAM PHILLIPS, Shff, and GEORGE GORDON, tr granted orig by NC to ROBERT KING by patent 340, on Caney creek, being 2500 acres, Gordon having paid $27.76 taxes due. Wit: DAVID NUTTING, JOSEPH CRAIGMILES.

Page 298   Sheriff's Deed Date and Parties as in above deed. Witnesses as above.

Page 299   Indenture 2 Oct 1812   WILLIAM RIDGE and CHRISTOPHER CATRON, $100 paid, 120 acres on Cane creek, part of tr of 2500 acres orig granted by NC to ROBERT KING, assee of JAMES WILLIAMS, Jr, Grant No 341 dated 1 Mar 1797. Wit: BENJAMIN GRIFFITH, JAMES MCCORMACK. Sworn by IRA BEDWELL.

Page 300   Indenture 27 Mar 1813 · THOMAS STONE and CHRISTOPHER CATRON, $1.00 paid, tr on Cane creek, a branch of Caney fork of Cumberland river, part of tr of 2500 acres. Wit: IREBY STONE, CORDEN STONE (relationships not stated).

Page 301   Indenture 18 July 1814   ANDREW MCBRIDE and GEORGE LONG, $222 paid, tr of 67 acres being on draught of Cherry creek. Wit: WILLIAM GLENN, JAMES CATES.

Page 302   Indenture 6 July 1814   DENNIS HARTY and JOHN BROWN, $300 paid, tr of 46 acres which was granted to Harty by Tennessee by Grant 533, tr including which Brown now lives. Wit: ANDREW GAMBER, DAVIS THOMPSON.

Page 303   Indenture 5 Jan 1814   DANIEL ALEXANDER and JAMES HUGGINS, $240 paid, 2 tracts as described therein. ___ HUNTER, Jr, CHARLES HUNTER (no relationship stated).

Page 304   Indenture 4 Aug 1812   THOMAS BOUNDS, BENJAMIN WEAVER, AARON ENGLAND, TURNER LANE, ALEXANDER LOWREY, JAMES FULKERSON and NICHOLAS GILLENTINE, Commissioners in trust of White County, one part, and HENRY LANCE, other part, $20.20 paid, Tract 80 in town of Sparta.

Page 305   Bill of Sale 6 May 1814   DAVIS SMYTH to MARGIT CHISUM, $425 paid, 1 Negro woman named CHARITY and her child named MATILDA, about 6 months old. Wit: ELIJAH CHISUM, Senr.

Page 305   Land Grant No 2247   20 May 1793   NORTH CAROLINA to JOSHUA DAVIS, assee of SIMON BAKER, a private in Continental line of sd state, 640 acres in Sumner County on Cany fork. THOMAS HICKMAN, DS, and JOSIAH PAYNE, and WM REED, CC.

Page 306   Indenture 23 Mar 1813   SETH DAVIS, Davidson Co, TN, Atty in fact for JOSHUA DAVIS, one part, and JAMES DAVIS of Williamson Co, TN, $250 paid, 640 acres granted by NC to Joshua on Caney fork. Wit: JOHN DAVIS, DARIEN DAVIS (relationships not stated), JOHN JONES. Ack in Davidson County before NATHAN EWING.

Page 307   Land Grant No 3910 2 Aug 1813   TENNESSEE by virtue of a Warrant No 536, dated 7 Apr 1812, issued by Commiss of W TN to JOHN RAINS, a hunter for the sur appointed by NC for laying off lands allotted officers and soldiers of Continental line of sd state, by No 8207, grants to GEORGE W SAUNDERS, assee of sd Rains, 50 acres on Caney fork, First Dist.

Page 307   Land Grant No 4911 Above date and Grantor, by virtue of part of

Certif 371, dated 16 Dec 1809, obtained by JOSHUA HADLEY and entered 31 Mar 1812 by No 7892, there is granted to GEORGE W SAUNDERS, Assee of Hadley, 10 acres on Caney fork, beg at NW cor of REUBIN P SAUNDERS 15 acre entry.

Page 308   Land Grant No 5478   16 Mar 1814   TENNESSEE by virtue Warrant dated 10 Jan 1794 issued to heirs of HARDY ASKEW, a private in Battallion of troops, grants GEORGE W SAUNDERS, assee of heirs of sd Askew, 50 acres on S side main Caney fork.

Page 309   Land Grant No 5556   26 Apr 1814 & of Independence of US the 38th TENNESSEE by virtue of part of a Warr dated 10 Jan 2794 issued to heirs of HARDY ASKEW, as above, to Grantee as above.

Page 310   Land Grant No 3011   16 Apr 1811   Grantor as above for military service performed by ROBERT BAKER to NC, to Grantee as above, as heirs of sd ROBERT CAKE(?), 300 acres in 1st Dist, 1st Range & 20th Sec on S side Caney fork, tr including improvements of said Saunders.   Surveyed 24 July 1808 by JOHN BOWEN, DS.

Page 311   Land Grant No 5479   16 Mar 1814   TENNESSEE by virtue Warr dated 10 Jan 1794, issued to heirs of HARRY ASKEW, a private in Battallion of troops NC, issues to GEORGE W SAUNDERS, assee sd heirs a tr of 50 acres in 3rd Dist on S side main Caney fork, beg at SE cor JOHN HILL.

Page 311   Land Grant No 4364   7 Nov 1812   TENNESSEE by virtue military service performed by HARDY HUNT to NC, Warr No 4618, dated 9 Feb 1797, entered 20 July 1809 by No 3660, grants to REUBEN P SAUNDERS, assee of heirs of Hunt, 30 acres part sd Warr in 1st Dist on waters on S side Caney fork near cabin on improvement of REUBEN CHAMBERS & adj NW cor JOHN SMALLMAN.

Page 312   Land Grant No 4913   2 Aug 1813   TENNESSEE by virtue part Certif 372 dated 9 Nov 1810 issued by Register of West TN to BENNET SEARCY and entered on 30 Mar 1812 by No 7885, grants to REUBIN P SANDERS, assee of sd Bennet Searcy, tr of 15 acres on Caney fork.

Page 313   Land Grant No 4912   Date & Grantor above, by Certif 371 dated 16 Dec 1809, to JOSHUA HADLEY, grants ELIJAH SANDERS, assee of Hadley, 50 acres on Caney fork beg at SE cor of JAMES LAXON occupant survey.

Page 314   Indenture   17 Oct 1814   JOSEPH WALLING and GEORGE W SAUNDERS, for $1200 paid, 163 acres being all land in grant issued by TN to Walling, No 1586.   Wit: ABEL HUTSON, DAVIS RUTLEDGE, BENJAMIN HAMLET.

Page 315   Indenture   23 Mar 1813   SETH DAVIS, Atty in fact for JOSHUA DAVIS of Davidson Co, TN, one part, and JAMES DAVIS, Williamson Co, TN, other part (no relationships stated), $250 paid, 640 acres granted by NC to JOSHUA DAVIS, lying on Caney fork river, adj WM REED, being 640 acres. Wit: JNO DAVIS, DARIUS DAVIS, JOHN JONES.   Ack in sd Davidson Co before NATHAN EWING.

Page 316   Indenture   23 Mar 1813   Parties as in above deed, $250 paid, 640 acres as granted to JOSHUA DAVIS on Caney fork river.   Wit: As above.

Page 317   Land Grant No 2250   20 May 1793   NORTH CAROLINA granted to

JOSHUA DAVIS, assee of AUGUSTINE HARRISON, a private in Continental line of sd state 640 acres on Caney fork. Certified on 4 Dec 1814 is true transcript from books of Military grants, JNO C MCLEMORE.

Page 317 Land Grant No 2282 20 May 1793 NC to above named Davis, assee of DANIEL GARRISON, private in Continental line, 640 acres in Sumner County. Also certified as above.

Page 318 Land Grant No 6048 21 Sept 1814 TENNESSEE as part of Certif 779, dated 9 Dec 1811, issued to JAMES TRIMBLE and entered on 3 Aug 1812 by No 1872, grants to WILLIAM BELCHER, assee of sd Trimble, 80 acres on Calf Killers fork of Caney fork.

Page 319 Sheriff's Deed 17 Oct 1814 ISAAC TAYLOR, Jnr, Esq, Shff, one part, and MOSES FISK, latter of Overton Co, TN, 2208 acres conveyed for $2.38 paid for taxes and costs.

Page 321 Land Grant No 5571 14 May 1814 TENNESSEE by virtue part Certif 162 dated 30 Oct 1810, issued to ANDREW M LUSKE , entered on 26 Jan 1811 by No 5817, grants to ISAAC MIDKIFF, assee of Luske, 25 acres on Taylor's creek of Caney fork beg ALEXANDER IRWIN 100 acre sur.

Page 321 Indenture 10 Sept 1813 ALEXANDER IRWIN and ISAAC MIDKIFF, $2000 paid, tr on both sides Wagon road leading from DANIEL ALEXANDER to Rock island 1/2 mile from where waggon road crosses S fork of Taylor's creek. Wit: HENRY NULL and JNO JETT.

Page 323 Indenture 26 Aug 1813 WILLIAM IRWIN and ISAAC MIDKILL, $300 paid, tr of 142 acres 1 rood & 21 perches, part of tr of 225 acres granted to JOHN RHEA and WILLIAM TERRELL by NC by Grant No 309, lying on Taylor's creek formerly Lick creek. Wit: SIMON ROSSEN, WILLIAM DUNCAN.

Page 324 Indenture 20 June 1814 WILLIAM MORRISON and JAMES SIMPSON, $100 paid, tr of 20 acres granted to William by TN, Grant No 1304, being on Caney fork on NW side of Morrison's mountain. Wit: ELY SIMS, HENRY LYDA.

Page 325 Indenture 19 July 1814 JAMES BOWEN and WILLIAM MCCOIN, $100 paid, tr of 50 acres in Grant 5590, beg at SW cor of DAVIS MITCHELL 100 acre sur. Wit: W P WHITE, JOHN WEAVER.

Page 326 Indenture 19 July 1814 JAMES BOWEN and WILLIAM MELVIN, $100 paid, 15 acres beg on SW cor DAVID MITCHELL. Wit: W P WHITE, JOHN WEAVER.

Page 327 Indenture 17 Oct 1814 Grantor above and DAVID HILLAYBOURN, $500 paid, 50 acres on N side Calf Killer fork of Caney fork and on Burdin Mill creek. Wit: JOHN W SIMPSON, WILLIAM SHAW.

Page 328 Indenture 5 Oct 1814 BENJAMIN HAMLETT and JOSHUA PENNINGTON, $125 paid, tr on waters of Calf Killer's fork & adj JAMES ISHAM 100 acre sur on his S bdy, being 72 acres. Wit: JACOB A LANE, ISHAM BRADLEY, JAMES ISHAM.

Page 329 Sheriff's Deed 3 Sept 1814 ISAAC TAYLOR, Junr, Shff, to WILLIAM HAWKINS by virtue of execution at instance of JOSEPH MORTON against goods & chattel lands of JOHN THAYER, $101 paid, 1 Negro boy child named

PATRICK about 2 yrs old.

Page 330   Land Grant No 2242   25 May 1810   TENNESSEE by virtue Certif No 42 dated 17 July 1807 obtained by JAMES MABANE, grants to BENJAMIN WEAVER, assee of sd James, 200 acres near DAVID WOMACK.   Surv 6 Aug 1808 by JAMES CHISUM, DS.

Page 331   Land Grant No 3972   17 June 1812   TENNESSEE by virtue Warr 1686 dated 19 Feb 1787 issued to DAVID ROSS, by Officer of claims for NC Western lands & entered on 13 Apr 1807 by No 362, grants to THOMAS MCBRIDE, assee sd Ross, 50 acres beg at beg cor of Esquire POTEET 200 acre tract.

Page 332   Indenture   17 Oct 1814   ISAAC TAYLOR, Jnr, and GUY SMITH, $100 paid, 201 acres on Cane creek of Falling water, it being moiety 1/2 tr granted by TN to Taylor by Grant No 4633.

Page 333   Land Grant No 4733   25 May 1813   TENNESSEE by virtue of part Warr No 536 dated 7 Apr 1812 issued to JOHN RAINS a hunter for the sur, for laying of lands allotted Officers and soldiers of Continental line of NC, entered 15 June 1812 by No 8283, grants to JOHN CHISUM, assee sd Rains, 25 acres in 1st Dist on waters of Caney fork.

Page 334   Land Grant No 334   17 June 1812   TENNESSEE by virtue part Warr 1079 dated 19 Feb 1787 issued to DAVIS ROSS by Officer of claims for NC Western lands, and entered on 5 Feb 1811 by No 1308, grants CHISUM, as above, 50 acres on waters of Calf killers fork of Caney fork.

Page 335   Land Grant No 6286   18 Nov 1814   TENNESSEE by virtue of part of Warr No 1686, dated 19 Feb 1787 issues to DANIEL ALEXANDER, assee of David Ross, 10 acres in 3rd Dist on Falling waters, a branch of the Caney fork.

Page 336   Land Grant No 6285   Date and parties as above, NC Warr 5090, 10 acres.

Page 337   Indenture   6 Dec 1813   JAMES BOWEN and CHRISTOPHER KUHN, $200 paid, tr in 3rd Dist on N side Calf killers fork of Caney fork entered 23 Sept 1812, No 2000, Warr 864, being 100 acres. Wit: WM ROBERTS, JOSEPH ANDERSON.

Page 338   Indenture   3 May 1814   SOLOMON JORDON of Madison Co, Terr of MS, one part, and BENJAMIN WEAVER, other part, $200 paid, tr on Cherry creek. Wit: THOS MCBRIDE, SAML JOHNSON, JOHN YOAKUM.

Page 339   Indenture   24 Sept 1814   EDWARD GLEASON and JOSEPH WALLING, $1600 paid, tr on Caney fork, being 400 acres the same tr conv by THOMAS K HARRIS to sd Gleason on 23 Dec 1811. Wit: ISAAC TAYLOR, Jr, THOMAS WALLING, THOMAS ROBERTSON, ELISHA WALLING (no relationships stated).

Page 340   Land Grant No 5714   15 June 1814   TENNESSEE by virtue part Certif 1263 dated 2 Oct 1812 issued by W TN to heirs of THOMAS WADE and entered on 5 Feb 1813 by 2281, grants to WILLIAM COCKE, assee sd heirs of Wade a tr of 30 acres in 3rd Dist on waters of main Caney fork on a back of a mountain, and beg W of sur where sd Cocke now lives.

Page 341   Land Grant No 3650   17 Jan 1812   TENNESSEE by part Certif 156 obtained by JAMES ROBERTSON and entered 24 Mar 1809 by No 26 as an occupant claim, grants to JAMES BARTLETT, assee sd Robertson 227 acres lying in Jackson County in 3rd Dist on the Falling waters of Caney fork.

Page 342   Land Grant No 4887   15 July 1813   Grantor above for military serv performed by WILLIAM WILLIAMS to NC, Warr No 3059, dated 30 Nov 1785, entered by No 897, grants to BERRYMAN HAMLETT, assee sd Williams, tr of 72 acres in 3rd Dist on Calf killers fork adj JAMES ISHAM 100 acre sur, and adj FREDERICK MILLER 151 acre sur.

Page 343   Land Grant No 5933   11 Aug 1814   Grantor above for military serv by DAVID JOYNER, a Captain in NC Warr 74 dated 18 Dec 1802, entered on 5 July 1808 by No 1996, grants to sd Joyner 640 acres, part sd warrant in 1st Dist on waters of Caney fork, beg at JOSEPH WALLINGS SE corner.

Page 344   Land Grant No 5584   23 May 1814   Grantor above by part of Certif 1441 dated 15 Mar 1813 issued by W TN to heirs of THOMAS WADE & entered 9 July 1813 by No 2349, grants to JESSE BABB, assee of sd heirs of Wade, 30 acres in 3rd Dist on Caney fork.

Page 345   Indenture   28 Dec 1814   JAMES BARTLETT and JOSHUA BARTLETT, $167 paid, 167 acres on Falling waters of Caney fork including where Bartlett now lives (relationship not stated).

Page 346   Bill of Sale   21 Feb 1814   ELISABETH WARREN to SPENCER MITCHELL, $300 paid, 1 Negro woman RACHEL and child TOW(?), the woman to continue to serve me during my life. Wit: WOODSON P WHITE, WILLIAM FOSTER.

Page 346   Bill of Sale   27 June 1814   JAMES BOWEN to JOHN CHISUM, $660 paid, 3 Negroes viz, 1 woman & 2 children, being SAL, aged 24, 1 sucking child a boy, named ELLICK, about 1 month old, the other a girl about 2 or 3 yrs old named ELISA. Wit: H H BROWN, JESSE WILSON.

Page 347   Indenture   16 Jan 1815   JOHN WALLING and WILLIAM HAMMOND, $400 paid, tr of 100 acres being where Hammond now lives, being part of tr of 640 acres orig granted to heirs of DAVID JOINER. Wit: WM GLENN, JOEL BRADSHAW.

Page 348   Indenture   5 Oct 1814   DANIEL HARTY and ENOCH ODLE, 24 acres near Green spring. Wit: DUNN DUFF, Junr, THOMAS DUFF.

Page 349   Land Grant No 5774   13 June 1814   TENNESSEE by virtue of part of Certif No 674 dated 23 Aug 1811, tr issued to Reg of W TN to GIDEON PILLOW, grants 49 acres on Calf killers fork of Caney fork.

Page 350   Land Grant No 6643   18 Feb 1815 Grantor as above by virtue part of Certif 229 dated 13 Aug 1810 issued to ROBERT KING and entered on 8 June 1813 by No 2507, grants to ELIJAH CHISUM, Senr, assee of sd King, tr of 30 acres in 3rd Dist on Calf killer fork.

Page 351   Land Grant No 7090   5 June 1815   TENNESSEE by part of Certif No 1831 dated 28 July 1814 issued to JOHN MCIVER on 28 Dec 1814 by No 3553, grants ELIJAH CHISUM, Senr, assee of McIver, 3 acres on Calf killers fork of Caney fork including a large fall in the spring branch that Chisum family uses water out of.

Page 352   Land Grant No 7089   5 June 1815   Grantor above by Certif No 359 dated 20 Nov 1809, grants to ELIJAH CHISUM, assee of ROBERT BURTON and JOHN MCIVER, 50 acres on Cherry creek in a cove of the rocky mountain.

Page 353   Land Grant No 5776   30 June 1814   Grantor above by Certif No 362, dated 5 Nov 1811 issued to JOHN MCIVER, tr of 25 acres in 3rd Dist on Calf killers forks of Caney fork.

Page 354   Land Grant No 5775   30 June 1814   Grantor above by Certif 959 issued to MCIVER as above, 50 acres in 3rd Dist.

Page 355   Land Grant No 6741   20 Mar 1815   Grantor above by Certif No 363 issued to Grantee above, 20 acres, 3rd Dist.

Page 356   Land Grant No 6761   23 Mar 1815   Grantor above by part Warr No 1724 dated 13 Jan 1809 issued to SAMUEL MCPHEETERS, entry made by him by No 1597, granted to ELIJAH CHISUM & WILLIAM P ANDERSON, assees sd McPheeters, 180 acres in 3rd Dist on NW side Calf killers fork of Caney fork & E of lands now occupied by LOWREY and FRALEY.

Page 357   Land Grant No 6762   23 Mar 1815   Grantor above for military service of THOMAS HART to NC, Warr 691, dated 27 Apr 1784 & entered 9 Oct 1810 by No 1167, grants to WILLIAM P ANDERSON & ELIJAH CHISUM, assees of PEGGY HART, heir of sd Thomas Hart, tr of 80 acres, part sd Warrant in 3rd Dist & on Calf killers fork.

Page 358   Land Grant No 5076   15 Oct 1813   Grantor above by part Certif No 1368 dated 15 Jan 1813, issued to JOHN C MCLEMORE, entered by No 2249, grants to MATTHEW BABB, assee sd McLemore, tr of 30 acres in 3rd Dist beg at SW cor 25 acre tr of JAMES BOWEN1, Entry No 1652.

Page 359   Land Grant No 5077   15 Oct 1813   Grantor above by part Certif 1368 (as above), to MATTHEW BABB, assee sd McLemore, 20 acres.

Page 360   Land Grant No 4742   25 May 1813   Grantor above by part Warr 536 dated 7 Apr 1812 issued to JOHN RAINS a hunter for the survey employed by NC for laying off lands for officers & soldiers of Continental line of sd state, grants to JOHN ENGLAND, assee sd Rains, tr of 37 1/2 acres in 1st Dist on S side Falling waters.

Page 361   Land Grant No 4477   30 Dec 1812 & of Independence of US the 37th Grantor as above by Warr dated 10 Jan 1794 issued to WILLIAM DALTON, a trumpeter in the Battalion of troops raised pursuant to act of Genl Assembly of NC for protection of inhabitants of Davidson Co, and entered on 24 Oct 1810 by No 5371, grants to JONATHAN WARD, assee sd Dalton, tr of 100 acres in 1st Dist on waters of Glade creek of the Falling waters.

Page 362   Indenture 7 Mar 1814   JOHN CLARY, Senr, and DAVIS PEARCE, $80.00 paid, tr of 100 acres granted to ZACHARIAH JONES by Grant 4474. Wit: ROBERT ARMSTRONG, JOHN CLARY.

Page 363   Indenture 9 Jan 1815   JOHN H BADGER, Monroe Co, KY(?), and WILLIAM HAWKINS, $430 paid, tr of 100 acres in 1st Dist 1st Range & 9th Sec. Wit: JOHN HAWKINS, BENJAMIN HAWKINS (relationships not stated).

Page 364 Indenture 17 Apr 1815 JAMES BOWEN and JOSEPH UPCHURCH, for $41.50 paid, tr in 3rd Dist on water of Caney fork, 32 1/2 acres & being land entered in name of ABNER HILL.

Page 365 Indenture 17 Apr 1815 JOHN ENGLAND and JONATHAN WARD, $100 paid, 37 1/2 acres on S side Falling water, beg at S bdy line of ANDERSON & MCIVER. Wit: ROBT ARMSTRONG, WM HITCHCOCK.

Page 366 Indenture 25 Aug 1814 WILLIAM IRWIN and JAMES MCCLURE, $320 paid by DARRITT OLIVER, tr on Taylors creek, a branch of Caney fork, 50 acres. Wit: ALEXANDER IRWIN, DAVID B CARTER.

Page 367 Indenture 19 Jan 1815 DAVID SMYTH and ISAAC THOMAS, $1.00 paid, Lot 3 in town of Sparta. Wit: JACOB A LANE, G W GIBBS.

Page 367 Bill of Sale 7 Feb 1815 JOSEPH ELLISON to ISAAC TAYLOR, Junr, a Negro woman slave named PHILLIS, aged 19. Wit: HERRON JOHNSTON, WILLIAM WHITE, JONATHAN WARD, JAMES ALLISON.

Page 368 Bill of Sale 30 Aug 1814 JAMES TAYLOR, Overton Co, TN, and THOMAS TAYLOR, to ISAAC TAYLOR, $400 paid, a Negro boy slave named LEE (?), aged 15 yrs. Wit: ISAAC TAYLOR, Senr, JAMES DUFEARN(?), THOS TAYLOR, Junr.

Page 369 Mortgage 26 July 1813 LAWSON HENDERSON, Lincoln Co, NC, by my agent JAMES HENDERSON, am bound to DAVID RUTLEDGE for $1000, with tract of 100 acres including farm & mill on Rutledge's Mill creek being the security.

Page 370 Indenture 10 Sept 1813 ISAAC MIDKIFF and ALEXANDER IRWIN, $1700 paid, tr of 142 acres 1 rood & 21 perches, it being part of tr of 225 acres which was granted JOHN RHEA and WILLIAM TYRRELL. Wit: HENRY NEILL, JNO JETT, ISAAC TAYLOR, Jnr, JOHN SULLIVAN. Ack before ELIJAH CHISUM, Reg of White County.

Page 371 Indenture 18 July 1814 ISAAC MIDKIFF to ALEXANDER IRWIN, $300 paid, 25 acres on waters of Taylor's creek of Caney fork adj Irwin 100 acre sur. Wit: ISAAC TAYLOR, Jnr, JOHN SULLIVAN.

Page 372 Indenture 20 June 1814 WILLIAM MORRISON and JAMES SIMPSON, $800 paid, tr of 130 acres granted to Morrison by TN by Grant No 565. Wit: ELY SIMS, HENRY LYDA.

Page 373 Indenture 2 Mar 1813 JAMES STINSON and WILLIAM STINSON (relationship not stated), $340 paid, tr of 640 acres purchased by Grantors from JOHN MCKEEVER and WILLIAM P ANDERSON. Wit: MACK LOWRY, CHARLES LOWREY.

Page 374 Indenture 27 May 1813 JAMES COLE and WILLIAM HOWARD, $31.00 paid, tr a part of tr Cole bought of WILLIAM P ANDERSON & JOHN MCIVER, 31 acres. Wit: WILLIAM PEGRAM, ISAAC HOWARD.

Page 375 Indenture 17 Apr 1815 JONATHAN WARD, one part, and SALLY HITCHCOCK, BETSY HITCHCOCK, POLLY HITCHCOCK, HENRY HITCHCOCK, REBEKAH HITCHCOCK, NANCY HITCHCOCK, SUSANNA HITCHCOCK and ELIJAH HITCHCOCK, (relationship not stated), tr on waters of Glass creek of Falling waters, being 100 acres of land, beg in S bdy of WILLIAM KING. Wit: ROBT ARMSTRONG, JOHN ENGLAND.

Page 376   Indenture   16 Feb 1815   JOHN KNOWLES, Junr, and JAMES KNOWLES, $390 paid, 130 acres being a moiety out of Grant 3501 issued by TN to RALEIGH RALLS for 300 acres. Tract begins at NW cor John Junr 95 acre sur. Wit: JAMES TOWNSEND, JOHN KNOWLES, Senr.

Page 377   Indenture   16 Feb 1815   Grantor above and JOHN KNOWLES, Senr, $225 paid, 75 acres out of above Grant 3501. JAMES TOWNSEND, JAMES KNOWLES. (Relationships not stated)

Page 378   Indenture   16 Feb 1815   JOHN KNOWLES, Senr, and JOHN KNOWLES, Junr, $90.00 paid, 30 acres being a moiety of Grant No 2569 issued by TN to JOHN KNOWLES, Senr, for 1295 acres, dated 29 Sept 1810, being on Caney fork beg at NW cor JOHN TEMPLETON survey. Wit: JAMES TOWNSEND, JAMES KNOWLES. (Relationships not stated)

Page 379   Power of Attorney   15 Aug 1815   JOHN PICKRELL of Champaign Co, OH, makes NICHOLAS PICKRELL, his Attorney to make deed for tract in White County to JACOB ROBISON. Wit: HARRY PICKRELL, ISAAC REA. (Relationships not stated) Ack in sd Champaign Co, OH before RALPH LOWE, Act Jus, and certif by WILLIAM WARD, Clk of Ct of Commiss.

Page 380   Indenture   19 Apr 1815   THOMAS STONE and JACOB ROBERTSON, $____ paid, 50 1/2 acres & 39 perches. (This is very dim microfilm)

Page 381   Sheriff's Deed   8 Sept 1815   ISAAC TAYLOR, Shff, one part, and GRAGE MATLOCK(?) and ROBERT ALLEN, second part, by writ against goods of ARMISTEAD STUBBLEFIELD, 514 acres on both side of Calf killer fork including the Harries Iron works on 137 acres adj above entered in name of BENJM ALEXANDER for the use of sd Stubblefield & 50 acres including iron oar bank on waters of Caney fork (and other lands).

Page 385   Indenture   9 Jan 1815   JOHN WILSON SHOCKLEY and SHADRACH ROBERTS, $60.00 paid, 30 acres on S side Caney fork. Wit: JOHN WARE, EPHRAIM SHOCKLEY.

Page 386   Indenture   18 Apr 1800   JOHN LOVE, Knox Co, TN, one part, and JOHN TAYLOR, Jr, of Buckland, Prince William Co, VA, $200 paid, 640 acres in the County of Middle Dist(?), on Caney fork of Cumberland River, including a plain where there has been an Indian Old Town and a large old field. Wit: STEPHEN HAYNES, JAMES TAYLOR, JAMES WATSON. Ack in District of Columbia, Washington County by WM BRENT, Clk, and certif in same place by WILLIAM CRAUCH, Chief Judge CC for DC. Proved in Knox Co, TN before CHA J MCCLUNG, Clk, by Dep ANDW HUTCHISON.

Page 387   Power of Attorney   10 Mar 1796   WILLIAM TYRRELL appoints STOCKLEY DONELSON, Esq, to be his atty in fact to convey, etc land. Executed in City of Raleigh, NC in Wake Co, NC. Ack before B SEAWELL & JNO MARSHALL, JPs. Certif by H LANE, CC, and proven before B L KING, CC, WCNC and certif by WILLIAM BOYLAN, Presid Magis, WCNC.

Page 389   Bill of Sale   15 May 1815   JOHN MCELHANEY and JAMES BOWEN for

$225 paid by WILLIAM M BRYAN, sell 1 Negro girl slave about 6 yrs of age named CALY. Wit: JOHN BRYAN, ANDREW BRYAN (relationship not stated).

Page 389 Bill of Sale Same date and Grantors as above, for $225 paid by STEPHEN WALLACE, 1 Negro girl slave about 4 yrs of age named MARY. Wit: As above.

Page 390 Bill of Sale 25 June 1815 Grantors as above, for $675 paid by ELIAS WALLACE, 2 Negro boys, one named JEFFERSON, about 12 yrs old, and other named DAVID, about 8 yrs. Wit: JOHN WALLIS, HENDERSON MCFARLIN.

Page 391 Bill of Sale 17 July 1815 Grantors as above, for $500 paid by Grantee above, 2 Negro slaves being 1 Negro woman named HANNAH about 32 yrs of age, the other a boy about 11 months old named WASHINGTON.

Page 391 Bill of Sale 1 July 1815 ALLEN CLARK and WILLIAM HUTCHINGS, Junr, of Hertford Co, NC, $320 paid by ROBERT PUCKET, $320 paid, 1 Negro girl named SUCK. Wit: THOMAS HARBUT.

Page 392 Bill of Sale 13 Apr 1813 MERRITT DILLIARD to JAMES TOWNSEND, $400 paid, 1 Negro woman named DILEY about 36 yrs of age and child. Wit: JOSIAH DILLIARD, ROBERT TOWNSEND.

Page 392 Indenture 18 July 1815 WILLIAM MARTIN, Warren Co, TN, one part, and JAMES CHARLES, other part, $325 paid, 1 tract in 1st Dist on N side Caney fork, 100 acres.

Page 393 Land Grant No 6413 19 Dec 1814 TENNESSEE for military service of THOMAS SCOTT to NC, Warr No 533, dated 20 Apr 1807, entered on 4 Dec 1809 by No 946 as an Occupant claim, grants to ROBERT HOWARD, assee of sd Thomas Scott, tr of 136 acres part of sd warrant lying in 3rd Dist on Cherry creek, a branch of Calf Killers fork of Caney fork.

Page 394 Land Grant No 5027 26 Sept 1813 TENNESSEE as part of Certif No 1109 dated 26 Aug 1812 issued to WOODSON P WHITE entered on 6 Nov 1812 by No 2078, then assigned by TN unto JOHN WILSON SHOCKLEY, assee, tr of 14 acres in 3rd Dist & on waters of main Caney fork.

Page 395 Land Grant No 2610 25 Oct 1810 TENNESSEE by Certif No 156 dated 16 Jan 1809 to JAMES ROBERTSON by No 21 on 18 Mar 1809, grants to NATHAN BARTLETT, assee of Robertson, tr of 183 acres lying in 3rd Dist on Falling waters of Caney fork.

Page 396 Indenture 29 Dec 1814 WOODSON P WHITE, one part, and CHARLES BOWEN and JOHN CUMMING, other part, $360 paid, tr conv to White by 2 grants issued by TN, Nos 5716 & 5709 being 110 acres.

Page 397 Indenture 11 Aug 1814 BENJAMIN WEAVER and SOLOMON YEAGER, latter of Washington Co, TN, $750 paid, tr on Cherry creek waters of Calf killers fork of Caney fork of Cumberland river. Wit: ELIJAH CHISUM, Senr, ABRAHAM BROYLES, THOS MCBURR(?).

Page 398 Indenture Same date and parties as in above indenture, $210 paid, 35 acres on Cherry creek, adj SE cor tr granted to SOLOMON JORDON by TN. Wit: As above.

Page 399 Indenture Date & parties as above, $252 paid, tr of 42 acres where Weaver now lives, beg in line of L H WEAVER & BENJAMIN WEAVER, also adj ELIJAH CHISUM. Wit: THOS MCBRIDE, ABRAHAM BRAYER, JOEL YEAGER.

Page 400 Indenture __ July 1815 WILLIAM HAYS and SOLOMON YAGER, $500 paid, tr of 50 acres being on Cherry creek a branch of Calf killers fork of Cany fork. Wit: THOMAS BROYLES, JOEL YEAGER, JAMES WILLHITE.

Page 401 Indenture 16 June 1815 ELIJAH CHISUM, Senr, and BENJAMIN WEAVER, $112 paid, 50 acres in Grant No 6741 containing 20 acres on waters of Calf killer waters of Caney fork, beg near SW cor WILLIAM P ANDERSON & sd Chisum survey of 180 acres known as Iron Ore tract. Wit: WILLIAM GLENN, ISAAC TAYLOR, Jr, ANTHONY DIBRELL.

Page 402 Indenture 22 July 1815 GEORGE W GIBBS and MATHIAS B ANDERSON, $38.00 paid, tr of 5 acres & 24 poles in or near town of Sparta.

Page 402 Land Grant No 5954 18 Aug 1814 TENNESSEE for military services performed by JETHRO SIMMONS(?) to state of NC, Warr No 4338, dated 18 Dec 1796, entered on 9 Sept 1813 by No 2678, grants to THOMAS WILSON, assee of heirs sd Simmons, tr of 10 1/2 acres, part of sd Warr lying in White Co in 3rd Dist in Hickory Valley, beg at NE cor sur made for ISAAC ANDERSON, surv 31 Jan 1814 by WOODSON P WHITE, DS.

Page 403 Indenture 12 Dec 1810 WILLIAM HAYS and SAMUEL THOMAS, $50.00 paid, tr of 35 acres in 3rd Dist on waters of Calf killers fork of Caney fork adj SHARP WHITLEY 115 acres. Wit: WILLIAM B USSRY, JOHN GRIGSBY.

Page 404 Indenture 26 Jan 1814 WILLIAM HAYS and THOMAS SHIRLY, $350 paid, 60 acres on NE side of Cherry creek, it being part of tr of sd Hays by Grant 4091. Wit: BENJN WEAVER, SIXTY WEAVER(?).

Page 405 Indenture 24 Mar 1815 HENRY HUTRON and WILLIAM HAWKINS, $50.00 paid, tr of 70 acres in 1st Dist on Cliff creek, adj line of JOHN JENKINS. Wit: JOHN HAWKINS, MILLS COOPER.

Page 406 Indenture 8 Dec 1813 JAMES RANDALS and WILLIAM ROGERS, $400 value paid in horse flesh at rates of 2 first horses, tr of 80 acres on Calf killers fork in 1st Dist 1st Range & 9th Sec, beg at line of JACOB MILLER and adj land of JOEL FOSTER and JOSEPH WALLING. Wit: ADAM HUMTSMAN, JACOB A LANE.

Page 407 Indenture 19 July 1815 ELIJAH CHISUM, Senr, and JAMES TURNER, $120 paid, tr of 40 acres granted to Chisum by Grant No 5771 on Calf killers fork in a cove of a mountain known as the Turkey cove.

Page 408 Indenture 30 Jan 1815 ELISHA WALLING and EDWARD GLEASON, $200 paid, tr on Caney fork being 58 acres as described. Wit: ANTHONY RICKITS, THOMAS ROBERTSON, JOHN ANDERSON, EDWARD HILTON.

Page 409 Indenture Date and parties as above, $600 paid, tr of 90 acres as described. Wit: JAMES GLEASON, ANTHONY RICKETS, THOMAS ROBERTSON.

Page 410 Indenture 5 Aug 1812 Commissioners of White County, being THOMAS ROUNDS, AARON ENGLAND, BENJAMIN WEAVER, TURNER LANE, ALEXANDER

LOWRY, JAMES FULKERSON & NICHOLAS GILLINTINE, one part, and ALEXANDER COOPER of other part, $9.12 1/2 paid, Lot 82 in Sparta.

Page 411 Indenture 12 May 1814 ROLAND LEE and THOMAS GAW, $10.00 paid, tr of 6 acres on Caney fork, it being part of a 640 acre tr of land sold to JAMES STINSON and WILLIAM STINSON (relationship not stated). Wit: JOSEPH MCBRIDE, REUBIN PERKINS.

Page 412 Indenture 17 July 1815 JOHN WALLING and WILLIAM HAMMOND, $158 paid, tr of 72 acres a part of 640 acres granted to heirs of DAVID JOINER, Warr No 74, and entered on 5 July 1808 by No 1996, being on Caney fork. Wit: WILLIAM GLENN, NICHOLAS GILLENTINE.

Page 413 Indenture 10 Mar 1815 ELISHA WALLING and THOMAS WALLING (relationship not stated), $300 paid, 135 acres in 1st Dist on E side Caney fork, it being part of Gum spring tr in Grant 640 for 640 acres, dated 8 Nov 1808. Wit: THOMAS ROBERTSON, WILLIAM FOX, JOSEPH WALLING.

Page 414 Indenture 30 Jan 1814 JAMES STINSON and WILLIAM STINSON (relationship not stated), one part, and ROWLAND LEE, other part, $200 paid, tr of 100 acres on Caney fork. Wit: JAS C MCBRIDE, JONAS ELLIOTT.

Page 415 Indenture 28 June 1815 GEORGE W RAYMAR, one part, and CHRISTOPHER MIDYETT and RICHARD MIDYETT, other part (no relationship stated), $300 paid, tr on waters of Caney fork (very dim microfilm). Wit: JOHN KNOWLES, Senr, JAS TOWNSEND.

Page 416 Indenture 16 May 1815 ELIJAH BATES, one part, and CHARLES BATES, Overton Co, TN (relationship not stated), $700 paid, 200 acres beg at NE cor of ELIJAH BATES 200 acre sur that he now lives on. Wit: JOSEPH BATES, JACOB BEESON, JOHN MCDONNERD, ROBERT BATES.

Page 417 Indenture 8 June 1815 ELIJAH BATES and NATHANIEL MARTIN, for $100 paid, tr of 200 acres on Caney fork. Wit: JOHN MAY, ROBERT BATES, GEORGE MARTIN.

Page 418 Indenture 8 June 1815 ELIJAH BATES and ROBERT (no relationship stated), $400 paid, 100 acres in 1st Dist in 10th Sec & 1st Range. Wit: GEORGE MARTIN, EZEKIEL BATES, JOHN MAY.

Page 419 Indenture 15 Mar 1815 WILLIAM B NEVIL, of one part, and SYLVESTER WILSON and WILLIAM WILSON (relationship not stated), other part, $500 paid, 150 acres, a part of Grant No 2873 granted by Tennessee to WILLIAM NEVIL, Sr, for 300 acres, line crossing road leading from Carthage to Sparta. Wit: JOHN MERRIL (?), RICHARD LUNDY.

Page 420 Indenture 17 July 1815 CURTIS MILLS and JONATHAN WARD, $300 paid, 200 acres on the Falling waters, being a moiety out of Grant 2701 issued by NC to JAMES EASTON, at one point adj lands of CURTIS MILLS and JONATHAN WARD. Wit: J THOMAS, WILLIAM CRUM.

Page 421 Indenture 20 June 1814 BIRD SMITH and SEABORN ODOM, $150 paid, tr in First Dist on Caney fork, 100 acres. Wit: JOHN WELCH, JOHN GAINA, WM J(?) SMITH.

Page 422   Indenture   31 Jan 1815   ABEL HUTSON to CASON SWINDELL, $60.00 paid, tr of 95 acres on Caney fork.   Wit: ISAIAH HUTSON, ARCHIBALD HUTSON.

Page 423   Indenture   28 Dec 1814   NATHAN BARTLETT and WILLIAM HUNTER, Senr, $91.50 paid, tr on fallen waters of Caney fork, including where Hunter now lives, part of tr granted by TN to Bartlett, Grant 2640 for 183 acres on 25 Oct 1810, tr conv 96 1/2 acres.

Page 424   Power of Attorney   7 Feb 1815   PATRICK DONAHO to friend JOHN CHISUM, power to assign my right to a plat and certif of survey founded on an entry made in my name for 100 acres, to JONATHAN HARRIS.   Wit: JACOB A LANE, GEORGE C HAMLETT.

Page 425   Bill of Sale   28 Sept 1815   JOHN PATE of Warren Co, TN, to ANTHONY PATE, (no relationship stated), $500 paid, 1 Negro boy named PETER, 16 years old, it being the boy that Anthony has had possession of for some time past.   Wit: THOS K HARRIS.

Page 425   Indenture   9 Jan 1815   JOHN WILSON SHOCKLEY and EPHRAIM SHOCKLEY, (no relationship stated), $30.00 paid, 14 acres on S side of Caney fork.   Wit: _____ GILLENTINE, SHADRACH ROBERTS, JOHN WARE.

Page 426   Land Grant   26 Sept 1813   TENNESSEE by virtue of part of Certif #421 dated 20 May 1812 issued by Reg of East Tennessee to JOSEPH WILLIAMS and entered on 18 Feb 1813 by No 2320, grants JOHN WILSON SHOCKLEY, assee of sd Williams, tr of 30 acres in 3rd Dist and on main Caney fork.

Page 427   Indenture   28 Dec 1812   JOHN HUTCHINGS and JESSE FINN, $65.00 paid, 84 acres on Caney fork, a part of 640 acre tr conv by WILLIAM P ANDERSON and JOHN MCIVER to Hutchings.   Wit: ROBT ARMSTRONG, JOHN ROPER.

Page 428   Indenture   18 Apr 1812   JAMES MCCLAIN and THOMAS GIST, of one part, and ALEXANDER LOWREY, other part, $5.00 paid, their interest in 1/5 & 1/2 of tr of 1 acre held by Grant No 3801, issued by Tennessee to JAMES MCCLAIN, ALEXANDER LOWREY and THOMAS GIST on 15 Mar 1812.   Wit: J A LANE, JOSEPH CRABB.

Page 429   Power of Attorney   6 Aug 1814   WILLIAM RIDGE, Bledsoe Co, TN, grants to JOHN MCBRIDE power of my agent to make entries or transfer any plat, certif, etc.   Wit: STEPHEN BRINDLEY, CHARLES HOLLOWAY, THOMAS RIDGE. Ack in Bledsoe County before JOSEPH B PORTER.

Page 429   Plat of Tract   Surveyed 14 June 1796 by THOS KING, Dist Surveyor, tr being in Territory S of Ohio, Middle Dist, TN, a Warr issued on 24 May 1784 to ROBERT KING, assee of JAMES WILLIAMS, 2500 acres on Camp creek, a branch of the falling water.

Page 430   Copy of Land Grant   1 Mar 1797   NORTH CAROLINA to ROBERT KING, assee of JAMES WILLIAMS, 2500 acres.   Certified by WM HILL, Secty, stating is copy of Grant 2253.   Also certif by WILLIAM HAWKINS, in NC.

Page 431   Land Grant No 5402   17 Feb 1814   TENNESSEE by part of Certif 1363, dated 11 Jan 1813, issued by Reg of W TN to JOHN C MCLIMORE, entered on 20 Jan 1813 by No 9938, then granted by sd state to DAVIS CUMMINGS, assee of McLimore, tr of 40 acres in White County in 1st Dist on S side

Caney fork, beg in N bdy line of JOSEPH CUMMINGS, surveyed 2 Jan 1813 by JAMES TOWNSEND.

Page 432   Land Grant No 1628   11 Sept 1809   TENNESSEE in consideration of Military service by STEPHEN MCDU__ to NC, No 2937, dated 30 Sept 1785, entered on 27 Aug 1807 by No 154, grants to WILLIAM CLAY, assee of sd Stephen, tr of 100 acres, part of sd warr lying in White County in 3rd Dist, 25 section, & on N side Calf Killers fork of Caney river.

Page 433   Land Grant No 2641   25 Oct 1810   TENNESSEE by virtue part of Certif No 156, dated 16 Jan 1809, obtained from W TN by JAMES ROBERTSON and entered on 24 Mar 1809, No 25, as an Occupant claim grants to JOSEPH HUNTER, assee of sd Robertson 184 acres in Jackson County in 3rd Dist, on falling water of Caney fork, adj NATHAN BARTLETT and Cumberland mountain.

Page 434   Land Grant No 2642   25 Oct 1810 and of Indepen of US the 35th TENNESSEE a part of Certif No 156 dated 18 Jan 1809 obtained from W TN by JAMES ROBERTSON and entered on 9 Oct 1809 by No 914, grants to JOSEPH HINTON, assee of sd Robertson, tr of 71 acres in Jackson County, 71 acres in 3rd Dist in the dry valley.

Page 435   Land Grant No 3970   17 June 1812   TENNESSEE by virtue of part of Warr 1648 dated 20 Nov 1784 issued to CHARLES ROBINSON by NC and entered on 5 Feb 1811, No 1309, grants to DAVID COWAN, assee of sd Robinson, 50 acres, 3rd Dist, on waters of the Calf Killer of Caney fork, beg where EDWARD DAVIS now lives, sur 12 Feb 1811 by W P WHITE, DS.

Page 436   Land Grant No 4886   15 July 1813   TENNESSEE in consideration of military service of WILLIAM WILLIAMS by NC Warr 3059, dated 30 Nov 1785, entered on 21 Aug 1809 by No 887, grants to GEORGE HAMLETT, assee of sd Williams, tr of 100 acres in 3rd Dist on Calf Killer fork, adj sur of JESSE DODSON on the East.

Page 437   Land Grant No 6550   25 Jan 1815   TENNESSEE as part of Certif 1604 dated 25 Sept 1813 issued by Reg of W TN to JOHN C MCLEMORE and entered on 5 Jan 1814 by No 3883, grants JOHN ANDERSON, assee sd McLemore, tr of 40 acres in 3rd Dist on W fork of Caney Fork on top of Cumberland mountain, beg at place known as JAMES ANDREWS camp.

Page 438   Land Grant No 1877   22 Jan 1810   TENNESSEE by part of Warr No 1588 dated 27 Mar 1799, issued to WILLIAM BLEVINS by JOHN CARTER, Entry taker for Washington County and entered on 15 Aug 1807 by No 52, grants to HENRY BOHANNON, assee of sd Blevins a tr of 100 acres in 3rd Dist on falling water of Caney fork in 16th Sec adj NATHANIEL TAYLOR Entry No 51 for 180 acres in the south.

Page 439   Land Grant No 4723   18 May 1813   TENNESSEE by virtue part of Certif 1207 dated 17 Sept 1812 issued by W TN to THOMAS DILLON, entered 24 Sept 1812 by No 8997, grants to ISAAC TAYLOR, Junr, assee sd Dillon, tr of 100 acres in 1st Dist on Caney creek, adj an entry of his own of 402 acres, Location No 6427, on his E bdy.

Page 440   Indenture   12 Nov 1814   JOHN HUTCHINGS, one part, and WILLIAM CAMERON, other part, $120 paid, 184 1/2 acres, part of a 640 acre tr conv to sd Hutchings by WILLIAM MCIVER, ANDERSON MCIVER, and JOHN MCIVER (relationship not stated), being on tr granted by NC to JAMES CARTER (description very dim). Wit: JOSEPH HUTCHINGS, ___ HUTCHINGS.

Page 441 Indenture 17 Jan 1815 JAMES BOWIN and JOHN STEWART, $100 paid, tr on Calf Killers fork, being 50 acres, beg near NE cor tr CLEM CLEMENTS formerly occupied. Wit: JOHN WEAVER, WILLIAM MELVIN.

Page 442 Indenture 6 Dec 1813 JAMES BOWER and JOHN STUART, $92.00 paid, tr on Caney fork on N side, entered 24 Nov 1812, No 2133, tr beg cor of JOHN CHISUM(?) --remainder very dim.

Page 443 Indenture Same Date and Parties as in above deed, $112 paid, tr on N side Caney fork, in Certif 1263, 56 acres. Wit: DAVID MITCHELL, CHRISTOPHER KUHN.

Page 444 Indenture 9 Nov 1814 HENRY LYDA and ROBERT PRIKET, $60.00 paid, tr in him vested by Grant 2809 issued by TN on 5 Jan 1811 for 120 acres on Calf Killers fork. Wit: J A LANE, JAMES SIMPSON.

Page 445 Bill of Sale (Tentative) 9 Sept 1815 RICHARD HORN to GEORGE DEFR__, $150 paid, a 1/5 interest in Negroes that is yet undivided, the Negroes deeded by RICHARD HORN, Sr, to five of his children, namely SARAH RIDGE, LETTE BREEDING(?), RICHARD HORN, Jr, ZACHEUS HORN, and WILLY HORN(?), said being called for in Deed of Gift, man slave called JIM, Negro woman AMY (?), and her child DILEY, 1 Negro woman named ACTS(?), and her child named HANNAH. Wit: JAMES COPE, JOHN WARRIN.

Page 445 Bill of Sale 19 Jan 1816 GEORGE W GIBBS to EDWARD GLEASON, a Negro boy named EMANUEL, $450 paid.

Page 446 Bill of Sale 4 Aug 1815 WILLIAM RIDGE and wife SARAH RIDGE, to GEORGE DEPRENE, $150 paid, (as described on above page 445 sale). Wit: WIL MCCANN, JAMES PERRYMAN, THOMAS RIDGE. Ack by JOSEPH B PORTER, CC (county is illegible).

Page 446 Bill of Sale 20 Oct 1815 JOHN SHROPSHIRE to JOHN WALLING, $274 paid, conveys 1 Negro girl named NANCY (or AMY), between 10 and 11 years of age. Wit: LAWSON NEWEL (?).

Page 447 Indenture 7 Aug 1815 JOHN HITCHCOCK and EZEKEIL HITCHCOCK (relationship not stated), $100 paid, tr beg at NE bdy WILLIAM HITCHCOCK of 110 acres & line running S of sd acreage, tr hereby conv being 50 acres. Wit: ROBT ARMISTON, JOHN CLARY.

Page 448 Indenture 5 Mar 1816 CHARLES BATES, Overton Co, TN, and NATHANIEL BOWMAN, $700 paid, 127 acres & 120 poles, a part of tr granted to ELIJAH BATES for 200 acres. Wit: JOHN JAMES, JAMES ROGERS.

Page 449 Indenture 31 July 1815 JAMES CHISUM, Overton Co, TN, and MARSHAL DUNCAN, $266 & 66 2/3 paid, tr on Calf killer's creek and on Cherry creek, including part of improvements where Duncan now lives, being 80 acres granted by TN to sd Chisum pr Grant No 5772 on 30 June 1811, beg at SW cor of HARVEY JARVIS(?) occupant sur of 100 acres. Wit: ELIJAH CHISUM, Senr, SOLOMON DUNCAN.

Page 450   Indenture   12 June 1815   ELIJAH CHISUM and WILLIAM E METCALF, $150 paid, 2 tracts of 50 acres & 25 acres, the 50 acres beg 60 poles from SE cor of WILLIAM HAYS entry 533, and other tr beg 4 poles E of SE line of 55 acre tr of WILLIAM P ANDERSON.   Wit: ABRAHAM BROYLE, SAMUEL LANE.

Page 451   Indenture   16 Oct 1815   WILLIAM ROBERTSON and WILLIAM MAY, $350 paid, tr being part tr granted sd Robertson of 120 acres, Grant 5591, Warr 4838, being in 3rd Dist on Calf Killers fork of Caney fork, including the farm and dwelling, and being 71 acres.   Wit: JONATHAN C DAVIS, STEPHEN K CHARLES.

Page 452   Indenture   15 Jan 1814   JACOB MILLER and JOSEPH CRABB, latter of ___ County, $400 paid, tr in first Dist on Caney fork, adj land of JOSEPH WALLING, 200 acres.   Wit: JOHN CHISUM, BENJ HAMLITT(?). (Very dim)

Page 453   Indenture   14 Jan 1814   JAMES STIMSON, WILLIAM STINSON (no relationship stated), one part, and JOSEPH C MCBRIDE, other part, for $200 paid, 100 acres on Caney fork, part of tr of 640 acres purchased by Stimsons from JOHN MCKEEVES(?) and WILLIAM P ANDERSON, tr adj land of ROLAND LEE.   Wit: ROLAND LEE, ___ ELLIOTT. (Very dim)

Page 454   Indenture   17 Oct 1815   JOHN ANDERSON and BLUFORD WARREN, $34.00 paid, tr on W fork Caney fork on top of Cumberland mountain, 40 acres granted by TN to sd Anderson by Grant No 6550 on 5 Jan 1815, tr adj JAMES ADERSON.   (Very dim)

Page 455   Indenture   16 Jan 1816   THOS H HARRIS and BENJAMIN WEBB, $600 paid, tr of 200 acres, it being tr whereon sd Thos now lives.

Page 456   Indenture   2 Jan 1812   THOMAS CRUTCHER and JAMES HILL, $120 paid, tr being part of 640 acres granted by NC to JAMES EASTON, and beginning at cor of WILLIAM ROBINSON, being 40 acres.   Wit: JACOB ROBINSON, HOWARD CASH.

Page 457   Indenture   7 Nov 1815   JOHN CHISUM and BONAPARTE CRABB, $300 paid, tr in 3rd Dist on Calf Killers fork of Caney fork, tr adj JOHN MILLER W cor, & being 50 acres.   Wit: JOSEPH UPCHURCH, JOHN SMITH.

Page 458   Indenture   9 Nov 1812   DAVID COWAN, Junr, one part, and JOHN CHISUM, other part, $150 paid, tr on Calf killers fork of Caney, adj tr where DAVID COWAN, Senr, now resides, 50 acres.   Wit: JOSEPH UPCHURCH, ELIJAH CHISUM, WILLIAM ROBERTS.

Page 459   Indenture   10 Jan 1814   FREDERICK MILLER and JOSEPH CRABB, $500 paid, tr in 3rd Dist being 5th Sec, 50 acres (very dim).   Wit: JESSE DEDSON.

Page 460   Indenture   7 Sept 1814   THOMAS TAYLOR, Senior, to SALLY L CARRICK, $100 paid, Lot No 61 in town of Sparta.   Wit: THOMAS TAYLOR, Junior, GEO CARRICK.

Page 460   Indenture   27 Sept 1815   (Very dim)   THOMAS WALLING and BENJAMIN GIBS, Hyde Co, NC, $300 paid, tr in White County lying near the Gum spring.   Wit: (Unreadable)

Page 461 Indenture 6 Jan 1816 DAVID NICHOLAS and JOHN DALE, $100 paid, tr conv to Nicholas by deed from THOMAS MCCORRY on 2 June 1808 for tr in the Hickory valley on S end of Nicholas sur. Wit: WILLIAM ROLING, JOHN YEATS.

Page 462 Indenture 7 Apr 1796 STOCKLEY DONELSON, of Raleigh, NC, one part, and JOHN LOVE of Prince William Co, VA, other part, $2000 paid, tr in Knox Co, TN, in the grassey valley on N side of Holston river, including a plain known as the Chinquipin patch, beg near line of THOMAS MARSHALL, and containing 1000 acres; also tr in same valley of 1000 acres; also tr in TN late the South Western Terr in Middle Dist, on Caney fork of Cumberland & including a place where there has been an old Indian town, 640 acres. Wit: (Unreadable). Ack before ANDREW JACKSON, Judge, Sup Court in the state on 21 Sept 1799.

Page 463 Release of Claim 16 Jan 1815 WILLIAM JONES to MATTHEW CLAY, $140 received, my claim in salt works or lick where I have been working in Jackson Co, TN, sd works are owned by THOMAS HARBERT and said Clay. Wit: JOHN MURRAY, JOHN M MURRAY, JOHN MCCORD.

Page 464 Land Grant No 6897 26 Apr 1815 TENNESSEE by virtue of part of Certif 1029, dated 30 May 1812, issued by Register of W TN to WILLIAM LYTLE and entered on 8 June 1812 by No 8247, grants to THOMAS GAW (?), assee of sd Lytle, tr of 30 acres in Jackson County in First Dist on Hutchings creek, tr conveyed including a cabin & 4 springs E of WILLIAM P ANDERSON survey.

Page 464 Land Grant No 7708 6 Sept 1815 TENNESSEE by virtue part Certif 1909, dated 11 Oct 1814, issued by Reg of W TN to DANNIE WILLIAMS, entered on 29 Oct 1814 by No 13663, grants to THOMAS GAW, assee sd Williams, 26 acres in White County in 3rd Dist on Hutchings creek of falling waters and beg SE cor Gaw's 50 acre sur, including all improvements made by SAMMIE SMITH.

Page 465 Land Grant 6896 26 Apr 1815 TENNESSEE by virtue part Certif 1082, dated 6 July 1812, issued to JOSEPH COLEMAN, entered on 4 Dec 1812 by No 9600 (or may be 9000), grants to THOMAS GAW, assee sd Coleman, tr of 50 acres in Jackson County in 1st Dist on Hutchings creek, and including Gaw's improvements.

Page 466 Land Grant No 5020 25 Sept 1813 TENNESSEE by virtue part Certif No 1007 dated 15 May 1812, issued to HUGH LEE__ (?), tr of 15 acres in 3rd Dist and in Milson's cove, issues to JOEL MILSON, sd land which also adj sur of DAVID THOMPSON.

Page 467 Land Grant 6398 17 Dec 1814 TENNESSEE by virtue part Certif 577 dated 17 Jan 1814, issued to WM HENRY and part Certif 1447, dated 23 Dec 1812, issued to JOHN C MCLENON and entered on 21 Feb 1814 by No 2915, grants to JOEL MILSON (or JOEL MELTON), assee sd Henry and McLemore, tr of 40 acres in 3rd Dist on waters of Town creek, beg near where Wilson now lives, and adj DAVID THOMPSON line.

Page 468 Land Grant 5431 1 Mar 1814 Grantor above by part Certif 1253, dated 29 Sept 1812, issued to JAMES TOWNSEND, entered 29 Sept 1812 by No 9108, grants to JOEL MELTON(?), assee sd Townsend, tr of 20 acres in 1st

Dist on Calf Killers fork, beg in head of Melton's Cove of the Town creek mountain.

Page 469   Land Grant No 5433   1 Mar 1814   Grantor above by part Certif 674, dated 23 Aug 1811, issued to GIDEON PILLOW, entered on 10 Sept 1812 by No 1984, grants to JOEL MILTON(?), assee sd Pillow, tr of 30 acres in 3rd Dist on Calf Killer's fork.

Page 470   Land Grant No 5715   15 June 1814 & of the Independence of the US the 38th   TENNESSEE by virtue part Certif 1007 dated 15 May 1812, issued to HENRY C LEEPER, entered on 30 Jan 1813 by No 3367, grants JOEL MELTON, assee sd Leeper, tr of 20 acres in 4rd Dist on Town creek.

Page 471   Indenture   7 Nov 1814   THOMAS STONE and WILLIAM DYER, $3.50 paid, tr on Cane creek, a part of tr of 2500 acres orig granted by NC to ROBERT KING, assee JAMES WILLIAMS by Grant 341, dated 1 Mar 1797, beg at cor of JACOB ROBINSON, 140 acres.   Wit: JOHN DYER, JAMES BRYANT.

Page 472   Indenture   10 Jan 1816   ISAAC TAYLOR, Junr, and JOSEPH ELLISON, $740 paid, 2 tracts on Cane creek, being 201 acres one moiety or half of tr of 402 acres granted sd Taylor on 27 Mar 1813 by Patent No 4633, and other tr being 100 acres granted by TN to Taylor on 18 May 1813, Patent 4723.

Page 473   Power of Attorney   4 Jan 1816   JAMES P TAYLOR, Carter Co, TN, appoints ISAAC TAYLOR as his attorney with power to sell his land, etc. Wit: THOMAS TAYLOR, Junr, JOHN TAYLOR.

Page 474   Indenture   15 Apr 1808   SAMMIE DUDLEY to MAY COX, $50.00 paid, tr vested in him by grant issued by TN No 5557, dated 30 Jan 1812, 10 acres.

Page 475   Indenture   29 May 1815   GEORGE C HAMBLET and ARCHIBALD CONNER, $132 paid, tr of 35 acres a part of Grant No 4888.   Wit: JOHN WALLING, JAMES MCMILLIN.

Page 476   Indenture   12 Nov 1815   GEORGE AILSWORTH, Esq, and LEONARD LAMBARON (?) of town of Sparta, $100 paid, part or parcel of 4 acres, part same land held by Grantor here by deed from GEO W GIBBS adj Sparta, being SE cor Lot 11. Wit: WILLIAM GLESON(?), ISAAC TAYLOR.

Page 477   Indenture   7 June 1815   DANNIE NEAL, Knox Co KY, one part, and MATTHEW ANDERSON and WILLIAM ANDERSON (no relationship stated), $20.00 paid, tr being Lot 40 in Sparta. Wit: WILLIAM GLENN and JAMES TURNER.

Page 478   Indenture   15 Sept 1814   JAMES COLE and GEORGE PARKERSON, $500 paid, tr of 145 acres on Post oak creek, a branch of falling waters.

Page 479   Indenture   15 Apr 1816   JOEL MILTON and WINNEFORD CLARKE, $230 paid, tracts of 52 3/4 acres. Wit: H DIBRILL.

Page 480   Land Grant No 4633   27 Mar 1813   TENNESSEE by virtue Certif No 547, dated 18 May 1811 issued by West Tennessee to WILLIAM RUSSELL and Certif No 594, No 595 & 596 issued to ISAAC TAYLOR, Junr, tr of 402 acres in 1st Dist on both sides of Cane creek on the falling water, tr conveyed adj JAMES CARTER and sur of 640 acres made for WILLIAM KING.

Page 481   Indenture 6 May 1815   JOHN CAMPBELL and GEORGE POTTS, $500 paid, 2 tracts on Taylor's creek, one adj SHADRACK GREEN SE cor of his occupant claim, each tract including approximately 100 acres. Wit: JESSE ALLEN, GEORGE W POTTS.

Page 482   Indenture 25 Dec 1815   JOHN JETT and MATTHEW ANDERSON and WILLIAM ANDERSON (no relationship stated), $400 paid, Lot 31 in town of Sparta. Wit: W P WHITE, CHARLES M SMITH.

Page 483   Indenture 20 Apr 1816   JOEL MELTON and FRANKY B THOMAS, $75.00 paid, tr of 27 1/3 acres, adj line of 2 3/4 of land conv by Melton to WINNIFORD CLARKE.

Page 484   Indenture 7 Apr 1816   WOODSON P WHITE and NICHOLAS GALLINTINE(?), $25.00 paid, tr in Grant No 5716, dated 15 June 1874, tr of 50 acres, beg at sd Giltentine's NW cor on THOMAS CLARK S bdy line, & adj DANIEL HARTIN W bdy line.

Page 485   Indenture 27 Jan 1816 & in 40th year of Am Indepen   BURRIL HUDSON and THOMAS HODSON, $6.25 paid, tr of 3 acres 16 roods, part sd Hudson's sur of 190 acres, tr adj Calf Killer. Wit: JAMES SCARBOROUGH, JAMES ROBISON.

Page 486   Deed of Correction 19 June 1815   JOSEPH ROBERTSON and JOHN JETT, $700 paid, 99 acres & 2 roods being on Calf Killer fork of Caney fork, being same land conv by deed made to Jett on 6 Nov 1812 purporting to convey 99 acres & 2 roods of land -- this deed is intended as a supplemental deed (see both deeds to compare land descriptions, if interested). Wit: ANDREW BLACKWOOD, WILLIAM GIST.

Page 487   Indenture 17 July 1815   WILLIAM ROBERTSON and JOHN JETT, $100 paid, tr on W side Calf Killer and being part Grant No 2840 issued by TN to Robertson and WILLIAM GIST for 200 acres on 20 Jan 2820, adj land of JOSEPH ROBERTSON, 23 acres & 1 rood. Wit: WILLIAM GLENN, ISAAC MIDKIFF.

Page 488   Deed 1 Nov 1813   MOSES FISK in consideration of the importance of religious worship and with a view of promoting the means thereof, gives to the Christian Society in about Kirkland(?) in White County, sd now under Pastoral care of the Reverend THOMAS MCBRIDE, to erect a meeting house near ___ creek, tr being 3 acres and to include the graveyard near the old meeting house. Wit: AUSTIN DEARING.

Page 489   Executor's Deed 17 Feb 1816   LILBURN L HENDERSON, Washington Co, VA, Executor of WILLIAM TRIGG, Decd, who was surviving Exr of WILLIAM KING, Decd, appoints WILLIAM J SMITH and JOHN J SMITH (no relationship stated) of White County, as my Exr to settle, liquidate, etc, all claims touching lands owned or claimed by sd King in White County. Wit: W E ANDERSON, JOSEPH SHAW.

Page 490   Indenture 1 Dec 1812   EDWIN L HARRIS and WILLIAM C BRITAIN, latter of Washington Co, TN, $200 paid, Lot 53 in town of Sparta. Wit: GEORGE AILSWORTH(?), JACOB A LANE.

Page 491   Indenture 6 Dec 1815   ROBERT BURTON, Granville Co, SC, and ISAAC TAYLOR, $325 paid, 1000 acres on Caney fork including a lick & on both sides of a small creek called by KING & CO, being tr granted by NC to STOCKLEY DONELSON, WILLIAM TYRELL & ROBERT KING by Patent 2579. Wit: WILLIAM GLENN, LAWSON NOUNE(?), LEONARD LAMBERSON.

Page 492 Indenture 8 Aug 1809   JOHN TAYLOR, Fauquier Co, VA, and PETER BEVERLY, Culpepper Co, VA, $12,000 paid, tr of 2445 acres on Cumberland and Ohio Rivers & being same tr conveyed by JOHN LOVE to JAMES TAYLOR, father of sd John on 12 July 1800, and certified by ARCHIBALD ROANE late a Judge of Super Ct of TN, James having since died intestate and left sd John his only child/heir. Wit: ISRAEL GLASCOCK, BIRKLEY WARD, NATHL SMITH. Ack in Fauquier County on 30 May 1811.

Plat of Survey by STOCKLEY DONELSON in Terr of USA, South of River Ohio, Middle Dist, by virtue of warr to me directed, No 100, dated 26 Feb 17__. Chainmen CHRISTIAN RHODES, ROBERT KING.

Page 494 Land Grant No 303   7 Mar 1796   NORTH CAROLINA for 2 pounds for every hundred acres being granted, paid by STOCKLEY DONELSON and WILLIAM TYRRELL, grant 640 acres in Middle Dist on Caney fork of Cumberland river, including a place where there has been an Indian old town and a large field.

Page 495 Indenture 15 July 1816   ELIJAH M WARD and JACOB ROBINSON, $4.00 paid, tr of 50 acres on headwaters of Post oak creek, it being part of same land that Ward holds by deed from JOHN KING and JAMES KING.

Page 496 Indenture 14 June 1816   JOHN KING, Junr, and JAMES KING (relationship not stated), and ELIJAH M WARD, $4.00 paid, tr of 2500 acres on Cane creek, a branch of Cany fork of Cumberland river. Wit: THOS BLAKE, J C MCNAIR, WILLIAM HILL, HENRY GOW.

Page 497 Land Grant No 2901 9 Feb 1811   TENNESSEE by virtue of Certif No 32 dated 18 Aug 1807 obtained by heirs of GEORGE RUSSELL, entered on 11 Aug 1808 by No 2161, part claim granted by TN (232 1/2 acres) in First Dist on Calf Killer fork.

Page 498 Indenture 8 Feb 1816   GEORGE C HAMLETT and WILLIAM HAMMOND, $300 paid, tr of 65 acres, part of tr of 100 acres granted to Hamlett and being on Caney fork, adj SW cor ARCHIBALD CONNERS, part of sd Grant of 100 acres, also adj JESSE DODSON on the military line. Wit: ANDREW COPE, ARCHIBALD CONNOR.

Page 499 Indenture 15 Jan 1816   JOHN WALLING and JESSE DODSON, $29.00 paid, tr on Caney fork of Cumberland river, a part of tr of 640 acres granted to heirs of DAVID JOINER.

Page 500 Indenture 13 Apr 1816   ELISHA SANDERS and JOHN HALLEMAN, $85.00 paid, tr in 3rd Dist on N side main Caney fork, being 50 acres. Wit: JOSEPH UPCHURCH, RHUBART P SANDERS(?).

Page 501 Indenture 24 June 1816 THOMAS STONE and DAVIS NORRIS, $1000 paid, tr of 386(?) acres, being on Cane creek a branch of Caney fork of Cumberland river, it being part of 2500 acres orig granted by NC to ROBERT KING, assee of JAMES WILLIAMS by Grant No 342, dated 1 Mar 1797. Wit: PINK HUDSON, IREBY W STONE.

Page 502   Indenture   23 Oct 1815   THOMAS H HARRIS and JOSEPH CLARK, $100 paid, tr of 100 acres on Jenkin's creek in White County, and adj DENNIS ALSTON tr of 457 1/3 acres. Wit: POLLY BADGER, JOHN KNOWLES.

Page 503   Indenture   13 July 1816   JAMES ROBINSON and JAMES SCARBROUGH, $26.00 paid, tr on waters of Calf Killers fork and being 13 acres, it being part of Grant No 4120 issued by TN to sd Robinson.

Page 504   Indenture   20 May 1816   BALEY CARTER and RUSSELL JOHNS, $200 paid, tr including the plantation whereon sd Johns now lives including 50 acres, beg at SE cor of 50 acres granted to WILLIAM IRWIN, and also including improvements made by ELY SIMS.

Page 504   Indenture   15 July 1816   ANDREW TOWNSEND and JOHN TOWNSEND (relationship not stated), and ISAAC TAYLOR, $302 paid, undiv 1/3 part tr of 1000 acres on Caney fork, including a lick & on both sides of a small creek called KING & CO little lick creek(now known as Taylor's creek), which tr was granted by NC to STOCKLEY DONELSON, WILLIAM TYRELL and ROBERT KING by Patent No 3579 on 7 Mar 1796. If title is later proven not good, Grantors agree to pay Grantee 93 cents an acre.

Page 506   Indenture   16 Jan 1816   WILLIAM CLARY and JAMES ROBERTS for $400 paid, tr of 100 acres in 3rd Dist & 25th section and on N side Calf Killer's fork of Caney fork, being same land Clary holds by Grant No 1628, dated 11 Sept 1809. Wit: TURNER LANE, JACOB A LANE.

Page 507   Indenture   1 Apr 1816   DAVIS DRUMMOND(?) and ISAAC GLENN, $60.00 paid, tr of 30 acres in 3rd Dist on Calf killers fork of the Caney fork, being tr sd David lives on himself, near tr of heirs of JOSEPH KINKAID, No 1157. Wit: JNO JETT, WILLIAM GIST, Senr.

Page 508   Indenture   15 July 1816   JOSHUA BARTLETT and JOHN BOHANNON, $100 paid, 12 1/2 acres, part of tr where sd Bartlett now lives, being part of Grant No 3650 for 12 acres, dated 17 Jan 1812.

Page 509   Indenture   24 June 1816   DAVID NORRIS and THOMAS STOWE, $1500 paid, tr in 1st Dist on headwaters of Town creek, orig granted by TN to Norris, assee of DAVID SHARES, by Grant No 8439, on 13 Jan 1816. Wit: PINK HUDSON, IREBY W STONE.

Page 510   Indenture   22 Sept 1815   JAMES TOWNSEND and JAMES ELLISON, $327 paid, tr of 140 acres (being a moiety out of Grant No 7032 issued by TN), being in 1st Dist on Cane creek of the falling water adj a sur of ISAAC TAYLOR, Junr, of 402 acres on his S bdy and including the farm and spring where LEVI SWEAT formerly lived. Wit: THOS K HARRIS, JOSEPH SMITH.

Page 511   Indenture   15 July 1816   DANIEL PARKESON(?), WASHINGTON PARKESON and GEORGE PARKESON (relationships not stated), first part, and JESSE CONWAY, other part, $400 paid, tr of 66 1/2 acres on falling water, it being part of grant issued by TN to THOMAS BOUNDS and THOMAS LOVELADY for 500 acres, No 1992, part Grant issued by sd state to sd Daniel and SAMUEL ENGLISH for 30 acres, No 3676 & part of Grant issued by TN to NATHANIEL TAYLOR for 99 acres, No 4357. Wit: TURNER LANE, JACOB A LANE.

Page 511   Power of Attorney   30 July 1814   JOHN MCDANIEL and ROBERT

MCDANIEL (relationship not stated) of Giles Co, TN, appoint ELISHA SANDERS as attorney with power to make to ISAAC DRAKE right as bond given by sd John & Robert to sd Elisha and ELIJAH SANDERS calls for. Wit: GEO W SANDERS, SAMUEL DENTON.

Page 512   Indenture   6 Dec 1813   JAMES BOWEN and MATTHEW BABB, $125 paid, tract in 3rd Dist on main Caney fork, entered 4 Feb 1812, No 1651, on Certif No 221, beg near plantation where JESSE MCGWIN did live, tr being 25 acres. Wit: ROBERT E LOWRY and CHRISTOPHER KUHN.

Page 512   Indenture   Date and parties as in above deed, $125 paid, tr in 3rd Dist on main Caney fork, entered 4 Feb 1812, No 1652, on Certif No 225, beg at NE cor of his entry 1651, being 25 acres. Wit: As above.

Page 513   Agreement   20 Nov 1806   THOMAS OVERTON and THOMAS DILLON agree that 1500 acres will belong to GEO OVERTON and 1500 to sd Dillon. Wit: ISAAC TAYLOR, Junr.

Page 514   Indenture   20 Jan 1816   WILLIAM BALCH and JOHN HOLLAND, $300 paid, tr on Caney fork, 100 acres, it being E end of Balch's 300 acre tr, beg in western bdy of ROLLY RALLS sur of 300 acres. Wit: ABEL HUTSON, HARRIS HOLLAND.

Page 514   Indenture   15 July 1816   JESSE WILLIAMS and CHARLES WILLIAMS (no relationship stated), $50.00 paid, tr of 10 acres in 1st Dist & on S side Caney fork, Grant No 8168, beg at NE cor JESSE KEATHLY. Wit: ROBERT DOWNING, GEORGE W SANDERS, REUBEN P SANDERS.

Page 515   Indenture   20 May 1816   ELY SIMS and JOHN KELLY, $450 paid, 100 acres Grant No 6684, 1st Dist on N side of Smarts mountain on the waters of Taylor's creek, and beg at NE cor JOHN RUSSELL 100 acre Occupant sur. Wit: J B HANCOCK, LAWSON NOURSE.

Page 515   Indenture   20 Jan 1817   JACOB A LANE, one part, and ELIZABETH M CAMPBELL, SOPHIA M CAMPBELL and MARIA W CAMPBELL, other part, $81.25 paid, convey 1 bay horse, saddle & bridle, and household goods, sold in Sheriff's sale, on the property of JAMES M CAMPBELL.

(This last instrument is acknowledged 20 Jan 1817 before JACOB A LANE, Clerk, White County Court, and Registered on 13 Feb 1817, ELIJAH CHISUM, Register, White County, TN.)

Volume F
May 1817 - June 1820

Page 1 Indenture 21 Apr 1817 PINK HUTRON and JULIAN HUTRON(?), his wife, GEORGE LONG and wife ELIZABETH LONG, IRA BEDWELL and wife BARBARA BEDWELL, and CHRISTOPHER CATRON and SOLOMON CATRON, one part, and JACOB CATRON of other part, $800 paid, tr on Cherry creek, part of tracts on which ELIZABETH CATRON now lives, being 167 acres. beg at NW cor GEORGE LONG sur of 220 acres that he now lives on, including the farm & dwelling of BENJAMIN HICKMAN, being part of 640 acre tr granted by NC to ROBERT KING, Grant 362, and also part of 2500 acre tr granted to sd King, Grant No 342. Grantors named above are heirs of JACOB CATRON, Decd. Ack on 25 Apr 1817 before JACOB A LANE, Clk of White Co, TN, and Registered by ELIJAH CHISUM, Reg sd county.

Page 2 Indenture 15 Nov 1814 WILLIAM STEWART and JOHN CURTER, $250 paid, tr of 80 acres on waters of Caney fork, tr conv by TN to sd Stewart on 3 July 1809, Grant 1290. Wit: SAMUEL MCCUTCHEN, HARDY HONEYCUTT.

Page 3 Land Grant No 6427 22 Dec 1814 & of Indepen of US the 39th TENNESSEE by virtue of part of Certif 1007, dated 15 May 1812, issued by W TN to HUGH LEEPER and entered on 4 Feb 1813 by No 2279, grants to NICHOLAS AVERY, assee of Leeper, 88 acres in 3rd Dist on Caney fork, beg at SW cor THOMAS WHITE 70 acres in military line, and also adj AMOS LACY line.

Page 4 Land Grant No 6428 Above date and Grantor, by virtue part Certif 866, dated 30 Jan 1812, issued to WILLIAM T LEWIS, entered on 3 Aug 1812 by No 1873, grants to NICHOLAS AVERY, assee of sd Lewis, 70 acres in 3rd Dist, beg at THOMAS CRUTCHER SW cor.

Page 5 Indenture 1 May 1816 JOHN HEATH and MILLERTON PETTYJOHN, $150 paid, tr of 40 acres on Nine lick creek where sd Pettyjohn now lives, being part of tr orig granted to JOSHUA DAVIS for 640 acres. Wit: JAMES DAVIS, LEVI BOSWORTH(?), WM HERRING.

Page 6 Indenture 21 Apr 1817 JAMES ANDERSON and JAMES MCKINNEY, $40 paid, 25 acres on W fork Caney fork and on Barren creek in 3rd Dist & on Cumberland mountain.

Page 7 Indenture 1 May 1816 WILLIAM HERRIN and JOHN HEATH, $150 paid, tr on Nine lick creek and near mouth sd creek, 25 acres, Patent 8283 granted to Herrin by TN, sd tr beg at NW cor 47 1/4 acre sur of FREDERICK DAVIS and transferred to Heath. Another tr of 15 acres granted to sd Herrin, beg on W bdy line of 640 acre sur granted to JOHN DAVIS. Wit: JAMES DAVIS, LEVI BOSATH(?), SAMUEL PETTYJOHN.

Page 8 Indenture 27 Jan 1817 ROBERT B PERKINS, one part, and IREBY W STONE and CORDER H STONE (no relationship stated),$500 paid, tr of 80 acres in 1st Dist on Ridge between Hutchings creek and Cane creek which was orig granted by TN to Perkins, assee of CALEB BERRY by Grant No 9525, dated 4 Aug 1816. Wit: THOMAS STONE, WILLIAM P STONE.

Page 9 Land Grant 6549 25 Jan 1815 TENNESSEE by Certif No 1604, 25 Sept 1813, issued to JOHN C MCLEMORE and entered on 24 Dec 1813 by No 2812, grants JAMES ANDERSON, assee of McLemore, tr of 25 acres in 4rd Dist on

Cumberland Mountain & on W fork Caney fork.

Page 10   Indenture   24 Feb 1817   RICHARD MIDYETT and CHRISTOPHER MIDYETT (no relationship stated), $2.00 paid, tr whereon my house and mill now stand, 1 acre land.   Wit: BENJN GIBBS, ARCHABAL HUTSON.

Page 11   Indenture   21 Apr 1817   NICHOLAS GILLENTINE and JOHN SMALLMAN, $200 paid, 50 acres on S side main Caney fork.

Page 12   Indenture   19 Apr 1817   WILLIAM GANOR and SMITTS HUTCHINGS, $300 paid, tr on Cain creek granted to Hutchings, being by 21 acres of land. Wit: JOSHUA WILLIAMS, JOHN HUTCHINGS.

Page 13   Bond   17 Mar 1815   ALEXANDER COOK binds himself to NATHANIEL BOWMAN for $200 to be void on condition that sd Cook makes to Bowman on 1 Jan next a deed for 50 acres of land, where Bowman now lives.   Wit: RALPH MATTHEWS.   Assigned to BENJAMIN BOWMAN but without any liability in case the bond should not be collected, 4 Feb 1817.   Wit: JAMES RODGERS.

Page 14   Land Grant No 7002   12 May 1815   TENNESSEE by virtue part Certif No 232, dated 10 Apr 1809, obtained from W TN by JOHN GRAY BLOUNT, entered on 10 Dec 1814 by No 2790, there is granted to WILLIAM HARGIS, assee of Blount, a tr of 10 acres dated 27 Aug 1814, in 3rd Dist, on waters of Calf killer fork, beg NW cor 19 acres of JAMES HUDSON.

Page 15   Land Grant No 6228   5 Nov 1814   TENNESSEE by part Certif 371, dated 16 Dec 1809, obtained from W TN by JOSHUA HADLEY, entered on 29 Dec 1811 by No 7327, grants to JESSEE KEATHLEY, assee sd Hadley, tr of 30 acres in 1st Dist on S side Caney fork.

Page 16   Land Grant No 7001   12 May 1815   TENNESSEE, by part Certif 298, dated 13 May 1811, issued by Register of E TN to JAMES P TAYLOR and entered on 6 May 1814 by No 3036, grants WILLIAM HARGIS, assee of sd Taylor, tr of 25 acres in 3rd Dist on Calf killers fork of Caney fork, beg E of the NE cor of an entry in name of JAMES HUDSON for 12 1/2 acres.

Page 17   Land Grant No 6677   1 Mar 1815   TENNESSEE by part of Certif No 607 dated 7 Dec 1812, issued to NICHOLAS AVERY, assee of WILLIAM T LEWIS, tr of 50 acres on Calf killers fork of Caney fork, beg at NW cor THOMAS TURNER.

Page 18   Land Grant No 8184   14 Nov 1815   TENNESSEE by part Certif No 42, dated 17 July 1807, obtained by JAMES MABANE, from West TN, entered on 6 Apr 1813 by No 2434, grants to JAMES HUDSON, assee of Mabane, tr of 12 1/2 acres on E side Calf killers fork, beg near NE cor of a field occupied by WILLIAM HARGIS.

Page 19   Indenture   27 July 1816   ROBERT G ANDERSON and SIMON DOYLE, latter of Pendleton Dist, SC, $10,500 paid, tract of 283 acres in Hickory valley, being part of sur of 400 acres conv to sd Anderson in 1808, part of grant from NC, No 310, dated 7 Mar 1796.   Wit: WILLIAM LEWIS, JOHN WHITE.

Page 20   Indenture   23 Dec 1816   JOHN JOWNSEND and ANDREW TOWNSEND, (relationship not stated) of one part, and BENJAMIN HAWKINS, of other part, $900 paid, 2 tracts of land, one of 300 acres, and other of 10 acres, being in 1st Dist on Caney fork, the 300 acre tr beg on side of the Gum spring mountain, being the beg cor of ARCHIBALD MCDANIEL Occupant sur, and having been granted to Townsend by TN by Grant 9661, on 30 Sept 1816. The 10 acre sur beg in head of McDaniel's cove, & being land granted by TN to Townsend by Grant No 9676. Wit: JOHN HAWKINS, ROBT TOWNSEND.

Page 21 Indenture 21 Jan 1817   ISAAC GLENN and JAMES CLARLES, $66.00 paid, tr of 33 acres on Caney fork about 1 mile N of the Rock Island.

Page 22 Bond 1 Feb 1815   THOMAS HARBERT, of Town of Sparta in White Co, TN, binds self for $100,000 to MATTHEW CLAY, this day selling Clay all his right in 6 surveys & 1 entry, 3 of surveys lying on dry fork of Mill creek & containing 25 acres, and the other 3 surveys lying on Hoppers creek and containing 40 acres of land, the entry containing 2 acres of land & lying on Blackburn's fork, all in Jackson CO, TN and all the surveys & entry made in name of Harbert & Clay. Wit: JOSEPH MURPHY, JOHN BOWEN, JNO B MURPHY, JOHN WILLARD.

Page 23 Land Grant No 9638 24 Sept 1816   TENNESSEE by part of Warrant No 167, dated 27 June 1780, issued to DAVID LOONEY by JOHN ADAIR, Entry taker for Sullivan County and entered on 24 Mar 1809 by No 783, grants to JOHN HILL, assee of sd Looney, tr of 50 acres by sur dated 1 Nov 1815, being in 3rd Dist on S side of main Caney fork and beg 5 poles above a Big Barron spring.

Page 24 Indenture 10 Jan 1817   NATHANIEL MARTIN and ELIJAH BATES, $600 paid, tr in 1st Dist on Caney fork, being 110 acres. Wit: JOSEPH UPCHURCH, GEORGE MARTIN, PLEASANT EARLS.

Page 25 Indenture 30 Mau 1812   JAMES MCCLANE and THEODORICK B RICE and GIDEON MORGAN, Junr, $800 paid, 1 undiv moiety or 1/2 of tr containing 1 acre on E side of Cane creek of Caney fork, which tr was granted by TN to McClane & ALEXANDER LOWERY & THOMAS GIST by Grant No 3801, dated 15 Mar 1812, and by deeds made by Lowery & Gist, 2 of orig grantees. Wit: THOMAS HARBERT, & ALEXANDER LOWERY.

Page 26 Indenture 15 Apr 1816   JAMES BOWEN and DAVID MITCHELL, $20.00 paid, Bowen having been granted tr for 50 acres, No 8176, dated 13 Nov 1815, tr of 18 acres on Calf killer. Wit: SML JOHNSON, JOHN BURDEN.

Page 27 Indenture 6 Nov 1815   JOHN HUTCHINGS and WILLIAM DODSON, $50.00 paid, 156 acres a part of a tr conv to Hutchings by WILLIAM P ANDERSON and JOHN MCIVER, situated on Town creek granted by NC to JAMES EASTON. Wit: DAVID NORRISS.

Page 28 Indenture 7 Apr 1817   BENJAMIN HAWKINS and ROBERT COOKE, $500 paid, 113 acre tr on Caney fork of Cumberland River on Rutledge's creek, adj sd Benjamin and his son WILLIAM HAWKINS, a part of claim of 211 acres as assee of DANIEL MCCLOUD. Wit: DANIEL NEWMAN, GEORGE PIRTLE, JNO CAMPBELL.

Page 29 Indenture 27 Jan 1817   ABRAHAM DENTON and ROBERT ANDERSON, latter of Buncombe Co, NC, $400 paid, tr of 100 acres in 1st Dist on S side of Caney fork. Wit: ELIJAH CHISUM, JAS D HOWARD, JOSEPH ANDERSON.

Page 30   Power of Attorney   20 May 1817   (Executed in Greenville Dist, SC)
WADDY THOMPSON and his wife ELIVIA B THOMPSON of Greenville Dist, SC,
appoints WADDY THOMPSON, Junr, as our attorney to dispose of all such land
warrants ours as heirs of ELIVIA THOMPSON, Decd, lands being granted to sd
Elivia in her lifetime in TN. Ack by W THOMPSON and ELIZA B THOMPSON, and
witnessed by JOHN H GOODLETT.

Page 31   Power of Attorney   24 June 1817   SARAH F CHATARD(?), one of heirs
at law of JAMES WILLIAMS, late of South Carolina, Decd, being a widow
residing in Natchez, MS Terr, has made my true friend WADDY THOMPSON, Jnr,
of South Carolina, but now in Tennessee, my attorney with power to sell
lands, etc, I have as heir of my father. Wit: JAMES DINSMORE, JOHN H
ROBINSON, R DUNBAR, Jr. Ack before JOHN HENDERSON, NP, for Natchez, MS
Terr, on above date.

Page 32   Power of Attorney   18 June 1817   JAMES WILLIAMS, of Orleans, LA,
appoints WADDY THOMPSON, Junr, of state of South Carolina, my attorney in
fact, to sell any tr belonging to me in TN. Ack in 1st Judicial Dist
Court, New Orleans, LA, before MARTIN GORDON, Clk.

Page 33   Indenture   11 July 1815   JOHN HUTCHINGS and JOHN RICHISON, $70.00
paid, tr on falling water & being 295 acres, a part of 640 acre tr conv by
WILLIAM P ANDERSON & JOHN MCIVER to sd Hutchings, being No 5 of a
connection of 10 surveys. Wit: ROBT ARMSTRONG, ROYAL ARMSTRONG.

Page 34   Indenture   19 June 1816   GEORGE W SANDERS and ISHAM RUSSELL,
latter of Warren Co, TN, $1200 paid, 163 acres, it being all the land
contained in a grant issued by TN to JOSEPH WALLING, No 1586 for 100 acres,
part of Grant No 1585 issued by sd state to MORGAN BRYAN for 100 acres,
containing 50 acres and part of Grant No 3790 issued to sd Walling for 93
acres, containing 13 acres, being in military Dist, adj WILLIAM ROGERS.
Wit: ROBT DOWNING, JOHN CHISUM.

Page 35   Indenture   27 Sept 1816   AARON PERRON and THOMAS LOVELADY, $200
paid, 1 tr of 55 acres in 1st Dist on W side of Pigeon Roost creek water of
the falling waters of the Caney fork, adj REUBEN RAGLAND, JOHN YOUNG &
JAMES BOUND, being part of a 560 acre tr granted by TN to BOUND & LOVELADY,
being dated 26 Feb 1810 for Grant 1992. Wit: JOHN LOVELADY, DAVID
HUDDLESTON, WILLIAM RAGLAND.

Page 36   Indenture   5 Oct 1817   JOHN SCOGGIN and JESSE SCOGGIN (no
relationship stated), $100 paid, his interest vested by virtue of Grant No
534 issued by TN to Scoggin for 21 acres, part of his 144 acres on N side
main Caney fork. Wit: JESSE SCOGGIN, W O WHITE(?).

Page 37   Indenture   17 Jan 1817   HERCULES OGLE, Senr, and ROBERT WATSON,
$300 paid, tr on Cane creek, being part tr granted by West TN to JOHN OGLE,
and a part of THOS DILLON 200 acre sur, beg at cor of JOSEPH HASTINGS, 65
acres. Wit: JOHN OGLE, JAS MOOR, WYATT OGLE.

Page 38   Indenture   26 Oct 1816   JOHN HILL and WILLIAM SHOCKLEY, for $900
paid, tr of 50 acres on S side Caney fork river. Wit: ALEXANDER COOK.

Page 39   Indenture   25 July 1817   WADDY THOMPSON, Senr, and ELIZA B
THOMPSON, his wife, of Greenville Dist, SC, JAMES WILLIAMS, of New Orleans,

LA, SARAH F CHATARD, of town of Natchez, MS Terr, and THOMAS B WILLIAMS, of Greenville Dist, SC, all the heirs of ELIZA WILLIAMS, Decd, by their Atty in fact WADDY THOMPSON, Junr, of one part, and ANTHONY DIBRELL of White Co, TN, and JOHN C MCLEMORE, of Davidson Co, TN, of other part, $240 paid, 640 acres granted by North Carolina to sd Eliza Williams by Grant No 2788, on 20 Dec 1796, which descended to sd Waddy Thompson, Senr, and ELIZABETH B WILLIAMS, his wife, and the others listed above. Tr is in Middle Dist on both sides of Caney fork of Cumberland River about 7 1/2 miles from the Roaring Spring. Wit: SAMUEL TURNEY, PLEASANT C FARLEY.

Page 40 Power of Attorney 12 June 1817 THOMAS B WILLIAMS, Greenville Dist, SC, appoint WADDY THOMPSON, Jr, to convey for me as one of heirs of ELIZA WILLIAMS, Decd, any land I may have interest in as such heir. Wit: ANTHONY DIBRELL, JACOB A LANE.

Page 41 Indenture 16 Oct 1816 REUBEN ROBARTS (REUBEN ROBERTS?), Warren Co, TN, and ISHAM RUSSELL, $200 paid, tr of 40 acres in 1st Dist in the Barrens, Grant No 5828. Wit: GEO W SANDERS, JOHN ROBARTS, WILLIAM ROBARTS.

Page 42 Indenture 16 Sept 1815 BENJAMIN WEAVER and DRURY SMITH, $40 paid, 20 acres, Grant No 6741, being 20 acres on Calf killers fork of Caney fork, beg W of SE cor of WILLIAM P ANDERSON sur of 180 acres known as the Iron aure trace. Wit: ANDREW BURK, EDWD CONNOR, ISAAC MCGUIAR.

Page 43 Indenture 10 Sept 1816 JESSEE KEATHELY and JOHN MEDLY, Sen, $150 paid, tr issued from TN No 6228, dated 5 Nov 1814, tr of 30 acres in 1st Dist on S side Cany fork, beg at NW cor DAVID H MABENS. Wit: JOHN CUMMINGS, JOSEPH CUMMINGS.

Page 44 Indenture 11 July 1815 JOHN HUTCHINGS and ENOCH ODLE, $240 paid, tr on falling water, being part 640 acre tr conv by WILLIAM P ANDERSON and JOHN MCIVER, 138 acres a part of Tr 5 of a connection of 10 tracts of 640 acres each. Wit: ROBT ARMSTRONG, ROYAL ARMSTRONG.

Page 45 Indenture 1 July 1815 JOHN HUTCHINGS and THOMAS DUFF, $62.00 paid, tr on falling water 204 acres, a part of 640 ac tr conv by Anderson & McIver (as above) to Grantor herein. Wit: As above.

Page 46 Indenture 21 Oct 1816 JOHN GREEN and JOHN FRYER, $500 paid, 96 acres in 3rd Dist on Lost creek, waters of Caney fork, a part of land he has by deed from TABER FITZGERALD and founded on a Grant for 320 acres dated 21 Apr 1810, No 2183.

Page 47 Land Grant No 5025 26 Sept 1813 TENNESSEE by virtue Certif 226, dated 23 Feb 1811, issued by Register of E TN to JOHN MCIVER, entered 18 Jan 1811 by No 1357, grants to PLEASANT WALLER, assee of sd McIver, tr of 100 acres in 3rd Dist & on Calf killers fork of Caney fork, beg in S bdy line of MOSES FISK in sight of ALEXANDER THOMAS field. Surveyed 6 Feb 1813 by W P WHITE, DS.

Page 48 Indenture 12 May 1817 JOHN ROSE and JOHN RUSSELL, $100 paid, tr of 16 acres granted to Rose by TN by Grant No 9046, being in 1st Dist on roads leading from the White place to Rock Island, tr including improvements formerly occupied by JACOB HARTZ by sur dated 18 Sept 1813.

Wit: BENJAMIN BROWN, RHODAM RUSSELL.

Page 49 Land Grant No 9453 4 July 1816 TENNESSEE for military service
of BOOKER PARISH to NC Warr No 529, dated 16 Dec 1797, entered on 20 July
1812 by No 1860, grants to JOHN JEFFRIES, assee of Parish, tr of 60 acres
part of sd warr by sur dated 10 Mar 1814 lying in 3rd Dist on falling water
of Caney fork, beg at SW cor of JESSE TERRY 20 acre entry. D MCGAVOCK, Reg
of W TN certif Jeffries is entitled to sd tract.

Page 50 Land Grant No 9452 4 July 1816 TENNESSEE for military serv
performed by BOOKER PARISH to NC Warr 5287 dated 16 Dec 1797, entered on 10
Nov 1812 by No 2084, grants to JOHN JEFFRIES, assee of sd Parish, tr of 10
acres part of sd warr in 3rd Dist on falling water, beg at NE cor entry of
Jeffries for 60 acres, No 1816, & adj W bdy of JESSE TERRY 20 acre entry.

Page 51 Land Grant No 4796 17 June 1813 (Executed at Nashville)
TENNESSEE by residue of Certif 176, dated 25 Dec 1810 issued by Reg of E TN
to JOHN MCIVER and entered on 4 Dec 1811, grants to FRANCIS WALLICE, assee
of McIver, tr of 40 acres in 3rd Dist & on Cane creek of main Cany fork.

Page 52 Indenture 10 Jan 1817 CHARLES BATES, Overton Co, TN, one part,
and ELIJAH BATES, $300 paid, 70 1/4 acre tr in 1st Dist on Caney fork, beg
at NE cor of sd Elijah 200 acre sur, & adj tr of NATHANIEL BOWMAN. Wit:
WILLIAM C BRITTAIN, NATHAN HAGGARD.

Page 53 Indenture 12 July 1816 ALEXANDER COOPER and WM J BENNETT,
$20.00 paid, grants lot of 60 sq perches in Town of Sparta bordering on
second main street & on back alley, being No 182 in plat.

Page 54 Indenture 16 July 1816 JOSEPH C MCBRIDE and GEORGE LANGE,
$50.00 paid, 25 acres on waters of Cherry creek and beg at SW cor of an
entry for 50 acres in name of CHRISTOPHER CATRON and transfered to ANDREW
MCBRIDE. Wit: WILLIAM C FITCH, SHADRACH PRICE.

Page 55 Land Grant No 5772 30 June 1814 TENNESSEE by part of Certif No
323 dated 25 Aug 1807 obtained from W TN by JOHN L MARTIN and SAMPSON
WILLIAMS, and entered on 5 June 1811(?) by No 499, grants to JAMES CHISUM,
assee of sd Martin & Williams, tr of 80 acres in 3rd Dist on Cherry creek,
a branch of Calf Killers fork, beg at SW cor HARDY ____, occupant sur of
100 acres which includes where he lives, and adj entry of ELIJAH CHISUM,
Junr.

Page 56 Indenture 23 Sept 1816 THOMAS CRUTCHER, of Bedford Co, TN, and
WILLIS MENEFEE, $1000 paid, 4 tracts all adj & totalling 400 acres (if
interested in these lands see the field notes in actual deed). Wit:
MANUEL PARKISON, JOHN SMITH.

Page 57 Indenture 31 Oct 1816 GEORGE W SANDERS and MOSES GODARD, $2.00
paid, part tr of 80 acres by grant No 3011 for 300 acres, sd tr adj cor
made by sd Godard and GEORGE SPARKMAN & consented to by EPHRAIM SHOCKLEY.
Wit: EPHRAIM SHOCKLEY, RICHARD MEDLEY.

Page 58 Indenture 31 Oct 1816 Grantor in above deed to RICHARD MIDLY(?),
part of 300 acre tr granted Sanders by Grant No 3011, on Caney fork River,
beg at mouth of the dry branch in the grant & with meanders of the bluff of

Caney fork River standing in a holler that is a conditional line between sd land & EPHRAIM SHOCKLEY, 30 acres. Wit: EPHRAIM SHOCKLEY, MOSES GODARD, REUBIN P SANDERS.

Page 59 Indenture 21 Dec 1816 JOHN HOLLAND and HARRISON HOLLAND (relationship not stated), $400 paid, tr on Caney fork, 100 acres, it being E end of WILLIAM BALCH 300 acre tr. Wit: JOSEPH FRANKS, JOSEPH CLARK.

Page 60 Indenture 17 Sept 1816 JOHN YOAKUM, one part, and JOHN BROYLES and REUBEN BROYLES (no relationship stated), other part, $700 paid, tr on S side Cherry creek, beg at SE cor of 2500 acre tr granted to ROBERT KING by Grant 342, 152 1/2 acres. Wit: JOHN W DEARING, JOEL YEAGAR, SOLOMON YEAGER, Sr.

Page 61 Indenture 15 Mar 1816 JESSE ENGLAND and SOLOMON COX, 108 paid, tr on falling water, a part of a connection of surveys orig granted by NC to JAS EASTON on 27 Mar 1796, beg in sd Coxe's field near old Rock Island road near Cox dwelling house, same being a cor of Major ISHAM RUSSELL, tr being 18 acres. Wit: ARON ENGLAND, ELIJAH WARD.

Page 62 Indenture 20 July 1815 JOHN ARMSTRONG and AMOS H LACY, $137 paid, tr of 50 acres in 3rd Dist and on Calf Killers fork, it being same land Armstrong holds by Grant 7019, and beg S of a mountain S of WILLIAM LEATHERS. Wit: JAMES DAVIS, HENRY BURTON.

Page 63 Indenture 18 July 1817 JESSE ENGLAND and WILLIAM R COLE, $56.00 paid, 30 acres on the falling water of the Caney fork of Cumberland River, beg on military line at NE cor 68 acres conv to Cole & SOLOMON COX, it being part of tr conv from THOMAS CRUTCHER to England.

Page 64 Sheriff's Deed 19 Apr 1817 THOMAS TAYLOR, Shff, and successor of ISAAC TAYLOR, late shff of White Co, and ELIJAH CHISUM, Senr, goods of WILLIAM P ANDERSON ordered sold, JOSEPH COLVILLE, lately of Warren County court recovers sum due, 55 acres in White county on Calf Killer's fork.

Page 65 Sheriff's Deed 16 July 1817 Grantor as in above conveyance, to ISAAC TAYLOR, satisfying debt of JOHN C HALL, being lot 40 in Town of Sparta.

Page 66 Land Grant No 7000 TENNESSEE by virtue part of Certif 1201, dated 16 Sept 1812, issued by W TN to heirs of THOMAS WADE and entered on 24 Nov 1812 by No 2132, grants to JAMES HUDSON, assee of sd heirs of Wade, tr of 19 acres by sur dated 26 Aug 1814, lying in White County in 3rd Dist on Calf Killers fork of Caney fork, beg on W bdy of BURRELL HUDSON 200 acre survey.

Page 67 Land Grant No 7004 TENNESSEE by virtue part Certif 485 dated 29 Jan 1811, to JOHN MCIVER from W TN & entered on 18 Aug 1811 by No 1477, grants to JOHN SUTTLE, assee of McIver, tr of 10 acres in 3rd Dist on headwaters of Calf Killers fork.

Page 68 Indenture 23 Apr 1817 IRA BEDWELL and BARBARA BEDWELL, his wife, CHRISTOPHER CATRON, JACOB CATRON and SOLOMON CATRON, of one part, and PINK HUTSON of the other part, $1500 paid, tr on Cherry creek, 330 acres. Tract is a part of 2500 acre tr pr grant No 342 assigned by NC to ROBERT

KING.

Page 69   Indenture   21 July 1817   WILLIAM GLENN and JOEL BRADSHAW, $50.00 paid, Lot 2 in Sparta.

Page 70   Indenture   24 July 1817   JOHN WALLING and ISHAM RUSSEL, Jnr, $100 paid, tr of 640 acres on Caney fork.

Page 71   Indenture   15 July 1817   Grantor above and JOSEPH HERD, $175 paid, 83 acres, part of 640 acre sur granted heirs of DAVID JOINER on Caney fork, adj at one point cor of P HAMMONS.

Page 72   Indenture   21 Apr 1817   WILLIAM MARTAIN of Warren Co, TN and RICHARD PHILLIPS, $40.00 pd, 20 acre tr in 1st Dist near Hickory nut mountain, including improvement of ISHAM PULLIAM. Wit: JOHN E CONN, WILLIAM SHAW.

Page 73   Indenture   18 Sept 1816   DANIEL VAUGHAN and JOHN SIMMONS, $215 paid, 30 acres on Grant No 5585 on main Cane fork. Wit: FRANCIS C WALLACE, JAMES OWEN.

Page 74   Indenture   9 Oct 1815   JOHN MILLER, Senr, and THOMAS WALLING, 50 acres in 1st Dist beg at SE cor of the Gum spring survey of 640 acres & including where ROBERT BATES now lives. Wit: JACOB MILLER, WILLIAM SHAW.

Page 75   Indenture   12 Mar 1813   THOMAS BOUNDS, AARON ENGLAND, BENJAMIN WEAVER, TURNER LANE, ALEXANDER LOWERY, JAMES FULKERSON and NICHOLAS GILLENTINE, Commissioners in trust for White County, one part, and BRADFORD ROSE, other part, $14.75 paid, Lot 79 in Sparta.

Page 76   Indenture   12 Dec 1816   MORGAN DEWEESE and MARY FITZGERREL, Widow, $60.00 paid, tr in 1st Dist, beg on a ridge near road leading from Sparta to Rock Island, & 1/4 mile from GARRETT FITZGERREL former dwelling house & adj line of survey whereon WILLIAM FITZGERREL, decd (___?), 30 acres. Wit: JOSEPH UPCHURCH, JOSEPH ANDERSON, GEO D HOWARD, ELIJAH CHISUM.

Page 77   Indenture   1 Apr 1817   WILLIAM C BRITTAIN and THOMAS WHALEY, $240 paid, Lot 31 in Sparta. Wit: LAWSON NOURSE, THOMAS G ROBERTS.

Page 78   Indenture   27 Jan 1817   SAMUEL DENTON and ROBERT ANDERSON, latter of Buncombe Co, NC, $800 paid, 102 acres in 1st Dist of 10th Sec of 1st Range, including improvement of Denton on S side of Caney fork, beg near connection formerly with JACOB DRAKE, & from LAXTON former dwelling house. Wit: ELIJAH CHISUM, GEO D HOWARD, JOSEPH ANDERSON.

Page 79   Indenture   5 Mar 1817   RICHARD MIDYETT and JOHN TEMPLETON, $160 paid, 89 acres in 1st Dist on Caney fork, adj Occupant sur of RAWLEIGH RALLS, part Grant 2421 to RAYMAN. Wit: CHRISTOPHER MIDYETT, CASON SWINDEL, CASON GIBBS, Jr.

Page 80   Land Grant No 7923   13 Oct 1815   TENNESSEE by Certif 1054, 15 June 1812, issued by Reg of W TN to JOHN CHISUM, entered 15 June 1812, grants sd Chisum 81 1/2 acres on Calf killers fork in 9th Sec of 1st Range, adj SE cor WILLIAM SHAW 100 acres.

Page 81   Land Grant 7924   13 Oct 1815   TENNESSEE by part Certif 53, dated 20 July 1807, issued to JOSEPH GRAY and JAMES GRAY (no relationship given), entered on 9 Feb 1811 by No 5912, grants to JOHN CHISUM, assee, tr of 50 acres by sur dated 14 July 1812, in 1st Dist, adj S line of FREDERICK MILLER 28 acres.

Page 82   Indenture   13 Aug 1816   DAVIS NORIS and ROBERT B PURKINS, $100 paid, 150 acres on Cane creek, part tr of 2500 acres orig granted by NC to ROBERT KING.   Wit: THOMAS STONE, CORDER STONE.

Page 83   Indenture   18 Mar 1817   THOMAS TRAPP, late of White Co, one part, and LEVI PERKINS, $44.00 paid, 5 1/2 acres in 1st Dist on W fork of Town creek.   Wit: JOHN DODSON, JOHN BARRON.

Page 84   Indenture   29 July 1816   HANNON LITTLE and THOMAS TOWNSEND, tr of 50 acres, sur 4 May 1814 by JAMES TOWNSEND, DS.   Wit: THOMAS CARTER, BAYLY CARTER.

Page 85   Indenture   24 Oct 1816   FRANKY B THOMAS and LARKIN BAKER, $100 paid to her, 27 11/4 acres, adj 2 3/4 acres conv by JOSEPH MELTON to WINNIFORD CLARK, tr including 1/2 of a spring & branch, this tr being same land she holds by deed from JOEL MELTON, dated 20 Apr 1816.   Wit: TURNER LANE, ARCHIBALD CONNOR.

Page 86   Indenture   2 Sept 1816   AARON PERRON and REUBEN RAGLAND, $300 paid, 30 acres in 1st Dist on E side of Pigeon Roost creek waters of the falling water of the Caney fork adj lands of THOMAS LOVELADY, JOHN YOUNG and THOMAS HOPKINS, it being part of a 560 acre tr granted by TN to THOMAS BOUNDS & THOMAS LOVELADY, Grant 1792.   Wit: JOHN LOVELADY, DAVID HUDDLESTON, WILLIAM RAGLAND.

Page 87   Indenture   17 Sept 1817   BENJAMIN HAWKINS, Senr, and JAMES SIKES, $25.00 paid, tr on N side Caney fork, beg near the big spring, the main head of S fork of Rutledges creek, 10 acres.   Wit: DANIEL NEWMAN, JAMES HAWKINS, CHRISTOPHER SWINDLE.

Page 88   Indenture   10 Nov 1816   WILLIAM WHITEACRE and WILLIAM HUNTER, $350 paid, tr on Caney fork in 3rd Dist, being tr granted by TN to Whiteacre on 4 Oct 1816, Grant 9688.   Wit: REUBEN RAGLAND, WILLIAM RAGLAND, THOMAS BARNES, JOSEPH HUNTER.

Page 89   Indenture   30 Sept 1817   DAVID THOMPSON and JAMES TURNEY, $700 paid, tr on Town creek, 174 acres, part of Grant 1296, dated 3 July 1809 to sd Thompson, tr adj JAMES TOWNSEND.   Wit: JAMES SIMPSON, J A LANE, JAS TOWNSEND.

Page 90   Indenture   15 Sept 1817   THOMAS WALLING and GEORGE AILSWORTH, $800 paid, 70 acres beg at SE cor BENJAMIN GIBBS survey.   Wit: CHARLES DIBRELL.

Page 91   Indenture   29 Apr 1817   JOSHUA WILLIAMS, one part, and SMITH HUTCHINGS and JOHN HUTCHINGS (relationship not stated), other part, for 400 Spanish milled dollars paid, tr on Cain creek, being 129 acres.   Wit: JOSEPH WILLIAMS, WM GARVER(?).

Page 92   Indenture   10 Apr 1817   JOHN CROOK and JANE GOOLSBY, $500 paid, 40 acre tr in 1st Dist orig granted by TN to Crook, assee of JOHN MCNARY and BENNET SEARCY, by Grant No 9240, on 7 __ 1816.   Wit: PETER GOOLSBY, JOHN CROOK, Junior.

Page 92   Indenture   Date and Parties as in above deed, $500 paid, 50 acres, 1st Dist, part Grant 9239.   Wit: AMOS RILEY, JOHN CROOK, Junior.

Page 93   Indenture   9 Oct 1817   DAVID THOMPSON and ANDREW GAMBLE, $40.00 paid, 100 acres part of 274 acre tr granted on 3 July 1809.   Wit: ANTHONY DIBRELL, WILLIAM GLENN.

Page 94   Indenture   21 Oct 1817   SMITH HUTCHINGS and JOHN HUTCHINGS (relationship not given), one part, and THOMAS CONANAY, other part, $400 paid, 200 acre tr on Town creek granted to Hutchings by TN.   Wit: JESSE CONWAY, WM BURTON.

Page 95   Indenture   23 Sept 1817   WILLIAM HAWKINS and JOHN TEMPLETON, $80.00 paid, 20 acres on Clift creek, beg at NW cor 100 acre sur of JOHN JENKINS.   Wit: JOHN KNOWLES, JAMES KNOWLES.

Page 96   Indenture   26 Dec 1816   NICHOLAS AVERY and WILLIAM BATES, $100 paid, 50 acres beg at NW cor THOMAS TURNER, in military line.   Wit: MANUEL PERKISON(?), ISAAC WILLIAMS, S L ALY(?).

Page 97   Indenture   6 Oct 1817   PINK HUTSON, late of White Co, TN, one part, and JOHN RUTLEDGE, $1500 paid, 330 acres on Cherry creek, adj land of ROBERT HOWARD, tr adj S CATRON tr, and being part of grant for 2500 acres from NC to ROBERT KING, Grant No 362.   Wit: ELIJAH WARD, JOHN W DEARING, JAMES HILL.

Page 98   Indenture   23 Sept 1817   WILLIAM HAWKINS and JOHN TEMPLETON, $420 paid, 100 acre tr in 1st Dist in 9th Sec of 1st Range, being same land entered by JOHN JENKINS.   Wit: JOHN KNOWLES, JAMES KNOWLES.

Page 99   Indenture   8 Feb 1816   JAMES LAXSON and WILLIAM VAUGHAN, $400 paid, 50 acres on S side Cany fork in 1st Dist, tr beg near cliff of mountain near JOHN J ROBERT MCDONALD 30 acre sur, Grant No 8417.   Wit: JOHN WILSON, JAMES EVANS.

Page 100   Indenture   27 Sept 1815   WILLIAM HAYS and JOHN W DEARING, $700 paid, tr of 80 or 90 acres on E side Cherry creek, adj BENJAMIN WEAVER Grant 2242.   Wit: SOLOMON YEAGER, THOMAS BROYLS, THOMAS SHIRLY(?).

Page 101   Indenture   15 Aug 1817   BENJAMIN HAWKINS and GEORGE PIRTLE, $350 paid, 180 acre tr in 1st Dist and on Cany fork, beg at E line of Benjamin's 211 acre tr, adj line of Benjamin's son WILLIAM HAWKINS.   Wit: ROBERT COOKE, DANIEL NEWMAN, POLLY NEWMAN (relationship not stated).

Page 102   Bill of Sale   25 Mar 1817   THEODERICK B RICE conveys to JOHN CATRON for $600 paid, a Negro boy JIM about 14 years of age.   Wit: JN DOUGHERTY.

Page 102   Indenture   20 Oct 1817   NICHOLAS GILLENTINE, Admr, and ISABEL COOK, Admrx, to estate of ALEXANDER COOK, Decd, of one part, and BENJAMIN

BOWMAN, other part, $100 paid, tr in 1st Dist on N side Caney fork entered 17 May 1814 on part of Certif No 1751, beg in SW cor of ELIJAH BATES 200 acre sur on part of which NATHANIEL BOWMAN now lives, tr being 50 acres.

Page 103 Indenture 21 Dec 1815 RICHARD M ROTTON, pf Warren Co, TN, of one part, and SHADRICK MOONEYHAM, other part, $200 paid, 57 acres in 3rd Dist on main Cany fork. Wit: JOHN A ROTTEN, GEORGE YEAT.

Page 104 Indenture 29 July 1817 WADDY THOMPSON, Senr, and ELIZA B THOMPSON, his wife, of Greenville Dist, SC, JAMES WILLIAMS of New Orleans, LA, and SARAH F CLIOTARD(?) of Natchez, MS Terr, and THOMAS B WILLIAMS of Greenville Dist, SC, all the legal heirs of ELIZA WILLIAMS, by Atty-in Fact, WADDY THOMPSON, Junr, of one part, and JONATHAN SCOTT, other part, $489.50 paid, 195 acres a part of 5000 acres granted by NC to ELIZA WILLIAMS, assee of JAMES WILLIAMS on 20 Dec 1796, and which descended to us from our decd ancestor. Wit: JOHN SCOGGIN, AMELIA BRADLEY.

Page 105 Indenture Date & Grantors as in above deed, and ANSELM BRADLY, $504 paid, 181 acres, part of the 5000 acre tract, as above. Wit: JOHN SCOGGIN, JONATHAN SCOTT.

Page 107 Indenture 23 Oct 1817 JOHN COTTON and DANIEL NEWMAN, 200 paid, 100 acres in 1st Dist on Caney fork, being land Cotton holds by Grant 9948, dated at Knoxville the 20 Apr 1817, tr adj JAMES RANDAL. Wit: TURNER LANE, GEO DAWSON.

Page 108 Land Grant No 7003 12 May 1815 TENNESSEE by virtue part Certif 485 dated 29 Jan 1811, obtained by JOHN MCIVER and entered on 27 Aug 1814 by No 3213, grants to JOHN TUTTLE, assee of McIver, 20 acres in 3rd Dist on Calf killer fork, beg in S bdy of BURRELL HUDSON 200 acre tr on W side sd fork.

Page 109 Petition 24 Mar 1817 SARAH HARBERT, widow of the late THOMAS HARBERT, Decd (who died in month of November last), to the County Court of White Co, TN, giving description of several tracts of land owned by Thomas, and asking that she may be endowed with sd property - some of persons owning adj land being Hariot Iron Works, ARMISTEAD STUBBLEFIELD, THEODORICK B RICE, BENJAMIN HUTSON (near salt petrecave which was partially owned by Thomas Harbert), JOSEPH ROBERTSON. Petitioner JOHN CATRON also signed.

Page 111 Notice 24 Mar 1817 SARAH HARBERT gives notice to THEO B RICE and wife POLLY RICE, JAMES HARBERT, WILLIAM HARBERT, JOHN HARBERT and NANCY HARBERT of her going to court to prove dower assigned her. Is followed by Writ by court that 1/2 of lands will be set apart for Sarah as dower, and by the division of sd land by Jurors THOS TAYLOR, Shff, ANTHONY DIBRELL, WILLIAM RODGERS, BENJMAN HAMBLETT, GASPER BARGER, JOHN MASSEY, ROBERT PUCKETT, JOHN SMITH, JOSEPH HEARD, DAVID THOMPSON, ISAAC MIDKIFF, HARDY JONES, A SAYER SIMPSON.

Page 113 Petition At Oct Session 1816 THOMAS TURNER & others by attorney ADAM HUNTSMAN, Esq. Said Thomas Turner, WILLIAM A TURNER (sons of DAVID TURNER, Decd), ABISHA TURNER, JAMES W CLARK, son & heir of CHRISTOPHER CLARK, Decd, who intermarried with HANNAH TURNER, & JOHN JONES, legal gdn for heirs at law of THOMAS THOMPSON, Decd, who was son of DAVID THOMPSON, who intermarried with MARY TURNER, all being heirs of THOMAS TURNER, the

Elder, & JAMES CHISUM, by Warr No 141 for 2500 acres issued to Thomas Turner as Heir of BENYAH TURNER(?). (Here are listed 6 Entries), sd land located & entered to sd Thomas Turner (who had no issue of his own body), and sd David Turner, Alisha Turner, Hannah Turner & Mary Turner were the brothers & sisters of sd Thomas - lists portions of estate to each. Commissioners listed are Esqr BARNES, Esq PRYOR, Major HAWES, ELIJAH ENGLAND, SAMUEL JOHNSTON & WOODSON P WHITE, Surveyor.

Page 114   Division of lands of THOMAS TURNER, Decd, late of Newbern, NC and JAMES CHISUM of Overton County.   17 Nov 1816.

Page 116   Indenture   26 Apr 1817   WILLIAM B NEVILL to ADAM HUNTSMAN, $200 paid, tr adj town of Sparta. Wit: SAYER STIMPSON, WM ROBERSON.

Page 116   Indenture   8 Aug 1803   ROBERT KING, Roane Co, TN, one part, and. JONATHAN WOOD and JAMES OSBURN, Russell Co, VA, other part, $1000 paid, 1000 acres in Smith County, being an undiv moiety of 2500 acres granted to sd King by NC by Patent 342, dated 1 Mar 1797, including Hopkins spring and being on Cumberland River. Wit: WILLIAM SMITH, ALEXR CARMICHAEL, JESSE BYRD. Ack in Roane Co before HENRY BRAZEAL, Clk, RCNC.

Page 117   Indenture   6 Sept 1816   WILLIAM JONES, one part, and WILLIAM ANDERSON and MATTHIAS ANDERSON, $10.00 paid, adj Lots 19 & 20 in Sparta. Wit: J A LANE, WILLIAM LAMPTON.

Page 118   Indenture   6 Sept 1816   Parties as in above deed, $10.00 paid, lot in Sparta. Wit: As above.

Page 119   Indenture   11 July 1812   THOMAS BOUNDS, AARON ENGLAND, BENJAMIN WEAVER, TURNER LANE, ALEXANDER LOWREY, JAMES FULKERSON and NICHOLAS GILLENTINE, Commissioners in trust, one part, and LEONARD LAMBERSON, of Sparta, other part, $10.00 paid, 1 lot in Sparta.

Page 120   Indenture 22 Dec 1814   GIDEON PILLOW, Giles County, one part, GEORGE MATLOCK and DANIEL ALEXANDER of Smith County, all of Tennessee, $1.00 paid, tr of 300 acres being DRURY PUCKET, occupant claim granted to ARMISTEAD STUBBLEFIELD by TN being on E side Calf killers fork of Cany fork, & being same tr Stubblefield conv to sd Pillow & same tr Matlock & Alexander bought from Sheriff of White County under execution against sd Stubblefield. Wit: J PICKETT, ROBERT ALLEN. Ack at office in Carthage, Smith Co, before ROBERT ALLEN, Clk.

Page 121   Indenture   8 Feb 1815   WILLIAM STINSON and THOMAS BURGAN, $300 paid, tr of 334 acres in Sec 7 as per conveyance from ISAAC TAYLOR to JAMES STINSON and WILLIAM STINSON Atty in fact for WILLIAM P ANDERSON, being adj JOHN LALLER cor, and JOSEPH W BRIDE(?) line. Wit: THOS BOUNDS, JOSEPH HUNTER.

Page 122   Indenture   11 July 1812   Commissioners of Sparta (as listed in deed on Page 119), and LEONARD LAMBERSON, latter of Sparta, $25.00 paid, Lot 72.

Page 123   Dissolution of Partnership   14 Jan 1817   Agreed to dissolve the partnership formed by ANDREW FULTON & SAMUEL FULTON, Merchants in Washington Co, VA, and WILLIAM GLENN in the mercantile business by name of

WILLM GLENN & CO & according to Article of Agreement the firm was to be for term of 5 years. SAMUEL FULTON, who is legal successor of the Fultons above, by his atty JOHN H FULTON & WILLIAM GLENN. Terms of settlement set out.

Page 124 Land Grant No 6592 13 Feb 1815 TENNESSEE by virtue part Certif 1065 dated 16 June 1812, entered on 16 June 8291, grants ISAAC TAYLOR, grants to ISAAC LUNDY, assee of sd Taylor, 10 acres in 1st Dist on Glade creek.

Page 125 Land Grant No 8253 27 Nov 1815 TENNESSEE by virtue Certif 1832, dated 16 Jan 1812, issued to CONSTANT QUARLES & entered on 27 July 1812 by No 8487, grants Heirs of WILLIAM CHRISTMAS, assee sd Quarles, tr of 304 acres dated 15 Oct 1814 in 1st Dist on Caney fork, beg at cor of WILLIAM WILLIAMS Occupant claim. Signed by JOSEPH MCMINN, Governor of TN, WM ALEXANDER, Secty.

Page 126 Indenture 17 Apr 1817 Executors of WILLIAM CHRISTMAS, Decd, of Williamson County & Rutherford County, one part, and WILLIAM WILLIAMS, $350 paid, tr of 304 acres, tr granted heirs of Christmas, Decd, lying in White County, the same tr where P WILLIAMS now lives. Signed by S(HERWOOD) GREEN, one of Exrs of William Christmas, Decd. Wit: SAMPSON SAWYERS, MARTIN CLARK, JNO E GREEN.

Page 127 Indenture 28 July 1817 WADDY THOMPSON, Senr, and ELIZA B THOMPSON, his wife, of Greenville Dist, SC, JAMES WILLIAMS, New Orleans, LA, SARAH F CLISTARD, Natchez, MS Terr, and THOMAS B WILLIAMS, Greenville Dist, SC, all legal heirs of ELIZA WILLIAMS, Decd, by their Atty in fact Waddy Thompson, Junr, one part, and JOHN C MCLEMORE, Davidson Co, TN, other part, $30.00 paid, several tracts of land. Wit: ANTHONY DIBRELL, ISAAC TAYLOR, JOHN SCOGGIN.

Page 130 Land Grant No 4736 25 May 1813 TENNESSEE by part Certif 421, dated 26 May 1812, issued by Reg of E TN to JOSEPH WILLIAMS, grants to ISAAC CATES, assee of JOSEPH WILLIAMS, tr of 13 acres in 3rd Dist on Cane creek.

Page 130 Land Grant No 9200 1 May 1816 TENNESSEE by part certif 459, dated 5 Feb 1811, issued to ANDREW TOWNSEND & entered on 21st Sept 1812 by 9003, grants to DAVID B CARTER, assee of sd Townsend, 20 acre tr, crossing Taylors creek & road leading from Sparta to Allins ferry on Caney fork.

Page 131 Land Grant No 9201 Date & Grantor as in above Grant, by virtue Certif 1868, dated 26 Aug 1814, issued to BENNET SEARCY & entered on 1 Mar 1815 by No 14634, grants DAVID B CARTER, assee of sd Searcy, 10 acres.

Page 132 Indenture 19 Jan 1818 SETH NORTON and JAMES G MURDOCK, one part, and FORRESTER MERCER, other part, $800 paid, 2 lots in Sparta. Wit: JOHN JETT, DENNY SMITH(?).

Page 133 Land Grant No 10,563 20 Aug 1817 TENNESSEE by virtue Certif 655, dated 5 Apr 1814, issued by E TN to JAMES P TAYLOR, entered on 26 Nov 1816 by No 4709, grants to sd Taylor tr of 200 acres, being in 3rd Dist on Caney fork, being at foot of a mountain, adj BURDEN line and also line of HARDY JONES.

Page 134   Indenture   22 Nov 1817   THEODERICK B RICE, surviving partner of THOMAS HERBERT, now deceased, who in his lifetime with sd Rice constituted firm of RICE & HERBERT, of one part, and WILLIAM CARROLL of Davidson Co, TN, other part, for trust & matters stated, confirms tr on Calf killer fork of Caney fork, Warr 106, beg NW cor JOSEPH ROBERTSON, adj ROBERT BURTON land, tr including HARRIET Iron Works. Refers to note executed at Nashville payable to THOS H FLETCHER. Wit: JNO DAUGHERTY, JOHN R DAUGHERTY.

Page 137   Indenture   7 Oct 1816   CHARLES BOWEN and JOHN CUMMINGS, one part, and JOHN MITCHELL, other part, $500 paid, 65 of 110 acres, part of land in Grant No 5716 & whole of Grant 5709. Wit: W P WHITE, WM DENNEY.

Page 138   Indenture   13 Jan 1817   JOHN SUTTLE and JOHN HENERY, $30.00 paid, tr on head waters of Calf killers fork of Caney fork, beg on Cumberland mountain, 10 acres including where sd Henry now lives. Wit: THOMAS HORNE, JOHN HORNE.

Page 139   Indenture   27 Dec 1817   WILLIAM BATES and EDMUND CARREL, $120 paid, 50 acres Bates holds by Grant No 6677, dated 1 Mar 1815, being on Calf Killers fork of Cany fork, beg at NW cor THOMAS TURNER. Wit: J A LANE, JOHN CATRON.

Page 140   Indenture   1 Jan 1818   ISHAM RUSSELL, Junr, and JAMES ANDERSON, $200 paid, tr on Cany fork, being part tr of 640 acres granted to heirs of DAVID JOINER (by Grant No 5933), and beg at SE cor of JOSEPH WALLING, 111 acres. Wit: WILLIAM WINTER, ISHAM RUSSELL.

Page 141   Indenture   26 Nov 1816   ISHAM SHOCKLEY and WILLIAM DENNEY, $200 paid, tr of 25 acres on Cany fork, beg on W bdy line granted to WILLIAM BROWN, No 3340 for 267 acres & dated 22 Aug 1811. Wit: W P WHITE, JOHN MITCHELL.

Page 143   Indenture   15 Nov 1816   ROBERT BATES and GEORGE D HOWARD, $440 paid, tr in 1st Dist on N side of Cany fork, beg at NW cor of 100 acre entry made to ALEXANDER COOK. Wit: JOSEPH UPCHURCH, ELIJAH CHISUM.

Page 144   Indenture   14 Jan 1818   GARRET FITZGEREL and ELIJAH CHISUM, tr in 1st Dist on N side Cany fork, a part of an entry made in name of WILLIAM FITZGERREL and by him bequeathed to sd Garret (no relationship given), tr beg at NW cor sd entry, being 22 1/2 acres. Wit: W P WHITE, JOSEPH ANDERSON.

Page 145   Indenture   20 Jan 1818   BLUFORD WARREN and WILLIAM MCKINNEY, $100 paid, tr on W fork of Caney fork on top of Cumberland mountain, containing 40 acres granted by TN to JOHN ANDERSON by Grant No 6550 on 5 Jan 1815, beg near JAMES ANDERSON Camp.

Page 146   Indenture   14 Jan 1815   JOHN WHITE, Senr, and PLEASANT WHITE, $200 paid, land received by White from THOMAS M CARY for 592 acres, tr conv being 160 acres. Wit: W P WHITE, JNO JETT.

Page 147   Indenture   30 Sept 1817   JOHN CLARY, Jnr, and JAMES COLE, $150 paid, tr of 35 acres on falling water crossing road leading from Carthage and Sparta. Wit: WM CRIM, ELIJAH BARNETT.

Page 148   Indenture   13 Sept 1815   JOHN SHROPSHIRE and ELIJAH CHISUM, Junr, $18.00 paid, tr on Cany fork in 1st Dist, beg on Rock Island Road, 12 acres. Wit: JOSEPH UPCHURCH, HICKS SHROPSHIRE, THOMAS HILL, JOHN MAY.

Page 149   Indenture   20 Jan 1818   WOODSON P WHITE and NATHANIEL AUSTIN, $600 paid, 175 acre tr beg at foot of the mountain.

Page 150   Indenture   21 Jan 1818   WILLIAM C BRIGHTWELL and GEORGE TUCKER, $500 paid, 100 acres he received by deed dated 21 Dec 1813 on waters of the hickory valley on the mountain, beg in S bdy line of FISH & CO, passing due N from a spring formerly occupied by JONATHAN BOSWELL.

Page 151   Indenture   22 Oct 1817   WILLIAM C BRIGHTWELL and JOHN AUSTIN, $80.00 paid, 20 acres on main Caney fork, granted by TN to JACOB A LANE by Grant No 4492 on 26 Jan 1813.

Page 152   Indenture   15 Jan 1811   ELIJAH CHISUM and ELIJAH HILL, tr of 1 acre on waters of N side of Caney fork, it being part of a Grant No 2087 issued to Chisum, beg in W bdy line of ABNER HILL Sur of 50 acres.

Page 153   Indenture   20 Oct 1817   JOSEPH GLENN and ROBERT GLENN (no relationship stated), for valuable consideration, 50 acres held by Grant No 8497, dated 22 Jan 1816, beg in W bdy of THOMAS TOWNSEND. Wit: ELY SIMS, ROBERT R GLENN.

Page 154   Indenture   19 July 1817   ISAAC PRUETT and CHRISTOPHER STECKLEY, $100 paid, 30 acres on S side Caney fork, beg on SW cor MEEKER, & ISAAC PRUETT NW cor, tr being part of tr granted to Pruet by Patent of 21 Sept 1812, No 4180. Wit: WM DENNEY, ARTHUR PARKER.

Page 155   Indenture   8 Apr 1816   ISAAC LUNDY and JOHN WILLIAMS, for valuable consideration, 10 acres on branch of Glade creek of the falling water, tr including an improvement made by Lundy, Grant No 6592. Wit: JESSE WILLIAMS, JOSEPH ROBERTS.

Page 156   Indenture   20 Jan 1818   ANTHONY DIBRELL and WOODSON P WHITE, one part, and JOHN AUSTIN of other part, $600 paid, 154 acres beg near survey of JACOB A LANE, and tr including tr where HOBBS formerly lived. Ack by A B LANE, Dep Clk.

Page 157   Indenture   5 Sept 1817   ISAAC PRUETT and ARTHUR PARKER, $500 paid, 120 acres in 3rd Dist on waters of main Cany fork, abutting cor of JOSEPH SMITH 100 acre sur, and being part tr granted to Pruett by Patent 4180, 21 Sept 1812. Wit: WM DENNEY, CHRISTOPHER STEAKLEY.

Page 158   Indenture   26 Aug 1816   JOHN HAWKINS and DANIEL NEWMAN, $300 paid, tr in First Dist of Caney fork, 150 acres, and beg at SW cor WILLIAM GLENN 50 acre sur, and adj E line JOHN CAMPBELL 50 acres. Wit: JOSEPH HAWKINS, JAMES HAWKINS, BENJAMIN HAWKINS and LINDSEY ARNOLD.

Page 159   Indenture   7 Aug 1817   JOHN M LITTLE and GEORGE PIRTLE, $600 paid, 2 tracts in first dist & on Caney fork, one containing 53 1/3 acres, & other being 30 acres. Wit: WILLIAM ERWIN, ROBERT COOKE, WILLIAM GLINN. Recorded 20 Jan 1818.

Page 160   Indenture   29 Aug 1817   DAVID B CARTER, Rutherford Co, TN, one part, and JOHN TAYLOR, other part, $46.00 paid, 2 tracts.   One tr contains 20 acres on Taylor's creek & at one point crossing road from Sparta to Allen's ferry.   Other tr of 10 acres is on waters of old Jacob's branch of Taylor's creek.   Wit: JAMES GLEASON, ISAAC TAYLOR, THOS TAYLOR.

Page 161   Indenture   18 Jan 1816   JESSE FAIN and JOHN PETTILOR, $65.00 paid, tr of 84 acres on Cany fork, it being part of 640 acre tr conv by WM P ANDERSON and JOHN MCIVER(?) to J HUTCHINGS (and) from him to Fain.   Also tr lying S of old tr, 10 acres.   Wit: REUBIN PERKINS, THOMAS BURGESS.

Page 162   Indenture   29 July 1817   WADDY THOMPSON, Senr, and ELIZA B THOMPSON, his wife, Greenville Dist, SC, JAMES WILLIAMS, New Orleans Co, LA, SARAH F CLIOTARD(?), Town of Natches, Mississippi Terr, and THOMAS B WILLIAMS, Greenville Dist, SC, all the heirs of ELIZA WILLIAMS, Decd, by their Atty in fact, WADDY THOMPSON, Junr, one part, and JOHN SCOGGON, Senr, of other part, $264 paid, 102 acres, being part of 5000 acres granted by NC to ELIZA WILLIAMS, assee of JAMES WILLIAMS by Grant No 326, dated 20 Dec 1796, which descended to sd Grantors as set out above.   Wit: ANTHONY DIBRELL, ISAAC TAYLOR.

Page 164   Indenture   7 Sept 1816   THOMAS CRUTCHER, Bedford Co, TN, and MANUEL PARKISON, $400 paid, 200 acres.   Wit: DANIEL LUNDY, WILLIS MENEFEE.

Page 165   Indenture   25 Apr 1817   PINK HUTSON and wife JULIAN HUTSON, GEORGE LONG and wife ELIZABETH LONG, CHRISTOPHER CATRON, JACOB CATRON and SOLOMON CATRON, of one part, and IRA BEDWELL, other part, $500 paid, tr of 120 acres on Cherry creek, granted by NC to ROBERT KING by Grant No 362, and coming to JACOB CATRON, whose heirs the above named Grantors are.

Page 166   Indenture   23 Apr 1817   PINK HUTSON and wife JULIANNA HUTSON, IRA BEDWELL and wife BARBARA BEDWELL, GEORGE LONG and wife ELISABETH LONG, CHRISTOPHER CATRON, JACOB CATRON, of one part, and SOLOMON CATRON, other part, $1000 paid, 162 acres on Cherry creek.   (Ira Bedwell and Pink Hutson quitclaim for support of their mother ELIZABETH CATRON, one half the mill and farm where she now lives for her support during her life, along with her house where she lives.)

Page 168   Indenture   23 Apr 1817   Grantors and Grantee as in above deed, $1000 paid, 206 acres on Cherry creek.

Page 169   Land Grant No 7235   23 June 1815   TENNESSEE by part of Certif 478 dated 28 Jan 1811, obtained from West TN by ROBERT J TAYLOR and THOMAS IRWIN, entered on 26 Dec 1810 by No 3541, grants to JOHN CATRON, assee of sd Taylor & Irwin, 50 acres in 3rd Dist on Town creek.

Page 170   Land Grant No 7236   Date and Grantor above by part Certif 478 dated 28 Jan 1811, grants JOHN CATRON (as above) 50 acres on waters of Calf Killers fork.

Page 170   Land Grant No 7237   Date and Grantor as above, by part Certif 666 dated 7 Apr 1814, grants JOHN CATRON 27 acres on Calf Killers fork, adj GEORGE W GIBBS Sur of 300 acres & just E of wagon road running North.

Page 171   Indenture   30 Dec 1817   MOSES FISK, of Overton Co, TN, and

THOMAS STORM, Esq, of City of New York, NY, land previously owned by RALPH THURMAN and sold by Sheriff to Fisk in 1810, $10.00 consideration, tract being 736 acres.

Page 172 Indenture 30 Dec 1817   MOSES FISK, as above, and SAMUEL DENTON of New York, NY, being 2208 acres in Fiskland, for $10.00 paid, 736 acres.

Page 174 Land Grant No 3030 17 Apr 1811   TENNESSEE for military service of RICHARD COPE to NC, Warr No 4528, dated 9 Feb 1797, grants to WILLIAM R COLE and SOLOMON COX, assee of sd Cope, tr of 228 acres in 1st Dist, on both sides of Falling water of Caney fork adj THOMAS BOUNDS & THOMAS LOVELADY 560 acres, tr beg at rock in field of JOHN CROOK, adj lands of HUTCHINGS and Pigeon roost creek, and WILLIAM P ANDERSON and JOHN MCIVER. R HUSTON, Secty. Certif eligible by D MCGAVOCK, Reg of W TN.

Page 175 Sheriff's Deed 21 Oct 1816   ISAAC TAYLOR, Shff, one part, and DANIEL ALEXANDER, GEORGE MATLOCK and JOHN JETT, other part, land of ARMSTEAD STUBBLEFIELD for $105 paid for debt which ARCHIBALD W OVERTON recovered against sd Stublefield, 300 acres land beg in line of FISK & CO, and adj C BURTON land.

Page 176 Indenture 23 Mar 1813 SETH DAVIS, Atty in fact for JOSHUA DAVIS of Davidson Co, TN, one part, and JAMES DAVIS, Williamson Co, TN (no relationship given), $250 paid, 640 acres granted by NC to sd Joshua on the Caney fork. Wit: JNO DAVIS, JOHN JONES, DARCUS DAVIS. Ack in Davidson Co CT before NATHAN EWING, Clk, 26 Apr 1814.

Page 178 Indenture 20 Apr 1818   CASON GIBBS and THOMAS ROBERTSON, $64.00 paid, 16 1/2 acres in 1st Dist on Caney fork, it being part of same land Gibbs now lives on and beg at stake made by JOSEPH WALLING and JOSEPH SMI__ on N line Gum Spring survey.

Page 179 Indenture 20 Apr 1818   JAMES DILDINE & JOHN ROBERTSON, $20.00 pd, 20 acres, Grant 6308, 10 Feb 1814, 1st Dist on N side river.

Page 180 Indenture 8 May 1817   AMOS JOHNSTON, of Maury Co, TN, and JOHN WELCH, $15.00 paid, tr beg at cor of WALSEY PEARCE 300 acre sur and adj WM RHODES 200 acre sur, which conveyed tr is part of WM RHODES 200 acre sur & same deeded by JAS T RHODES, heir at law to sd Wm Rhodes, to LEWIS JOHNSTON and by him to sd Amos. Wit: JEREMIAH PRYOR, CHARLES HUNTER.

Page 181 Indenture 16 Oct 1815   WILLIAM PARKISON and ELIJAH ENGLAND, $800 paid, tr on Post oak creek, a branch of falling water of Caney fork of Cumberland, being 209 3/4 acres. Wit: THOMAS STONE, IREBY W STONE, JOHN ENGLAND.

Page 182 Indenture 13 Apr 1818   JAMES DILDINE and ALEXANDER STEEL, for valuable consideration, 20 acres in 1st Dist & on S side of falling water, beg W of an Entry of JAMES TOWNSEND, tr granted to Dildine by Grant No 6307, by TN, 29 Nov 1814.

Page 183 Indenture 21 Apr 1817   JOHN WALLING and WILLIAM HAMLETT, $340 pd, tr part of 640 acres granted to heirs of DAVID JOINER on Caney fork, by Warr 74, tr adj ISHAM RUSSELL, being 87 1/2 acres.

Page 184 Indenture 27 Mar 1818 JOHN TRAP and JOHN COLLON(?), $1,000 paid, 183 acres on Town creek. Wit: THOMAS STONE, CORDER STONE.

Page 185 Indenture 18 Mar 1818 JOHN COLLAR(?) and JOHN TRAP, $1000 pd, tr on falling water a branch of Cany fork of Cumberland river, being part of half section that REUBEN PURKINS bought of WILLIAM P ANDERSON and JOHN MCKEEVER(?), also a part of section JAMES STINSON bought of sd Anderson & McKeever, being 175 acres hereby conveyed. Wit: THOMAS STONE, CORDER STONE.

Page 186 Indenture 14 Mar 1818 ANDREW COPE and JOHN CHISUM, $400 paid, 2 tracts in 1st dist on N side Caney fork, tracts including improvements where sd Cope now lives, being in whole 124 3/4 acres.

Page 187 Indenture 18 Sept 1817 WILLIAM DODSON and JAMES WELCH, 137 acres, being a part of tr conv to WILLIAM P ANDERSON and JOHN MCIVER, on Town Creek and having been conv by NC to JAMES EASTON, beg near line between Dodson and EPRIAM PERKINS. Wit: EPHRIAM PERKINS, ABSALOM PERKINS.

Page 188 Indenture 25 Sept 1817 JOEL MELTON and WILLIAM TILMON, $300 paid, tr of 35 acres on Cumberland mountain on waters of Lost creek, being tr granted to Melton by Grant No 10467, dated 1817. Wit: JOHN ROSE, LEWIS FLETCHER.

Page 190 Indenture 1 Apr 1818 ISHAM RUSSELL and JAMES ROBERTS, $1200 paid, tr of 163 acres, being all the land in grant from TN to JOSEPH WALLING, No 1586, 100 acres, part Grant No 1585 issued to MORGAN BRYAN for 100 acres, tr conv being 50 acres.

Page 191 Indenture 28 Feb 1818 ELIJAH WARD and CALEB JOB, $60.00 paid, 120 acre tr on Cane creek, a branch of Cany of Cumberland river, being part tr of 2500 acres orig granted by NC to ROBT KING, assee of JAMES WILLIAMS, by Grant 341, dated 1 Mar 1797. Wit: JAMES H PASS, ROBERT B PERKINS.

Page 192 Indenture 16 Dec 1817 ELIJAH SANDERS, of Warren Co, TN, and SAMUEL MILLER, $125 paid, 2 tracts in 3rd Dist N side of main Cany fork, being part of 50 acre Sur granted to sd Sanders by Certif 832, being 43 acres. Wit: THOMAS MILLER, SOLOMON DODSON.

Page 193 Indenture 16 Feb 1818 Grantor as above to SOLOMON DODSON, $40.00 paid, 15 acres by Grant 8223, in Warrant 832. Tract is on main Cane fork on N side, beg at cor GEORGE SUGG 32 acre tr. Wit: THOMAS MILLER, SAMUEL MILLER.

Page 194 Indenture 16 Sept 1815 BENJAMIN WEAVER, Sen, and ANDREW BURK, $60.00 paid, 30 acre tr in Grant 6643, being on Calf Killers fork, beg at NW cor ELIJAH CHISM, Senr, 20 acre survey. Wit: DRURY SMITH, EWARD CONNER, ISAAC MCGUIER.

Page 195 Land Grant No 10,525 13 Aug 1817 & the Independence of the US, the 42nd   TENNESSEE by Certif 173, dated 25 Dec 1810, issued by Register of E TN to JOHN MCIVER & entered on 25 Feb 1811 by No 1332, 100 acres by Sur dated 10 May 1814, lying in 3rd Dist on a branch of Caney fork of Cumberland river, adj bdy of DAVID ROSS 65 acre Entry.

Page 196 Indenture 19 Jan 1818 JONATHAN WARD and DAVID NOBLETT, for $300 paid, tr of 37 1/2 acres on S side of falling water, beg in ANDERSON and WILLIAM CRIM lines.

Page 197 Indenture 15 Sept 1817 JOHN WALLING, one part, and WILLIAM TAYLOR, other part, $310 paid, 100 acres granted Walling by Grant 594, 100 acres in 1st Dist, 1st Range, 9th Section, & on Caney fork; also 9 1/2 acres being a part of sur of 228 acres & Grant No 592. Wit: _____, J W SIMPSON.

Page 198 Indenture 8 Jan 1818 JAMES TURNEY and SETH NORTON, tr on Town creek and being 175 acres, being part Grant 1296, dated 3 July 1809, issued by TN to DAVID THOMPSON and deeded to Turney by Thompson on 13 Sept 1817.

Page 199 Indenture 22 Jan 1818 JOSEPH COPHER and THOMAS HOPKINS, $70.00 paid, Lot 75 in town of Sparta. Wit: JOHN CATRON, W B HESLEY.

Page 200 Indenture 6 Mar 1813 THOS K HARRIS and CHARLES SULLIVAN, $1100 paid, Lot 9 in town of Sparta.

Page 201 Indenture 11 Nov 1817 AMOS JOHNSTON, Maury Co, TN, and JEREMIAH PRYOR, $685 paid, 263 acres in 1 tract at foot of Cumberland Mountain and another tr of 192 acres & 136 poles, being near JOHN WELCH and WILREY PEARCE corners, both grants being in name of WILLIAM RHODES heirs, and by them granted to GENL JAS T RHODES, and by him conv to LEWIS JOHNSTON, who conv to Grantor. Wit: ELIJAH WARD, JACOB ROBINSON.

Page 202 Indenture 12 June 1817 GEORGE C HAMLETT, of one part, and SETH NORTON and JAMES G MURDOCK, other part, $400 paid, 2 lots in Sparta being hereby granted (Lots 28 and 29). Wit: WILLIAM SIMPSON, MOSES NORMON.

Page 204 Indenture 4 Dec 1816 JOEL MILTON and DANIEL CLARK, $350 paid, 20 acres granted to Milton by TN by Grant 1258, dated 29 Sept 1812, and also by part certif 1007, dated 15 May 1812, tr being in 3rd Dist in Milton's cove. Wit: DAVID THOMPSON, SAMUEL LANCE.

Page 205 Indenture 22 Sept 1817 SOLOMON COX and WILLIAM R COLE, $1000 paid, tr on falling waters of Caney fork of Cumberland river, being 270 acres, beg on JOHN CROOK, Senr, conditional line, and adj WILLIAM P ANDERSON and JOHN MCIVER lines. Wit: REUBEN RAGLAND, ELIJAH ENGLAND.

Page 207 Indenture 19 Jan 1818 JAMES ANDERSON and WILLIAM MCKINNEY, $50.00 paid, tr of 3 acres on Cumberland mountain, on Caney fork, beg cor of 50 acre tr of DANIEL ALEXANDER.

Page 207 Indenture Date and parties as above, $300 paid, tr of 40 acres on Cumberland mountain granted by TN to sd Anderson by Grant dated 5 Jan 1815, beg at SW cor of an entry in name of DANIEL ALEXANDER for 50 acres.

Page 208 Indenture 29 July 1817 WADDY THOMPSON, Senr, and ELINOR B THOMPSON, his wife, Greenville Dist, SC, JAMES WILLIAMS, New Orleans, LA, SARAH F CLIOTARD(?), Natchez, MS Terr, and THOMAS B WILLIAMS, also of Greenville Dist, SC, all legal heirs of ELIZA WILLIAMS, Decd, by their Atty in fact WADDY THOMPSON, Jnr, of one part, and JAMES ANDERSON, Junr, of White County, TN, of other part, sd WADDY THOMPSON, Senr, and ELIZA B

THOMPSON, his wife, JAMES WILLIAMS, SARAH F CLIOTARD and THOMAS B WILLIAMS, for $625 paid, 273 acres, part of Grant No 326 for 5000 acres issued by NC to ELIZA WILLIAMS, assee of JAMES WILLIAMS by 20 Nov 1796. Wit: ISAAC TAYLOR, ANTHONY DIBRELL, JAMES COLE.

Page 210   Indenture   15 Apr 1818   JAMES DILDINE and EZEKIAH DILDINE, of one part (relationship not stated), $100 paid, tr of 100 acres on Rum creek and on both sides of road leading from White plains to Rock Island, tr granted by TN to sd James Dildine on 18 Feb 1815 by No 9881.

Page 211   Sheriff's Deed   20 Jan 1817   THOMAS TAYLOR, Shff, one part, and ELIJIAH WARD, one part, on order of court of Anderson County for JOHN TERRY, Judg having been issued against ROBERT KING, JOHN KING, JAMES KING, WILLIAM KING, ABNER UNDERWOOD and wife MARY UNDERWOOD, EDWARD KING, ROBERT KING and ANN KING, Heirs at law of ROBERT KING, No of Grant 341, dated 1 Mar 1797.   Conveys 2500 acres on creek orig known as Cane creek, now part Oak creek.   (Also includes plat of tracts signed by JAS TOWNSEND, ISAAC MIDKIFF, ELIJ SIMS, JAMES TOWNSEND, dated 18 Dec 1816, and ack on 24 Jan 1817.)

Page 215   Indenture   21 Oct 1816   THOMAS BOUNDS, AARON ENGLAND, TURNER LANE, ALEXANDER LOWRY, JAMES FULKERSON and NICHOLAS GILLENTINE, Commissioners of White Co0, one part, and WILLIAM GLENN, $41.00 paid, Lot 52 in Sparta, beginning on Turnpike Street.

Page 216   Indenture   6 Mar 1813   THOMAS K HARRIS, one part, and CHARLES SULLIVAN and GEORGE W SANDERS, other part, $350 paid, Lot 10 in Sparta.

Page 217   Indenture   20 Jan 1817   ELIJAH WARD and DANIEL LUNDY, $200 paid, tr on a fork of Caney fork beg in S bdy of 2500 acres ROBERT HOWARD bought of THOMAS DILLAN.

Page 218   Indenture   21 Apr 1817   PINK HUTSON and his wife JULIA HUTSON, IRA BEDWELL and wife BARBARA BEDWELL, CHRISTOPHER CATRON, JACOB CATRON, and SOLOMON CATRON, heirs of JACOB CATRON, Decd, of one part, and GEORGE LONG, other part, $1000 paid, tr on Cherry creek, being part of tr on which ELISABETH CATRON now resides, being 200 acres.

Page 219   Indenture   Same date and parties as in above deed, $500 paid, 180 acres on Cherry creek, part of 2500 acres.

Page 220   Indenture   28 Feb 1818   DAVID NORRIS and JOHN PISTOLE, $950 paid, tr on headwaters of Cherry creek including place now occupied by Norris being a part of 2500 acres granted by NC to ROBT KING, Patent 341 and dated 1 Mar 1797. Wit: JAMES H PASS, BRICE BYRNE.

Page 221   Land Grant No 2571   7 Mar 1796   NORTH CAROLINA grants to JOHN GRAY BLOUNT, assee of JOHN MCNEESE, a captain in Continental line of sd state, 3840 acres on Caney fork including a camp made by ROBERT KING & CO and a place where they killed a remarkable fat bear.

Page 222   Land Grant No 3142   14 Sept 1797   Grantor above grants RICHARD BARBOUR, assee of heirs of STEPHEN ARTHUS, a private in Continental line of sd state, 640 acres in Sumner County on S side Caney fork of Cumberland river in a valley known as the Caney fork valley.

Page 222   Land Grant No 3144   14 Sept 1797   Grantor above grants RICHARD BARBOUR, assee of heirs of NIMROD TERRELL, a drummer in Continental line of sd state, 1000 acre of land in Sumner County on Flat creek, a branch of Muirs fork of the Caney fork. DAN DAVIDSON, HENRY WOODS, CC. Certified copy from book of Military Grants certif by WILLIAM WHITE, Secty of NC. Signed by JNO C MCLEMORE in Nashville, 10 Aug 1818.

Page 223   Land Grant No 3145   14 Sept 1797   Grantor granted RICHARD BARBOUR, assee of WILLIAM LIPPENCUT, a private in Continental line sd state, 640 acres in Eastern Dist. Certif & signed as above, same date.

Page 224   Land Grant No 3146   Date & grantor to sd BARBOUR, assee of FREDERICK DAVIS, a private in sd line sd state, 365 acres in Eastern Dist on Spring creek. Certif on 22 Aug 1818.

Page 224   Land Grant No 3147   Above date & Grantor to sd BARBOUR, assee WILLIAM MORRISON, a Lieutenant in sd line, 197 acres in Sumner County, being Warr No 4069, signed by JONATHAN WOOD, DS, and HENRY WOOD and FRANK LEEPER, CC (Chain Carriers, and signed as above.)

Page 225   Land Grant No 3143   14 Sept 1797   NC grants sd Barbour, assee of heirs of STEPHEN ARCHER, a private in Continental line sd state, 640 acres in Sumner on S side Caney fork of Cumberland river. Warr No 3851.

Page 225   Land Grant No 3144   Date as above, NC grants Barbour, assee NIMROD TYRRELL, a drummer in Continental line sd state, 1000 acres in Sumner Co on Flat creek. Warr 4758, DANIEL DAVIDSON, HENRY WOODS, CC.

Page 226   Land Grant No 3147   14 Sept 1797   NC to RICHARD BARBOUR, assee, WILLIAM HARRISON, a lieutenant in Continental line sd state, 197 acres in Sumner County. Warr No 4069.

Page 226   Land Grant 2252   20 May 1798   NC grants to JOSHUA DAVIS, assee of ROBERT BLANSHOT(?), a private in Continental line sd state, 640 acres in Sumner County of E side Caney fork.

Page 227   Indenture   20 July 1818   EZEKIEL BATES and ELIJAH CHISUM, $100 paid, 39 acres.

Page 228   Indenture   6 July 1818   GARRET FITZGERRAL of the Alabama Territory, one part, and ELIJAH CHISUM, other part, $800 paid, tr in first dist on Cany fork. Wit: ABNER HILL, WILLIAM HILL.

Page 229   Indenture   4 Mar 1817   DAVID JACKSON and WILLIAM SHOCKLY, $0.25 pd, 24 acres on S side main Cany fork, beg on N bdy line JACKSON Claim, it being SW cor small sur of GEORGE W GIBBS.

Page 230   Indenture   3 Oct 1816   JOSEPH WALLING and CASON GIBBS, Jr, $500 paid, 212 acres on Caney fork. Wit: BENJN GIBBS, JESSE GIBBS.

Page 231   Indenture   6 July 1818   GEORGE G TAYLOR and wife ELIZABETH TAYLOR, WILLIAM N LANE and wife SALLY LANE, of Clark Co, KY, and WESLEY W KEAS and wife, SARAH KEAS, of county aforesd, one part, and SAML LONGSTREET and JOSHUA BAILEY of City of Philadelphia, PA, other part, $2,000 paid, Lot 30 in Sparta. Wit: ROBT GRIFFING, JNO WARD. Ack in sd Clark Co, KY before sd witnesses, being JP's. Certif by JAMES P BULLOCK, Court Clk, and BENJ J LANE, Presid Magis, Co Court.

Page 232   Indenture   24 July 1818   MORGAN DEWEESE and PLEASANT EARLS, $35.00 paid, tr on Caney fork being 17 1/2 acres and beg in N bdy of GARRETT FITTSGERALD 100 acres.

Page 233   Indenture   20 July 1818   Grantor above and EZEKIEL BATES, tr in First Dist on Caney fork, beg at cor of GARRETT FITTSGERALD, 39 acres. Wit: ABNER HILL, JOSEPH UPCHURCH.

Page 234   Indenture   20 July 1818   WILLIS MENEFEE and GEORGE DEPREESE, $800 paid, 12 acres adj Lodderdale's gap, and adj tr of 145 acres granted to THOMAS CRUTCHER, and MANUEL PARKISON corner.

Page 235   Indenture   18 Dec 1816   ALEXANDER GLENN, Senior, and ALEXANDER GLENN, Junr, $250 paid, 82 acres in 1st Dist on Caney fork on S side of Taylor's creek, and both sides of the wagon road leading from DANIEL ALEXANDER, Esqr, to Rock Island. Wit: CHRISTOPHER SWINDLE, JESSE GLENN.

Page 236   Indenture   24 Jan 1818   NATHAN HAGGARD, Jackson Co, TN, one part, and WILLIAM J BENNETT, other part, $25.00 paid, Lot 83 in Town of Sparta. Wit: ARON OVERTON, JACOB A LANE.

Page 238   Indenture   23 July 1818   ANDREW BURK and LEWIS BOHANNON, $262 paid, 40 acres on headwaters of Calf Killers fork of Caney fork excluding RIDING CRISP(?) cabin at the fork of the creek.

Page 239   Indenture   28 Feb 1818   ROBERT A PIRKINS and JOHN PISTOLE, $450 paid, tr being on headwaters of Cherry creek, a part of tr of 2500 acres granted by NC to ROBT KING, Patent No 341, dated 1 Mar 1797. Wit: BRICE BYRNE, REUBEN ROBINSON, JAMES H PASS.

Page 240   Indenture   1 Aug 1817   ELIJAH SAUNDERS, Warren Co, TN, and RANDOLPH ROSS, of Virginia, $1.00 paid, 50 acres beg SE cor JAMES LAXTON Occupant sur, tr adj GEO W SAUNDERS and REUBIN P SAUNDERS. Wit: RICHARD WITHROW, JNO MILLER.

Page 241   Indenture   22 July 1818   THOMAS BOUNDS and WILLIAM MITCHELL, latter of Sparta, Lot 10 in said town. Wit: WILLIAM H CAMPBELL, THOS TAYLOR.

Page 242   Indenture   3 Jan 1817   HARRIS BURK and ISAAC MIDKOFF, $131 paid, tr on Caney fork including place where sd Burk now lives, and being 50 acres. Wit: JACOB A LANE, JOHN ROBISON.

Page 243   Indenture   16 July 1818   JOHN WALLING and JAMES WILLIAMS, $1000 paid, 176 1/2 acres in 1st Dist on Caney fork, beg N of SE cor 228 acre tr entered to sd Walling.

Page 244   Indenture   30 Sept 1817   JOHN S CLARY and DAVID PEARCE, $40.00 paid, 10 acres on waters of the falling water, beg on SW cor ZACHARIAH JONES entry. Wit: JOHN RICHMOND, JAMES RICHMOND.

Page 245   Indenture   5 Jan 1814   JOHN MCBRIDE and ARTHUR BOWIN, $100 paid,

25 acres on S side main Caney fork. Wit: NICHOLAS GILLENTINE, CHARLES BOWIN, THOMAS MEEK.

Page 246 Indenture 1 Dec 1815 The two JOHN GRIGGS, Senr & Junr, one part, and DAVID JACKSON, $600 pd, 4 tracts in 3rd Dist on S side main Caney fork: 45 acres, 12 acres beg NW cor ALEXANDER COOK 45 acre sur, 10 acres beg SW cor JOHN GRIGGS 12 acre tr, and 10 acres. Wit: JOHN MCELHINEY, WILLIAM SHOCKLEY.

Page 247 Indenture 21 July 1818 JOHN TOWNSEND and BRITAIN JOHNSON, $60.00 paid, 50 acres granted by TN to sd Townsend in Patent 10205, on 20 June 1817. Wit: HENRY BURTON, WILLIAM ERWIN.

Page 248 Indenture 22 July 1818 ANDREW TOWNSEND and JOHN KELLY, $600 paid, 300 acres in 1st Dist on Caney fork, beg on S side of Smarts mountain, and including Townsend's improvement, being all of Grant 2326.

Page 249 Indenture ___ ___ 1817 LEVI SWEET and HAMBLETON ELLISON, $75.00 paid, tr lying on W side Cane creek on Walnut branch of sd creek, 50 acres. Wit: JAS TOWNSEND, JAS ALLISON, WILLIAM ELLISON.

Page 250 Indenture 21 July 1818 WILLIAM BELCHER and JOSEPH KERR, Junr, $325 paid, 80 acres on waters of Calf killer fork in the Caney fork, 3rd Dist.

Page 250 Indenture 20 July 1818 ISAAC MIDKIFF and WILLIAM LISK, $1300 paid, 5 tracts, being in all 322 acres in 1st Dist & on Taylor's creek.

Page 252 Indenture 2 May 1818 ISAAC TAYLOR, Junr, and JAMES TOWNSEND, of one part, and JOHN KELLY, other part, $250 paid, 201 acres, being 1 moiety of Grant No 6601 issued by TN to sd Taylor & Townsend for 402 acres, being on Taylor's creek, beg at cor of HENRY LYDA on W bdy line of DAVID THOMPSON.

Page 253 Indenture 15 Sept 1817 JOHN BROWN and JOHN RICHMOND, $200 paid, tr of 46 acres in 1st Dist on waters of the falling water. Wit: JOHN HASH, DAVID PEARCE, JAMES RICHMOND.

Page 254 Indenture 12 June 1818 JOHN HAWKINS and DANIEL NEWMAN, $100 paid, tr of 50 acres in first Dist on waters of Taylor's creek, it being same land which Hawkins holds by grant from TN, his improvement being included in this sale. Wit: JOSEPH HAWKINS, BENJAMIN HAWKINS.

Page 255 Bill of Sale 8 Sept 1818 THOMAS YATES, JESSE DADSAN(?), and POLLY HAMLETT to BERRY HAMLITT, $300 paid by Hamlitt, grant him the power to bring suit against JAMES CHAMBERS to recover a Negro woman and her increase named CHARITY, who formerly belonged to Est of GEORGE COMBS of Halifax Co, VA, which woman was formerly owned by PHEBE COMBS (widow of sd George Combs), above named Grantors being heirs of sd George. Wit: JOHN CATRON, HENRY LYDA, WILLIAM CHISM, ARCHIBALD CONNOR.

Page 256 Power of Attorney 8 Aug 1818 THOMAS T THOMSON, Green Co, NY, appoints SAMUEL DENTON of City of New York, Merchant, the power to convey any land owned by Grantor in White Co, TN. Wit: THOMAS S BURRALL.

Page 257   Land Grant 7758   22 Sept 1815   TENNESSEE for military service performed by NICHOLAS BODEN to NC, Warr 5090, dated 6 Dec 1797, & entered to CORDER STONE, assee of heirs of sd Boden, tr being 15 acres in 3rd Dist on headwaters of Cherry creek.

Page 257   Land Grant No 9963   30 Apr 1817   TENNESSEE by virtue part of Certif 277, dated 17 Aug 1807, to JAMES SHARP and entered on 24 Mar 1809 by No 782, grants CORDY STONE, assee of sd James, 81 acres dated 22 Apr 1814, being in 3rd Dist on headwaters of Cherry creek.

Page 258   Indenture   20 Oct 1817   SAMUEL DENTON of New York City, and MARY DENTON, his wife, one part, and THOMAS T THOMSON of Catskill, NY, merchant, second part, $8000 paid, undiv half part of land in White Co, TN, being 2204 acres. Wit: ABRAHAM P GIBSON, SAML TURMAN. Ack in New York State on 21 Oct 1817, before THO BOTTON, and in New York City on 30 Oct 1817, before R SWANTON, Justice of Jus Ct for NY.

Page 261   Bill of Sale   24 Jan 1818   LEONARD LAMBERTSON to ISAAC TAYLOR, a Negro boy named JACK, aged 18 years. Wit: WILLIAM GLENN, JOHN M HANNAH.

Page 262   Power of Attorney   22 July 1818   ISAAC MIDKIFF appoints ISAAC TAYLOR his attorney to act for him in re 50 acres on head of Caney fork, being place where HARRIS BIRK formerly lived and by him conveyed to me, and tr I bought at sheriff's sale, a tr of GEORGE W SANDERS being 100 acres, and other lands.

Page 263   Indenture   1 Aug 1818   ANTHONY DIBRELL and WILLIAM MITCHELL, one part, and THOMAS LYONS, other part, $2650 paid, 2 lots (8 & 9) in Sparta. Wit: WILLIAM SIMPSON, J B HANCOCK, JNO ALLEN.

Page 264   Indenture   31 July 1818   WILLIAM MITCHELL, of Sparta, TN, and THOMAS LYONS, Rutherford Co, TN, $100 paid, Lot 10 in Sparta. Wit: JNO ALLEN, J B HANCOCK, ANTHONY DIBRELL.

Page 265   Indenture   31 July 1818   WM SO MITCHELL and THOMAS LYONS, as in above deed, $50.00 paid, tr contiguous to Sparta, being same orig conv by CALEB FRALEY to BENJAMIN WEAVER, now owned by sd Mitchell. Wit: JAS ALLEN, J B HANCOCK, ANTHONY DIBRELL.

Page 266   Indenture   6 Mar 1817   JOHN DYSON and WILLIAM MITCHELL of Sparta, $28.00 paid, tr orig conv by Fraley to Weaver, as above. JACOB A LANE, JOHN R FOSTER.

Page 267   Indenture   2 Sept 1816   WILLIAM BURDEN, Sen, and WILLIAM LAMPTON, latter of Sparta, $2000 paid, Lot 11 in Sparta.

Page 268   Indenture   1 June 1818   ISHAM RUSSELL and JAMES ANDERSON, $200 paid, 40 acres in first Dist in the Barrens Grant No 5828. Wit: JNO JETT, ARCHIBALD CONNOR.

Page 269   Indenture   31 Jan 1814   GEORGE W GIBBS and ANTHONY DIBRELL, $800 paid, 70 acre tr on Calf Killers fork of Caney fork. Wit: TEMPLE PARTON.

Page 270   Indenture   9 Sept 1818   GEORGE TUCKER and JOHN AUSTIN, $400 paid, tr of 1 acre on waters of Hickory valley, on the mountain, being part of 100 acre sur conv from WILLIAM C BRIGHTWELL to sd Tucker. Wit: A DIBRELL, MOSES NORMAN.

Page 271 Indenture 10 Jan 1818 REUBEN P SANDERS, of Madison Co, Alabama Terr, one part, and RANDOLPH ROSS, Rockbridge Co, VA, other part, $1.00 paid, 15 acres granted to Sanders by Grant No 4913, dated 2 Aug 1813. Wit: JOHN ANDERSON, JAMES ANDERSON, JNO MILLER.

Page 272 Indenture 19 Sept 1816 ANTHONY DIBRELL and GEORGE W GIBBS, $1000 paid, tr of 87 acres & 35 poles, beg 2nd cor to GEORGE AILSWORTH & adj line WILLIAM GRACY land & being where he now lives. Wit: CHARLES DIBRELL, LAWSON NOURSE(?).

Page 273 Bill of Sale 9 Sept 1818 HOWEL G HARRIS to JOSEPH WALLING, $700 paid, a Negro boy named HERCULES, about 14 yrs old. Wit: WILLIAM GLENN, ISHAM BRADLEY. Ack by ANTHONY DIBRELL, Clk White Co CC, by his deputy JACOB A LANE.

Page 273 Bill of Sale 24 Sept 1816 THOMAS HERBERT to ELI SIMS, $500 paid, a Negro woman named MARCY and her child MARRIAH. Wit: ROBERT PUCKETT.

Page 274 Bond & Assignment 10 Oct 1815 BENJAMIN DENTON bind himself to WILLIAM MUNKES(?), $300 paid, Denton to make deed for 50 acres on Caney fork, beg on ALEXANDER COOK NW cor. Wit: ALEX COOK. Assigned to THOS CRAWLEY on 31 Aug 1816. Wit: EPHRAIM SHOCKLEY.

Page 275 Indenture 3 July 1816 THOMAS USSERY, Warren Co, TN, and DAVID HUDSON, for $100 paid, 30 acre tract. Wit: ISAAC MIDKIFF, ELY SIMS.

Page 276 Indenture 19 Oct 1818 JOSHUA BARTLETT and ISAAC WELCH, $200 paid, 12 1/2 acres on falling water of Cany fork in edge of the Dry valley, including where JOHN BOHANNON now lives, being part tr granted by TN to JAMES BARTLETT.

Page 277 Indenture 8 Oct 1817 JAMES CARTER and RHODA SMITH, $1,000 paid, tr on Cane creek of falling water, 202 acres, beg in N bdy line sur orig claimed by WILLIAM KING for 640 acres. Wit: HAMBLETT ALLISON, LEVI SWEAT.

Page 278 Indenture 24 Mar 1817 ROBERT WALKER and EDMOND CUNNINGHAM, being all claim vested in Walker by Grant No 4167, dated 21 Sept 1812, being 100 acres on waters of Lost creek of main Cany fork. Wit: W P WHITE, WM GRAHAM.

Page 279 Indenture 6 Aug 1817 MATTHEW BABB and NATHAN EARLES, $200 paid, 4 tracts in 3rd Dist on main Caney fork on N side. Wit: WILLIAM SHAW, JACOB MILLER.

Page 280 Indenture 25 Sept 1818 LARKIN BAKER and DANIEL CLARK, $200 paid, 25 1/4 acres on Town creek, and beg on conditional line between WINNIFORD CLARK and sd Baker, and near 30 acre sur of JOEL MILTON. Wit: A B LANE, P H MIDKIFF.

Page 281 Indenture 29 Sept 1818 GASPER BARGER and WILLIAM ANDERSON,

$138 paid, tr of 154 1/2 acres, a part of 511 acre tr granted to Barger by Grant No 5713, dated 15 June 1814, Warr 5298, dated 16 Dec 1797, & entered on 9 May 1812 by No 1767, being at head of Town creek, and including farm occupied by PHILLIP BARGER.

Page 282   Indenture __ Oct 1818   ROBERT TOWNSEND and SAMUEL GLENN, $200 paid, tr on Caney fork, being 50 acres sd Townsend holds by Grant No 10348, dated 14 July 1817. Wit: PHAROAH H MIDKIFF, DANIEL NEWMAN.

Page 283   Indenture 19 Oct 1818   WILLIAM SHAW and ANDREW CAPE, $800 paid, 2 tracts in 1st Dist, 1st Range, & 9th Sec on waters of Cany fork, 120 acres.

Page 284   Indenture 19 Oct 1818   BENJAMIN SHAW and Grantee above, $300 paid, 50 acres in 1st Dist on Calf killers fork, beg SE cor JACOB MILLER. Wit: JOSEPH UPCHURCH, WILLIAM SHAW.

Page 285   Indenture 21 Oct 1818   ANDREW BURK, Snr, and ISAAC BRUMBELOW, Junior, $29.00 paid, 15 acres on Calf killers fork.

Page 286   Indenture 14 June 1817   HENRY FRANKS and LEMUEL FRANKS, $40.00 paid, tr of 70 acres by sur of 17 Dec 1818, tr being in 1st Dist & including tr where LEMUEL FRANKS now lives. Wit: WILLIAM LAURENCE, EZEKIEL ELLEDGE.

Page 287   Indenture 30 July 1818   JAMES MCCLEARN and JAMES DILDINE, $50.00 paid, 25 acres in 1st Dist on waters of falling water as per Grant No 10798, dated 10 Nov 1814, tract conv including the spring & improvement where TOLBET DALTON(?) did live. Wit: WILLIAM ERWIN, EZAKIAH DILDINE.

Page 288   Indenture 30 July 1818   JAMES MCCLEARN and JAMES DILDINE, $40.00 paid, 20 acres in 1st Dist on the falling water. Wit: WILLIAM ERWIN, EZAHIAL DILDINE.

Page 289   Indenture 30 July 1818   Parties as in above deed, $9.00 paid, 4 acres in first Dist adj his(?) 25 acre tr on S. Wit: As above.

Page 290   Indenture 5 May 1818   THOMAS TOWNSEND and HENRY LIDEY(?), $500 paid, 300 acres granted to sd Townsend by TN by Grant 9886, being in 1st Dist, 1st Range & 8th Sec on the Caney, beg on SE cor of 20 acre tr of WILLIAM MORRISON, now conv to JAMES SIMPSON. Wit: JAMES SIMPSON, WILLIAM LYDA.

Page 291   Indenture 1 Oct 1818   WILLIE FARROW and JOHN CUNNINGHAM, latter of Warren Co, TN, $55.00 paid, 20 acres in 1st Dist on Caney fork.

Page 292   Indenture 6 Feb 1818   LARKIN BAKER and WINIFRED CLARKE, $15.00 paid, 2 acres on Town creek, it being a part of tr Baker bought of FRANCIS B THOMAS. Wit: WM B NEVILL, DANIEL CLARKE.

Page 293   Indenture 12 June 1818   CORDER H STONE and IREBY W STONE, (relationship not stated), $80.00 paid, 40 acres in 1st Dist between Hutchings creek and Cane creek which was orig granted by TN to ROBERT B PERKINS, assee of CALEB BERRY by Grant No 9525. Wit: THOMAS STONE, JOHN CALLAS.

Page 294   Indenture   13 June 1818   DANIEL NEWMAN and RICHARD CROWDER $600 paid, tracts on Caney fork, 50 acres granted to JOHN HAWKINS by TN & conv to Newman by deed, 150 acres adj JOHN CAMPBELL, and 20 acres beg at Hawkins NW cor; also 40 acres beg at WILLIAM HAWKINS NW cor, tr adj EDWARD HOOPER sur. Wit: ISAAC TAYLOR, JAMES RANDAL.

Page 295   Power of Attorney   18 Oct 1816   JAMES CARTER appoints JAMES TOWNSEND as his Attorney in fact to convey to RHODA SMITH(?), tr of 20 acres. Wit: HAMBLETON ALLISON, LEVI SWEAT.

Page 296   Indenture   20 Aug 1817   WILLIAM DODSON and JOHN RICHARDSON, one part, and EPHRAIM PERKINS, other part, $150 paid, 93 acres 17 poles, part tr conv by WM P ANDERSON and JOHN MCIVER to JOHN HUTCHINS, being on Town creek granted by NC to JAMES EASTON. Wit: ABSALOM PERKINS, JAMES WELCH.

Page 297   Land Grant No 4167   21 Sept 1812   TENNESSEE by virtue of Certif 630 dated 22 July 1811, issued to ISAAC TAYLOR, Jr, entered on 8 Oct 1811 by No 1537, grants to ROBERT WALKER, assee of sd Taylor, a 100 acre tr in 3rd Dist on Loss creek(?), waters of main Caney fork, being surv 4 Jan 1812 by W P WHITE, D S.

Page 297   Bill of Sale   22 Jan 1814   JOHN E DALE, Smith Co, TN, to LEONARD AMBERSON, 1 Negro boy named JACK, aged 14 or 15 yrs, $250 paid. Wit: ISAAC WARREN, WILLIAM ANDERSON, THOS WHALEY.

Page 298   Indenture   21 July 1817   JESSE ALLEN, Warren Co, TN, one part, and COUNTY OF WHITE, for benefits accruing to public in general, as well as to himself, tr as a place of public Inspection, being 2 acres beg near edge of water of Caney fork 6 poles just below where sd Allen's boat now lands.

Page 299   Plan of Allenville   18 Oct 1818   (Plat of 6 lots) Signed by Commissioners ISAAC MIDKIFF, JAMES TOWNSEND, and GEORGE ALLEN who are to proceed to build a warehouse on a small scale.

Page 300   Indenture   19 Oct 1818   Commissioners as above and THOMAS TAYLOR, $20.00 paid, Lot 2 in town of ALLENVILLE.

Page 301   Indenture   Date and Commissioners as above, and JESSE ALLEN, latter of Warren Co, TN, $26.00 paid, Lot 2 in Allenville.

Page 302   Indenture   Date & Commissioners as above, and sd JESSE ALLEN, $23.00 paid, Lot 4 in above named town.

Page 303   Indenture   Date & Commissioners as above, and JOHN TAYLOR, $29.00 paid, lot in above town, adj Lots 4 & 6.

Page 304   Indenture   Date & Commissioners as above, and JOHN KELLY, $31.00 paid, Lot 6 in Allenville.

Page 305   Power of Attorney   20 Nov 1818   THOMAS INGRAM, heir of WILLIAM INGRAM, Decd, Hawkins Co, TN, having heretofore sold to RICHARD MITCHELL of same place, all land entered in my name as heir of WM INGRAM, or in name of WILLIAM INGRAM, I do appoint WILLIAM MITCHELL, the brother of sd Richard, my atty, to sell my land. Wit: BENJM SPYKER, JAS MILLER. Certif in Hawkins Co, TN before S D MITCHELL, Clk, and JOSEPH W CARDIN, JP.

Page 306   Indenture   29 July 1817   WADDY THOMPSON, Senr, and ELIZA B THOMPSON, his wife, of Greenville Dist, SC (by their attorney WADDY THOMPSON, Junr), and JAMES WILLIAMS, New Orleans Co, LA, and SARAH F CHOTARD, and THOMAS B WILLIAMS, to THOMAS LINVILLE, $200 paid, 100 acres being part of 5000 acres granted by NC to ELIZA WILLIAMS, assee of JAMES WILLIAMS, dated 20 Dec 1796 which descended to us from our decd ancester, tr beg in ANSELM BRADLEY.   Wit: ANTHONY DIBRELL, H DAVIS.

Page 307   Power of Attorney   24 Sept 1810   JOHN KINKEAD, Montgomery Co, KY, constitute and appoint WILLIAM MCCLELLAND of Fayette Co, KY, my atty with power to transfer my interest in a Warrant 261 which was entered in name of JOSEPH KINKEAD, Decd, on 400 acres on S side of Holston river and opposite mouth of North fork, granted me by sd Joseph, my decd father, by his last will & tes, the other moiety to ELIZABETH MCCLELLAND, wife of sd William McClelland; to ALEXANDER LOWRY of White County.   Ack in Fayette Co, KY before RICHARD HIGGINS, presiding JP.

Page 308   Power of Attorney   19 July 1817   WILLIAM MCCLELLAN, Fayette Co, KY, heir of his decd wife (formerly ELIZABETH KINKEAD) & as atty in fact for JOHN KINKEAD, being heirs of JOSEPH KINKEAD, Decd, appoints as atty-in-fact ALEXANDER LOWRY of White County, with power to assign all plats founded on Warr 251, issued by Comm of E TN for 400 acres entered in office of surveyor of 3rd Dist of sd state.   Ack in Fayette County before J C RODES, Clk, and OLIVER KEEN, JP.

Page 309   Indenture   9 Jan 1819   JOHN TEMPLETON and WILLIAM BLACKBURN, $550 paid, 100 acres, 1st Dist, 9th Sec, 1st Range, beg near THOMAS K HARRIS, & being same land entered by JOHN JENKINS.   Wit: WILLIAM LAWRENCE, ELY HILL.

Page 310   Indenture   13 Nov 1818   WILLIAM E AIKMAN, Howard Co, MO Terr, and WILLIAM DEWEESE, $200 paid, 2 tracts of 45 acres.   Wit: JAMES FRISBY, SAMUEL GLENN.

Page 311   Indenture   9 Jan 1819   JOHN TEMPLETON and WILLIAM BLACKBURN, $150 paid, tr of 20 acres, 1st Dist, on waters Clift creek, beg NW cor 100 acre sur of JOHN JENKINS.   Wit: WILLIAM LAURENCE, ELIJAH HILL.

Page 312   Indenture   16 July 1818   JOHN WALLING and SHARP WHITLEY, $1000 paid, 176 1/2 acre tr in 1st Dist on Cany fork.   Wit: JAMES JARRELL, JAS SIMPSON, THOMAS WALLING.

Page 313   Indenture   10 Sept 1818   JOSEPH PRYOR and JOHN BOHANNON, $350 paid, 50 acres in Dry valley, beg NE cor WM PRIOR Sur.   Wit: WILLIAM PRYOR, ELIJAH WARD.

Page 314   Indenture   14 Jan 1819   ABEL HUTSON and MATTHEW HUTSON, son of sd Abel, for love & affection, 194 acres & on Cany fork.   Wit: WILLIAM KNOWLES, ISAIAH HUTSON.

Page 315   Indenture   19 Oct 1818   SHARAD HORN and LEWIS BOHANNON, $200 paid, 100 acre tr of GEORGE RUSSELL, tr being on both sides Calf killers fork of Caney fork.   Wit: WILLIAM STAMPS, SANDFORD STAMPS.

Page 316   Indenture   19 Oct 1818   SHAROD HORN and LUIS BOHANNON, $200 paid, 25 acre tr on both sides Calf killers fork of Caney, adj 30 acre tr of sd Horn per Grant 4889. Wit: As in above deed.

Page 317 Indenture 14 Jan 1819 ABEL HUTSON and JULIANNA LAURENCE, daughter of sd Abel, for love of sd daughter, 25 acres on Cany fork, beg NW cor of 20 acre entry of JOHN TEMPLETON.

Page 318 Indenture 12 Jan 1819 MATTHEW HUTSON and WILLIAM LAURENCE, $60.00 paid, 18 acres on Cany fork, adj JOHN TEMPLETON 24 acre sur, part of Certif 1699. Wit: WILLIAM KNOWLES, ISAIAH HUTSON.

Page 319 Indenture 18 Apr 1819(?) JOHN CROOK, Senr, and JOHN CROOK, Jnr, $500 paid, tr on falling water of Caney fork, a part of grant by TN to THOS BOUNDS & THOS LOVELADY, dated 26 Feb 1810. Wit: AMOS SHIRLEY, JAMES BOUNDS.

Page 320 Indenture 15 Oct 1817 LEWIS SPARKMAN and GEORGE MORGAN BROWN, $60.00 paid, 10 acres on S side Caney fork, beg at JESSE KEITHLEY NE cor. Wit: MICAJAH SIMMONS, MOSES GODARD, WILLIAM SPARKMAN.

Page 321 Indenture 6 Sept 1816 ELIHU SANDERS, one part, and ISAAC DRAKE and JACOB DRAKE, Warren Co, TN, other part, $60.00 paid, 30 acres on N side Cany fork river Grant No 5558, beg upper cor REUBEN P SANDERS 10 acre survey. Wit: ALX COOK, HAREL SUGG, RICHARD LANE.

Page 322 Indenture 6 Sept 1816 ELIHU SANDERS, Attorney for ROBERT MCDONALD, one part, and ISAAC & JACOB DRAKE (as above), other part, $50.00 paid, 18 acres, Grant 3985, on N side Cany fork river. Wit: HAZEAD SUGG (?), ELIJAH DRAKE, RICHARD LANE.

Page 323 Indenture 6 Sept 1816 ELIHU SANDERS, Atty for ROBERT MCDONALD and JOHN MCDONALD, one part, and Drakes as in above deed, $50.00 paid, 10 acres on N side Caney fork river, Grant 2627. Wit: ALX COOK, HAYAL SUGG(?), ELIJAH DRAKE, RICHARD LANE.

Page 324 Indenture 13 Jan 1819 JACOB MILLER and ANDREW COPE, $450 paid, 100 acre tr in 1st Dist on Cany fork, 1st Range & 9th Sec, beg at cor of JOHN MILLER entry of 160 acres, No 482, & adj WILLIAM SHAW 100 acre survey. Wit: JOSEPH UPCHURCH, RICHARD WALLACE.

Page 325 Indenture 13 Jan 1819 FREDERICK MILLER and RICHARD WALLACE, $200 paid, 50 acres in 1st Dist on Caney fork, beg near SW cor JOSEPH DODSON entry. Wit: JOSEPH UPCHURCH, ANDREW COPE.

Page 326 Indenture 16 Jan 1819 WILLIAM GLENN, Admr of ALEXANDER GLENN, Decd, one part, and ALEXANDER GLENN (relationships not stated), $280 paid, tr of 55 acres by survey of 8 Feb 1814 in 1st Dist on Rutledge's mill creek.

Page 327 Indenture 16 Jan 1819 Parties as in above deed, $120 paid, 24 1/4 acres.

Page 328 Indenture 12 Jan 1819 ARCHIBALD HUTSON and JULIANNA LAURENCE, $37.50 paid, tract on Caney fork E of the Hickory nut mountain, containing 10 acres, adj ABEL HUTSON.

Page 329   Power of Attorney   13 July 1818   SOLOMAN COX, Howard Co, MO, appoints ELIJAH WARD to take the papers out of the office and get the grant of tr of 50 acres & convey to THOMAS BOUNDS. Wit: GRAY BYNUM, WM E AIKMAN. Ack in sd Howard County before GRAY BYNUM, Clk, and by NATHANIEL BEVERLEY TUCKER, Judge of St Louis Co, MS Terr.

Page 330   Power of Attorney   13 July 1818   CHRISTOPHER CATRON, Terr of MO, appoint ELIJAH WARD my atty-in-fact to convey to CALEB JOBE, tract on Cherry creek 30 acres adj ROBERT HOWARD and other lands as set out in deed. Wit: GRAY BYNUM, WM C AIKMAN. Ack as in above deed.

Page 331   Indenture   20 Apr 1818   MARVEL SUGG by his attorney GEORGE SUGG, Cabarrus Co, NC, and JOHN GRAHAM, $300 paid, 50 acres in Grant No 8335 & Warr 49, being on S side of main Cane fork. Wit: NICHOLAS GILLENTINE, WM GRAHAM.

Page 332   Indenture   18 Jan 1819   JAMES CHISUM, Overton Co, TN, and JOHN CHISUM, White County, Exrs last Will & Tes of ELIJAH CHISUM, Senr, one part, and JOHN RUTLEDGE, other part, $2500 paid, secured by note, tr on Calf Killers fork of Caney fork, including late residence of sd Elijah, Decd, being part 450 acre tr granted by TN to sd Elijah, Patent No 1858, 300 acres, reserving space for graves of late proprietors.

Page 333   Bill of Sale   15 Dec 1817   JAMES TAYLOR and THOMAS TAYLOR (relationship not stated), Admrs of Est of THOMAS TAYLOR, Decd, for $286 paid, to REBECCAH TAYLOR (widow of sd Taylor, Decd), a Negro woman named NANN, aged about 38 yrs. Wit: WILLIAM TAYLOR, JOHN TAYLOR.

Page 334   Bill of Sale   28 Oct 1818   REBEKEY TAYLOR to JAMES MCCLARN, $286 paid, a Negro woman named NANN, aged 38 yrs. Wit: WILLIAM TAYLOR, WILLIAM ERWIN.

Page 335   Deed   27 Dec 1817   CHRISTOPHER MIDYETT to URIAH GIBBS, $400 paid, 111 acres on Caney fork & beg at foot of Gumspring mountain, and adj land of RICHARD MIDYETT. Wit: CASON GIBBS, BENJN GIBBS.

Page 335   Indenture   3 Apr 1819   THOMAS LYON of Sparta, and JACOB ROBINSON, Lots 8 & 9 in said town. Wit: ALEXANDER B LANE, JAMES B ROBINSON.

Page 337   Indenture   Same date and parties as in above deed, $80.00 paid, 1 tract (No 10). Wit: As above.

Page 338   Indenture   Same date & parties as on p 335, $120 paid, tr adjoining Sparta, being land conv to Lyon by deed from WILLIAM MITCHELL on 31 July 1818.

Page 339   Indenture   __ Apr 1819   CHARLES HUTCHINGS and HENRY NEILL, $400 paid, tr on Rutledge's Mill creek, being 100 acres, including sd Hutchings improvement survey. Wit: JAS TOWNSEND, AARON HUTCHINGS.

Page 340   Indenture   12 Apr 1819   HENRY NEILL, one part, and THOMAS BURGESS and THOMAS H BURGESS, other part, $800 paid, 140 acres, by sur dated 9 Nov 1814, 1st Dist on N side Caney fork. Wit: JAS TOWNSEND, WM A KIRBY, JAS WILMOUTH.

Page 341   Indenture   27 Feb 1819   JOHN RUSSELL and RICHARD BROWN, $250 paid, 20 acres including crossroad where JAMES EASON now lives on little Cany fork, being tr granted Russell by Warr No 533 on 31 Mar 1812.   Wit: ZACHARIAH SULLINS, JNO BROWN.

Page 342   Indenture   Date and parties as in above deed, $300 paid, 15 acres on little Caney fork, including part road leading from White Plains to Rock Island ford, Warr 1214, dated 17 Sept 1812.   Wit: ZACHARIAH SULLINS, JOHN BROWN.

Page 343   Indenture   WILLIAM B NEVILLE, one part, and GEORGE W GIBBS, latter of town of Nashville, Davidson Co, TN, $200 paid, 235 acres on Town creek.   (Very dim)

Page 344   Indenture   19 Aug 1814   BURRELL HENDERSON and JOHN HENDERSON(?), $355 paid, tr on Calf Killers fork of Caney, 100 acres.   Wit: JAMES MOORE, SAMUEL JOHNSON, WM HARGIS. (Very dim)

Page 345   Indenture   14 Dec 1818   WILLIS KEITHLEY, Lawrence Co, IN, and ELIJAH HILL, $125 paid, tr on N side Caney, 50 acres including spring & improvement where JOHN KEITHLEY now lives.   Wit: JOSEPH UPCHURCH, JOSEPH CUMMINGS, HENRY KEATHLEY.

Page 346   Bill of Sale   28 Nov 1818   JOHN PATE, Warren Co, TN, to JARAMIAH PATE, after my decease, for love I have for Jaramiah, my son, a certain Negro boy FRANK.   Wit: LEONARD ADCOCK, ANTHONY PATE.

Page 346   Power of Attorney   FAUCHE GARNER(?) appoints friend JOHN HUNTER, with power to procure grants from TN on Entry 10310 for 14 acres (former Jackson Co), & also 11 acres, & to convey to WILLIAM MAINARD.   Wit: REUBIN RAGLAND, JOHN MANOR.   Ack 19 July 1817.

Page 347   Power of Attorney   13 Apr 1819   HENRY NEILL appoints JAMES TOWNSEND as my atty to delived deeds to ISAAC ADCOCK for 50 acres in Warren County adj SAMUEL WILLIAMS, JOSEPH JADWIN(?), JOHN HOWARD, JOHN WATSON.   Wit: JOHN CLOUSE, WILLIAM KIRBY.

Page 348   Indenture   22 Sept 1817   JAMES FULKERSON and ALEXANDER S SIMPSON, $1200 paid, 170 1/3 acres on Calf killer, part of Grant 310.   Wit: GEO AINSWORTH, WILLIAM HARBERT, THOS TAYLOR.

Page 349   Indenture   12 July 1814   BRADFORD ROSS of Anderson Co, TN, one part, and LEVI L MCBEE, $30.00 paid, Lot 79 in Sparta.   Wit: ROBERT W AYLOTT, JAMES DAVIS.

Page 349   Indenture   10 Apr 1819   JAMES TURNER and WILLIAM BROWN, $350 paid, tr of 49 acres granted by TN to ELIJAH CHISUM, Senr, by Grant 5774. Wit: A DIBRELL, ISAAC TAYLOR.

Page 350   Bill of Sale   17 July 1819   ZACHARIAH JONES to ISAAC TAYLOR, $875 paid, a Negro named DINAH, about 36 yrs, and her son GEORGE, about 9 yrs. Wit: HENRY BURTON, JOHN YOUNG, WILLIAM WHITE, ARCHIBALD H NAPIER.

Page 351   Indenture   ___ ____ 1818   GEORGE PARKISON and ROBERT B PURKINS, $700 paid, 147 1/2 acres that sd Parkison now lives on, being on Post Oak creek, a branch of the falling water. Wit: ELIJAH ENGLAND, SIMPSON CASH.

Page 352 Indenture 17 July 1819 JAMES HOLLAND and THOMAS BRIDGMAN, $175 paid, 100 acres on Jenkins creek, beg at SE cor WILLIAM ALSTON tr of 457 1/3 acres. Wit: WM LAURENCE, AMOS MCGOWEN.

Page 353 Indenture 28 May 1819 BENJAMIN HAWKINS, Senr, one part, and JAMES HAWKINS, other part, (relationship not stated), 100 acres in 1st Dist on Caney fork.

Page 354 Indenture Date and Grantor above and BENJAMIN HAWKINS, Junr, $300 paid, 100 acres in 1st Dist on Caney fork, beg on N bdy line of 300 acres granted by TN to JOHN TOWNSEND, Grant No 9661, 30 Sept 1816.

Page 355 Indenture 19 Jan 1819 GEORGE PATILLA and JOHN CHISUM, $30.00 paid, tr in 1st Dist on Calf killer. Wit: JOHN ANDERSON, THOMAS RIPLEY.

Page 356 Indenture 25 Dec 1818 REUBEN PERKINS and SAMUEL HARDESTER, $300 paid, 83 1/2 acres on Cany fork, being part tr orig granted by NC to JAMES EASTON, assee of heirs of MATTHIAS DUEL(?) by Grant No 2705. Wit: THOMAS STONE, IREBY W STONE.

Page 357 Indenture 9 Apr 1818 MICHAEL SAILERS and REUBEN PERKINS, $300 paid, 320 acres on Cainy fork, 1/2 of a tr orig granted by NC to JAMES EASTOR, assee of heirs of MATTHIAS DUDLY, Patent No 2705. Wit: SILAS HARRIS,SAMUEL HARDISTER.

Page 358 Indenture 23 Oct 1817 GEORGE AILSWORTH, of town of Sparta, and JOHN B GARRET of same place, $70.00 paid, our equal moiety of 2 lots in Sparta, being Nos 71 & 72.

Page 359 Indenture 30 Apr 1818 JAMES BOUNDS and JOSEPH TERRY, $1000 paid, tr on falling waters of Caney fork of Cumberland River, 130 acres, adj THOMAS LOVELADY line. Wit: THOS BOUNDS, WILLIAM WARRENER(?).

Page 360 Indenture 24 Aug 1811 SPENCE MITCHELL, of one part, and the minister and people of congregation of the UNION MEETING HOUSE and all other of God's people who make an open profession of the Christian religion and are by good standing in their own church (Shakers and others excepted), other part, for love, etc, 1 tract of land for a house for preaching, being on Caney fork. Wit: TURNER LANE, ___ LANE.

Page 361 Indenture 25 July 1818 ABNER HILL and EZEKIEL BATES, $525 pd, 97 acres beg at foot of Town mountain, being NW cor sd Hill's 60 acre sur, & adj THOMAS HILL field. Wit: ELIJAH HILL, WINKFIELD HILL.

Page 362 Indenture 23 Mar 1819 WILLIAM WINTER and JAMES WALLING, latter of Scott Co, VA, $1300 pd, 200 acres on Calf killers fork joining line of JOHN MILLER. Wit: THOMAS WALLING, JOSEPH WALLING, JACOB MILLER.

Page 363 Indenture 5 Sept 1818 JOHN WALLING, Senior, and JOHN WALLING, Junior, $400 paid, 100 acres beg at NW cor Sur in name of heirs of DAVID JOINER. Wit: JAS SIMPSON, JAMES WILLIAMS, THOMAS WALLING.

Page 364 Indenture 10 Oct 1818 ALEXANDER GLENN, blacksmith, one part, and ISAAC GLENN, other part, $100 paid, tr of 24 acres in 1st Dist, N side of Caney fork, watering Rutledges mills creek, beg at E side of path leading from ALEXANDER GLENN to WILLIAM GLENN.

Page 365 Indenture 28 Feb 1818 ELIJAH WARD and DAVID NORRIS, $62.00 paid, 284 acres on Caney fork, being part of 2500 acres orig granted by NC to ROBERT KING, assee of JAMES WILLIAMS, Grant #341. Wit: JACOB JOHNSON, JAMES H PASS.

Page 366 Bill of Sale 15 Dec 1817 JAMES TAYLOR and THOMAS TAYLOR, Admrs in part of Est of THOMAS TAYLOR, Decd, to JOHN TAYLOR, $248 paid, a Negro girl named DINA, aged 5. Wit: JAMES MCCLARIN, WILLIAM TAYLOR.

Page 366 Indenture 9 Oct 1815 WILLIS ALSTON, Halifax Co, NC, one part, and DANIEL MCAULY, Smith Co, TN, $300 paid, 357 1/3 acres beg at JOHN JENKINS cor, being part of grant of 457 1/3 acres deeded me by THOMAS K HARRIS. Wit: JOHN M WILLIAMS, JACOB ALLINON. Ack in sd Smith County before ROBERT COLLIN, Clk, 18 May 1816.

Page 368 Indenture 20 July 1819 RICHARD PORTERFIELD and ZACHARIAH JONES, $1200 paid, 260 acres granted Grantor herein by Grant No 2024. Wit: JOHN FOOCHEE, WM ERVIN, JOHN A FOUSHEE.

Page 369 Power of Attorney 20 July 1819 RICHARD PORTERFIELD, having heretofore made his friend JAMES TOWNSEND his atty, transfers title to 40 acre tr near road leading from Sparta to Allens ferry on Caney fork. Wit: ZACHARIAH JONES, JOHN TANHILL(?), WM ERVIN.

Page 369 Indenture 16 Sept 1819 ROBT WEBB and ELISHA WEBB, one part, and HARRISON HOLLAND, other part, $1550 paid, part of 640 acres granted to heirs of DAVID JOINER (Grant 5733) and another 40 acres granted by No 5828, totalling 255 acres. Wit: J C DAVIS, WM HAMMOND.

Page 371 Indenture 20 July 1818 ABNER HILL and ELIJAH HILL (no relationship stated), $300 paid, 50 acres in 1st Dist & on N side Caney fork. Wit: WINKFIELD HILL, EZEKIEL BATES.

Page 372 Indenture 28 Oct 1817 DANIEL KEITH and JAMES SCOTT, $350 pd, 100 acres on S side main Cane fork, beg at NW cor JAMES MEEKS Sur. Wit: RICHARD EVINS.

Page 373 Indenture 9 Mar 1818 ARTHUR BOWEN and JAMES SCOTT, $170 pd, 25 acres on S line main Cany fork. Wit: ARTHUR PARKER, ROBERT BRIAN.

Page 374 Indenture 5 Aug 1819 THOMAS INGRAM, heir of WILLIAM INGRAM, Decd, of Hawkins Co, TN, by WILLIAM MITCHELL, his atty in fact, one part, and CHARLES HUDDLESTON and JOHN C HUDDLESTON (no relationships stated), $2000 pd, 2 tracts being 340 acres total, on waters of falling water, & granted by TN to WILLIAM INGRAM, Decd, by Grant No 13252, for 140 acres & Grant No 13253 for 200 acres, beg at SW cor of WALKY W PEARCE Occupant Sur. Wit: A B LANE, BASHFORD IRVIN(?).

Page 375 Indenture 15 May 1819 ROBERT HOWARD and JOHN MCGEE, $70 pd, tr on Cherry creek, beg at line of tr IRA BEDWELL sold to McGee, 15 1/2 acres. Wit: REUBEN WILLHITE, THOS WILLIAMS.

Page 376   Indenture   4 May 1817   IRE BEDWELL(?) and JOHN MCGEE, $500 pd, 120 acres on Cherry creek. Wit: REUBEN WILLHITE, THOS WILLIAMS.

Page 377   Indenture   10 Aug 1819   JOHN HUDSON and JAMES OFFICER, $1000 pd, tr on Calf killers fork, being 110 acres adj BURREL HUDSON tr and THOMAS HORN. Wit: WILLIAM HARGIS, JAMES J HARGIS, JAMES SCARBROUGH.

Page 378   Bill of Sale   14 Oct 1819   HARDY JONES to NANSEY MAHAN, _____ Co, AL, $5,020 paid, 9 Negroes, man named HARRY & woman named PATSEY, girl named COLFERN, boy named SIMON, girls named GINNEY and PAT, boys named ANDREW, ROBBIN and TOM. Wit: JAMES BRAY, HARDY JONES, Jr.

Page 378   Bill of Sale   Date & parties as above, $500 paid, sorrel horse, 15 head cattle, etc, household items, 40 acres corn, etc. Wit: As above.

Page 379   Indenture   21 July 1819   HARRISON HOLLAND and JOSEPH MCGOWEN, $1200 paid, 200 acres on Caney fork. Wit: AMOS MCGOWEN, CALEB MASON.

Page 380   Indenture   3 July 1819   HARRISON HOLLAND and JOHN MASON, $600 paid, 100 acres in 1st Dist on Caney fork, beg in W bdy line ROLLY ROLLS 300 acre sur. Wit: BENJN GIBBS, RICHARD MIDYETT.

Page 381   Indenture   16 Oct 1819   JAMES HEMBREE and GEORGE KEESE, $500 pd, 100 acres including where Keesee now lives, granted by TN to sd Hembree on 18 May 1814 by No 5579, beg on side of mountain WILLIAM NEVILL SW cor, & also adj LOWREY line. Wit: A DIBRELL, ABRAHAM BROYLE.

Page 382   Indenture   29 Sept 1819   JOHN MERRILL and ANDREW GAMBLE, $180 pd, 40 acres being same granted to Merrill by Grant 5074, in 1st Dist & on Calf killers. Wit: JONATH C DAVIS, JAMES S LINN.

Page 383   Indenture   30 Apr 1817   JACOB CATTRON and BENJAMIN HICKMAN, $850 pd, tr on Cherry creek granted to ROBERT KING by Grant 342, assigned by NC 7 Mar 1797. Tr includes 167 acres and farm & dwelling of sd Jacob. Wit: SOLOMON YEAGER, JOHN W DEARING, THOMAS CHIRLY, Senr.

Page 384   Indenture   29 July 1818   HAZEL SUGG and JOHN DALL, $500 pd, tr of 121 acres on dry fork of Caney fork, granted to Sugg by Grant 4023, 11 July 1812. (Signature looks like HAZEAIE SUGG) Wit: JACOB A LANE, ALEXANDER B LANE.

Page 385   Indenture   25 July 1818   ABNER HILL and WINKFIELD HILL, $150 pd, 50 acres. Wit: EZEKIEL BATES, ELIJAH HILL.

Page 386   Indenture   5 Aug 1819   THOMAS INGRAM, heir of WILLIAM INGRAM, Decd, Hawkins Co, TN, by his atty in fact WILLIAM MITCHELL, one part, and BASHFORD IRWIN, other part, $1000 pd, tr of 300 acres in White (formerly Jackson County, TN, on Caney fork, including land surv in 1808 for WOOLSEY W PEARCE as our occupant claim, granted by TN to WILLIAM INGRAM. Wit: A B LANE, CHARLES HUDELLSTON.

Page 387   Indenture   17 Nov 1817   DAVID NICHOLS and WILLIAM MOONEY, $800 pd, 100 acres in Hickory valley, being land he holds by deed from THOMAS M CORRY for 200 acres, dated 2 June 1808. Wit: TURNER LANE, WILLIAM BARTON.

Page 388 Indenture 21 July 1818   JACOB DRAKE and ISAAC DRAKE, Warren Co, TN, one part, and RANDOLPH ROSS, latter of Virginia, $200 paid, 30 acres on N side Caney fork Grant 5558, beg at upper cor REUBEN P SAUNDERS 10 acres. Wit: M R LYON(?), JNO MILLER.

Page 389 Indenture 17 Nov 1817   DAVID NICHOLS and WILLIAM MOONEY, $800 paid, 100 acres in Hickory valley, part of 200 acres he holds by deed from THOMAS MCCORRY. Wit: TURNER LANE, WILLIAM BARTON.

Page 390 Indenture 21 July 1818   ISAAC DRAKE and JACOB DRAKE, Warren Co, TN, and RANDOLPH ROSS of Virginia, $200 paid, 10 acres Grant No 2627. Wit: M R LYON, JNO MILLER.

Page 391 Indenture 21 Oct 1818   JOHN SHROPSHIRE and RANDOLPH ROSS, latter of Rockbridge Co, VA, $275 paid, 100 acres, 2 roods & 7 perches by deed from Sheriff of White County on 20 Oct 1815, including Big horse cave, also sundry furnaces containing 36 kettles, property sold by Shff as property of TUCKER M WOODSON. Wit: ROBT ANDERSON, JESSE BABB.

Page 392 Indenture 10 Sept 1819   GEORGE W GIBBS, Town of Nashville, and JOHN WALKER, $1800 pd, tr on Town creek. Wit: ANTHONY DIBRELL, CHAS DIBRELL, JOHN DUNNISTON.

Page 393 Land Grant No 3345 24 Aug 1811 & of Indepen of US the 31st TENNESSEE by virtue part Certif No 235, dated Apr 13 1809, obtained by THOMAS DILLON, grants to GEORGE W RAYMAN, assee sd Dillon, 250 acres in 1st Dist on Caney fork, tr surveyed 2 Aug 1808 by JOHN BOWEN, DS.

Page 394 Land Grant No 3346 Date as above, parties as in above Grant, 288 acres in 2st Dist, on S side Caney.

Page 395 Indenture __ Mar 1819   GEORGE W RAYMOND, Jackson Co, TN, one part, and HIRAM S COOK, ELIZABETH HAWKINS (wife of JOHN HAWKINS), GEORGE L COOK, MARY C COOK, JAMES COOK, AMANDA COOK and GREENVILLE COOK, heirs of ALEXANDER COOK, Decd, other part, $5.00 pd by sd Alexander, 250 acres being same land conv to sd Raymond by TN by Grant 3345 on 14 Aug 1811, adj conditional lines of DAVID ELKINS and JAMES LARSON. Wit: ALEX DILLIAN, KINSEY POOLE.

Page 396 Indenture __ Mar 1819   Parties as in above deed, 288 acres as in Grant No 3346, $5.00 paid as above. Wit: ALEX DILLION, D KINNEY POOLE, JAMES DILLION.

Page 397 Indenture 12 Sept 1815   ELIJAH CHISUM, Junr, and JOHN SHROPSHIRE, $150 paid, 100 acres on Cany fork, entered on Warr No 229 in 1st Dist, beg on SE cor of JAMES MARTIN 100 acre entry in S bdy line of JOSEPH UPCHURCH Occupant Sur. Wit: JOSEPH UPCHURCH, HICKS SHROPSHIRE, THOMAS HILL, JOHN MAY.

Page 398 Indenture Same date and parties as in above deed, $150 paid, 100 acres on Caney fork, entered as Warr 1908, beg on S bdy line of ABNER HILL Sur of 87 acres & beg cor of JOSEPH UPCHURCH Occupant sur. Wit: As in above deed.

Page 339 Indenture 8 Sept 1819   JOHN SHROPSHIRE and THOMAS HOPKINS, latter of Sullivan Co, TN, $600 pd, 2 tracts on Caney fork of Cumberland river, first entered on Warr 229, beg at SE cor JAMES MARTIN 100 acre entry & S bdy JOSEPH UPCHURCH, being 100 acres; other tr entered on Warr 1908, beg in S bdy of ABNER HILL, adj ROBERT ANDERSON, & adj 100 acres reserving 12 acres conv to ELIJAH CHISUM. Wit: HICKS R SHROPSHIRE, ELIJAH HILL.

Page 400 Indenture 9 Sept 1819   JAMES HUDGINS and JAMES GRACE heirs, $800 paid, 93 acres in 5 lots. Wit: JOHN ROGERS, GEORGE GRACE.

Page 401 Indenture 22 Oct 1818   WILLIAM WHITE, one part, and RICHARD MIDYETT, other part, $80.00 paid, 20 acre tr on Caney fork. Wit: SAMUEL JARVIS, THOS MAYS, BENJN GIBB.

Page 402 Indenture 29 Oct 1819   JOHN COOTS and WILLIAM GLEN, $200 paid, tr on waters of Ceder creek emptying into Caney fork, including sd Coots improvement surv 15 July 1810 by JAMES TOWNSEND, D S, being 100 acres granted by TN to sd John, founded on Warr 100, dated 22 Oct 1783, entered on 9 July 1811 by No 6517, and assigned to John by JAMES PORTERFIELD, heir of DENNY PORTERFIELD. Wit: JOHN WATSON, JOHN HICKS.

Page 403 Indenture 11 Feb 1819   JOSEPH CLARKE and JAMES HOLLAND, $150 paid, $85.00 cash & bal in one loan(?), 100 acres on Jenkins creek, beg at SE cor WILLIAM ALSTON tr of 457 1/3 acres. Wit: HARRISON HOLLAND, DERIUS CLARK.

Page 404 Indenture 31 July 1818   JOSEPH ANDERSON and JOHN JERVIS, $400 paid, tr in 1st Dist on Caney fork N side, adj JOSEPH & GEORGE ANDERSON conditional line, 75 acres. Wit: JOHN ANDERSON, JOHN MAY.

Page 405 Indenture 10 Jan 1820   JOHN MILLAR and JAMES DAVIS, $100 paid, 25 acre tr in Grant 6642 & Warr 230, being on S side main Cany fork.

Page 406 Indenture 9 Sept 1819   JOHN GOODPASTURE, Overton Co, TN, and WILLIAM M BRYAN, $215 paid, 21 1/2 acres in Hickory valley on Caney fork, adj TURNER LANE corner. Wit: TURNER LANE, ROBERT E LOWEY.

Page 407 Indenture 15 Feb 1816   JAMES BOWEN and JAMES MULHANY, $500 paid, 100 acres in 3rd Dist on main Caney fork & on S side of it, beg at foot of Cumberland mountain. Wit: GEORGE W LEDBETTER, ISACK COUNTS.

Page 408 Indenture 12 Jan 1820   JOSEPH RODGERS and THOMAS USERY, $415 paid, 20 acres granted by TN in Grant 10762, dated 21 Sept 1817 granted to sd USERY, beg at JOHN WALLING SW cor on EQUILLO GREER line, and 1 other tr of 25 acres granted by TN to JONATHAN C DAVIS by No 10921, dated 18 Nov 1817. Wit: A DIBRELL.

Page 409 Indenture 21 July 1818   JACOB DRAKE, ELIJAH DRAKE, & ISAAC DRAKE, all of Warren Co, TN, one part, and RANDOLF ROSS of State of Virginia, $112 paid, all their interest vested in Grantors by virtue of Deed of Transfer from RICHARD C CRADOCK who holds title by Sheriff deed dated 19 Oct 185 to 1 furnace, 3 kettles, 15 acres of land including Big Bone cave(?), and 100 acres between sd cave and JAMES HOLMAN Survey, which property was sold by Shff on 14 Apr 1815 as property of TUCKER WOODSON, and purchased by sd Cradock, by his agent ROBERT B MITCHELL. Wit: ELIHU SANDERS(?), JOSEPH MEDLEY.

Page 410 Bill of Sale 24 Sept 1819 BARTEE GIBBS, Hyde Co, NC, to BENJN GILLS, Sen, $327 paid, a Negro girl named LUE(?). Wit: URIAH GIBBS, CORNELIUS JARVIS.

Page 410 Gift Deed 25 Nov 1819 EDWARD CLARK, Grainger Co, TN, for love borne my daughter FRANCI BROWN and her husband, ISAAC BROWN, 1 Negro girl named ROSE, now about 7 yrs old. Wit: JAMES CANTWELL, JERAMIAH CANTWELL.

Page 411 Indenture 6 Feb 1819 WILLIAM BALCH and CORNELIUS JARVIS, $150 paid, tr of 60 acres on Caney fork, adj ARCHA MCDANIEL Sur. Wit: JOHN TEMPLETON, URIAH GIBBS.

Page 412 Indenture 23 Jan 1819 ELIJAH SANDERS, Warren Co, TN, and JOHN DALE, $50.00 paid, 6 acres on N side of main Caney fork. Wit: JOHN DODSON, JOHN GILLENTINE, GEORGE SUGG.

Page 413 Indenture Date & Grantor above, and JOHN DODSON, $130 pd, 100 acres on N side of main Caney fork. Wit: JOHN DALE, JOHN GILLENTINE, GEORGE SUGG.

Page 414 Indenture 16 Dec 1813 NATHANIEL TAYLOR, Carter Co, TN, one part, and WILLIAM PARKINSON, other part, $250 paid, 99 acres in 3rd Dist on falling water of Cany fork, joining his entry of 90 acres which he holds by Grant from TN, No 3257. Wit: ALEX COOK, WILLIAM GIST.

Page 415 Bill of Sale 31 July 1818 CASON GIBBS, Jnr, of one part, and JOHN JETT, other part, $1010 paid, a Negro woman named AGNES, 30 yrs, her 2 children SABRE, 4 yrs, and NANCY, 2 months old. Wit: BENJN GIBBS, JAMES OWENS.

Page 416 Indenture 1 Oct 1819 WILLIAM LAWRENCE and ABEL HUTSON, $60.00 pd, tr of 18 acres on Caney fork. Wit: MATTHIAS HUTSON, ISAIAH HUTSON.

Page 417 Plat and Land Annexation to Town of Sparta 20 Mar 1820 Commissioners of Sparta annex 8 1/2 acres of land the property of JACOB A LANE, and being Lots 92 & 93. Signed by WM S MITCHELL, WILLIAM GLENN, LAWSON NOURSE, GEO DAWSON, JACOB A LANE.

Page 418 Indenture 18 Dec 1819 DRURY SMITH and WILLIAM BROWN, $100 paid, 20 acres known as Grant 6740, which tr was conv by BENJAMIN WEAVER to sd Smith, tr being on Calf killers fork of Caney fork, beg W of SW cor of WILLIAM P ANDERSON Sur of 180 acres known as the Iron Ore tract. Wit: W H CAMPBELL, A B LANE.

Page 419 Indenture 22 Jan 1820 Parties as in above deed, $300 paid, tr of 38 acres known by Grant No 13412, being on Calf killer. Wit: CHARLES DIBRELL, ARCHIBALD CANNON.

Page 420 Sheriff's Deed 21 Apr 1820 THOMAS TAYLOR, Shff, one part, and ANTHONY DIBRELL and ISAAC TAYLOR, other part, due to Writ of Green Co, TN, dated 5 Feb 1820, ordering Sheriff to sell interest of heirs of WILLIAM KING, Decd, namely THOMAS CLABOURN and wife SARAH CLABOURN, late SARAH KING, widow and relict of JAMES KING, Decd, WILLIAM KING, THOMAS KING and ELIZA KING, infant children of JAMES KING, Decd, JOHN MITCHELL, SALLY MITCHELL and RACHEL MITCHELL, infant children of JOHN MITCHELL, Decd, by his wife, ELIZABETH MITCHELL, Decd, WILLIAM KING, JAMES KING and THOMAS KING, infant children of SAMUEL KING, by ALEXANDER BROWN, Junior, their guardian, JOHN MITCHELL, WILLIAM THEGHILL(?) and wife ELIZA THEGHILL, CONNALLY FINDLEY and wife NANCY FINDLEY, JOSEPH TRIGG and wife ELIZABETH TRIGG, late ELIZABETH FINDLEY, JOHN ALLEN and wife HANNAH ALLEN, WILLIAM CONNALLY, DANIEL TRIGG, LILBOURN TRIGG, infant children of WILLIAM TRIGG, Decd, by his wife RACHEL TRIGG, by their Guardian LILBOURN L HENDERSON, any interest they had in a tr on Salt river formerly, now the falling water of the Caney fork, granted by NC to WILLIAM KING, by No 2535, dated 10 Dec 1795, $64.00 being highest bid. Wit: WM H CAMPBELL, ADAM HUMTSMAN.

Page 421 Indenture 2 Mar 1819 THEODORICK B RICE, of Sparta, and JAMES EASTHAM, other part, $900 paid, 7 lots being Nos 24, 42, 43, 44, 64, 65. Wit: TURNER LANE, A B LANE.

Page 422 Indenture 21 Apr 1819 WILLIAM MOONEY and ANDREW BRIANT, $65.00 paid, tr in 3rd Dist on main Caney fork, being land he holds by Grant 11810, beg 20 poles E of beg of THOMAS FRASER 30 acres. Wit: HARTWELLL WILSON, JAMES HOLLOWAY.

Page 424 Indenture 21 Apr 1819 THOMAS FRASER and ANDREW BRYAN, $175.00 paid, 30 acres granted Fraser 21 Sept 1812. Wit: JAMES GALLOWAY, JAMES PURVEYAR(?).

Page 425 Indenture 18 Jan 1820 ABIJAH CRANE and ROBERT GAMBLE, $100 paid, 50 acres on Cane creek, adj WILLIAM BROWN 100 acres, tr adj DARBER T CRAIN line. Wit: JESSE BROWER.

Page 425 Indenture 6 Apr 1820 DAVID PEARCE and GEORGE PRICE, $400 pd, 4 tracts in 1st Dist on falling water of Cany fork of Cumberland river, beg on SE cor of 100 acre tr granted ZACHARIAH JONES, No 4484, and 3 other tracts. Wit: THOMAS WILSON, EBENEZER JONES, SAMUEL WILSON, JESSE DAVIS, ROBERT CATE.

Page 429 (out of order) Indenture 9 Mar 1819 ANTHONY DIBRELL and JOHN C MCLEMORE, one part, and GEORGE PRICE, other part, $125 pd, 124 acres granted to NC to ELIZA WILLIAMS by Grant 326, beg at cor of JOHN BROWN. Wit: JNO ALLEN, WILLIAM C BRITAIN.

Page 430 Indenture 10 Apr 1820 ANTHONY DIBRELL and JOHN C MCLEMORE, by A DRIBRELL, his agent, one part, and LEVI SWAIN, other part, $150 paid, 200 acres on Rum creek, including plantation Swain now lives on, beg at cor of ISAAC HUTSON, and tr being part of large tr granted by NC to ELIZA WILLIAMS, by Grant No 326, dated 20 Dec 1796.

Page 427 (Out of order) Indenture 22 Feb 1820 SMITH HUTCHINGS and WILLIAM P RHEA, $50.00 pd, moiety of 1/9th part of tr on Town creek on branch of falling water, being 200 acres, beg in E bdy line of WILLIAM KING 640 acre survey. Wit: WM J SMITH, ROBERT RHEA, JAMES RUSSELL.

Page 427 Release of Dower Rights 22 Feb 1820 BETSEY HUTCHINGS, $5.00 paid, releases dower right in tr of 200 acres, heir to WM P RHEA, granted by TN to EZEKIEL RHEA, my former husband, Decd, and which my present husband SMITH HUTCHINGS has this day sold. Wit: As in above Indenture.

Page 428 Indenture 23 May 1818   JOHN ANDERSON and JAMES OWENS, $100 paid, 50 acre tr adj ARCHABALD MCDANIELS Sur. Wit: JOHN ELLIS, JASON GIBBS. Registered and examined on 26 June 1820, TURNER LANE, Register of White County.   (Last entry in volume)

ABBOTT
   JONATHAN, 7
ACADEMY
   PRIESTLY, 27
ACUFF
   SPENCER, 64
ADAIR
   JOHN, 91
ADCOCK
   ISAAC, 119
   LEONARD, 119
ADERSON
   JAMES, 82
ADIE
   JAMES M, 25
AIKMAN
   WILLIAM E, 116
   WM C, 118
   WM E, 118
AILSWORTH
   GEORGE, 84, 85, 97,
      113, 120
AINSWORTH
   GEO, 119
ALEXANDER
   CHARLES, 13
   DANCEL, 15
   DANIEL, 21, 29, 49,
      51, 57, 68, 70,
      71, 100, 105,
      107, 110
   DANL, 36
   DAVID, 19
   PETER, 42
   WM, 101
ALLEN
   GEORGE, 115
   HANNAH, 126
   JAS, 112
   JESSE, 53, 85, 115
   JNO, 112, 126
   JOHN, 33, 48, 126
   ROBERT, 9, 36, 75,
      100
ALLIE
   DANL, 4
ALLINON
   JACOB, 121
ALLISON
   HAMBLETON, 115
   HAMBLETT, 113
   JAMES, 74
   JAS, 111
ALLY
   WALTER, 14

ALSTON
   DENNIS, 87
   WILLIAM, 120, 124
   WILLIS, 121
ALY
   S L, 98
AMBERSON
   LEONARD, 115
ANDERSON, 74, 107
   CHARLES, 13
   GEORGE, 124
   ISAAC, 17, 30, 31,
      36, 56, 65, 77
   JACOB, 13, 17
   JAMES, 1, 48, 56,
      89, 102, 107,
      112, 113
   JOHN, 17, 31, 36,
      77, 80, 82, 102,
      113, 120, 124,
      127
   JOHN A, 29
   JOSEPH, 13, 48, 71,
      91, 96, 102, 124
   MATHIAS B, 77
   MATTHEW, 84, 85
   MATTHIAS, 35, 65,
      100
   ROBERT, 91, 96, 124
   ROBERT G, 1, 13,
      26, 50, 90
   ROBT, 123
   ROBT G, 16
   W E, 85
   W P, 10
   WILLIAM, 35, 65,
      84, 85, 100,
      113, 115
   WILLIAM P, 23, 24,
      26, 28, 30, 31,
      36, 48, 56, 66,
      73, 77, 79, 82,
      83, 91, 92, 93,
      95, 100, 105,
      106, 107, 125
   WM P, 104, 115
   ZACHARIAH, 41
ARCHER
   STEPHEN, 109
ARMISTEAD
   JOHN B, 46
ARMISTON
   ROBT, 81
ARMSTRONG
   JOHN, 9, 15, 21,

      49, 95
   JOHN C, 52
   MAR C, 8
   MARTIN, 6, 28, 31,
      48
   ROBERT, 36, 53, 65,
      73
   ROBT, 35, 53, 67,
      74, 75, 79, 92,
      93
   ROYAL, 92, 93
ARNOLD
   LINDSEY, 103
ARTHUS
   STEPHEN, 108
ASHE
   SAMUEL, 1
ASKEW
   HARDY, 69
   HARRY, 69
AUSTIN
   JOHN, 103, 112
   NATHANIEL, 103
   STEPHEN, 11, 12
AVERY
   NICHOLAS, 89, 90, 98
AYLOTT
   ROBERT W, 119
BABB
   JESSE, 63, 64, 72,
      123
   MATTHEW, 64, 73,
      88, 113
BADGER
   JOHN H, 48, 73
   JOSHUA, 24, 48
   OLLIVER, 42
   POLLY, 87
BAGGAN
   JAMES, 15
   PATRICK, 15
BAGLEY
   ISAAC, 60
BAILEY
   BRITAIN, 45
   JOSHUA, 109
BAINBRIDGE
   JOHN T, 58
BAKER
   JACOB, 4
   LARKIN, 97, 113
   ROBERT, 69
   SIMON, 68
BALCH
   WILLIAM, 88, 95, 125

BALSH
  WILLIAM, 57
BARBOUR
  RICHARD, 108, 109
BARGER
  GASPER, 65, 99, 113
  PHILLIP, 114
BARNES, 100
  THOMAS, 97
BARNET
  ROBERT, 45
BARNETT
  ELIJAH, 41, 102
  ROBERT, 49
BARRON
  JOHN, 97
BARROW
  SHERROD, 17
BARTEE, 125
BARTLETT
  JAMES, 72, 113
  JOSHUA, 72, 87, 113
  NATHAN, 76, 79, 80
BARTON
  HUGH, 50
  WILLIAM, 55, 122,
    123
BATES
  CHARLES, 78, 81, 94
  ELIJAH, 53, 57, 64,
    78, 81, 91, 94,
    99
  EZEKIEL, 78, 109,
    110, 120, 121,
    122
  JOSEPH, 78
  ROBERT, 53, 78, 96,
    102
  WILLIAM, 98, 102
BAYGIN
  GRISSEL, 15
BEAN
  EDMUND, 52
  HENRY, 26
  JOHN, 38, 53
BEARD
  JAMES, 10
  LEWIS, 24, 42
BEDWELL
  BARBARA, 89, 95,
    104, 108
  IRA, 68, 89, 95,
    104, 108, 121
  IRE, 122
BEEBEE

ANNUL, 63
BEESON
  JACOB, 78
BELCHER
  WILLIAM, 70, 111
BENNETT
  PETER, 63
  WILLIAM J, 110
  WM J, 94
BENSON
  ELY, 9
BENTON
  ROBERT, 24
BERRY
  CALEB, 89, 114
BERTON
  WILLIAM, 16
BEVERLY
  PETER, 86
BIBBY
  EDMOND, 22
BILDO
  J M, 56
BILLINGS
  PETER, 34
BIRDEN
  BENJAMIN, 33
BIRK
  HARRIS, 112
BLACKAMON
  GEORGE D, 67
BLACKBORN
  R, 18
BLACKBURN
  WILLIAM, 116
BLACKWOOD
  ANDREW, 85
BLAGG
  SAMUEL, 63
BLAGGE
  BENJ, 12
  JOHN, 12
  SAMUEL, 2, 19, 22
  SARAH, 12, 22
  THOMAS, 12
  THOS W F, 19
BLAIR
  ALEXDR, 26
  SO, 2
  TO, 6
BLAKE
  THOS, 86
BLAKEMORE
  JAS, 17
BLAN

JO, 21
BLANSHOT
  ROBERT, 6, 109
BLARE
  JAMES, 14
BLEVINS
  WILLIAM, 80
BLITHE
  ROBERT, 14
BLOUNT
  JOHN GRAY, 36, 90,
    108
  THOM, 8
  THOMAS, 8
  WILLIAM, 2, 3, 4,
    12, 63
  WILLIE, 28
BODEN
  NICHOLAS, 112
BOHANNON
  HENRY, 47, 80
  JOHN, 87, 113, 116
  LEWIS, 110, 116
  LUIS, 116
BOSATH
  LEVI, 89
BOSWELL
  JONATHAN, 103
BOSWORTH
  LEVI, 89
BOTTON
  THO, 112
BOUND, 92
  JAMES, 92
BOUNDS
  JAMES, 46, 117, 120
  THOMAS, 36, 39, 46,
    48, 55, 68, 87,
    96, 97, 100,
    105, 108, 110,
    118
  THOS, 9, 23, 30,
    40, 100, 117, 120
BOWAN
  J H, 14
BOWEN
  ARTHUR, 121
  CHARLES, 76, 102
  JAMES, 32, 34, 40,
    55, 64, 70, 71,
    72, 74, 75, 88,
    91, 124
  JOHN, 11, 69, 91,
    123
BOWEN1

JAMES, 73
BOWER
   JAMES, 81
BOWERS
   WILLIAM, 23
BOWIN
   ARTHUR, 110
   CHARLES, 111
   JAMES, 81
BOWMAN
   BENJAMIN, 90, 98
   GILBERT, 33
   NATHANIEL, 81, 90,
      94, 99
   WILLIAM, 56
BOYD
   WM, 40
BOYED
   MARGARET, 44
BOYLAN
   WILLIAM, 75
BRADLEY, 23
   AMELIA, 99
   ANSELM, 116
   ISHAM, 20, 21, 48,
      70, 113
BRADLY
   ANSELM, 99
   ISHAM, 23, 31
BRADSHAW
   JOEL, 32, 72, 96
BRAHAN
   JOHN, 9
BRAHAW
   JOHN, 28
BRASEL
   RICHARD, 49
   ROBERT, 54
BRASELTON
   ISAAC, 50
BRASIL
   RICHARD, 57, 64
BRAY
   JAMES, 122
BRAYER
   ABRAHAM, 77
BRAZEAL
   HENRY, 100
BREEDING
   BRYANT, 12, 24
   LETTE, 81
   LETTUCE, 3
BRENT
   WM, 75
BRIAN

ANDREW, 13
ROBERT, 121
BRIANT
   ANDREW, 13, 126
   MORGAN, 51
   WILLIAM, 13, 17
   WILLIAM M, 13
BRIDE
   J M, 24
   JOSEPH W, 100
BRIDGMAN
   THOMAS, 120
BRIGHTWELL
   WILLIAM C, 103, 113
BRILES
   ABRAHAM, 54
   REUBEN, 54
BRINDLEY
   STEPHEN, 79
BRITAIN
   WILLIAM C, 85, 126
BRITTAIN
   WILLIAM C, 94, 96
BROCK
   JESSE, 38, 64
   JOHN, 64
   ZEDIKIAH, 19
BROOKS
   HENRY, 48
BROWER
   JESSE, 126
   WILLIAM, 44
BROWN
   ALEXANDER, 126
   B, 32
   BENJAMIN, 94
   ELEBETH, 15
   FRANCI, 125
   GEORGE MORGAN, 117
   H H, 72
   ISAAC, 20, 47, 125
   ISAACK, 64
   JACOB, 1, 55
   JNO, 119
   JOHN, 40, 68, 111,
      119, 126
   MARYIN, 15
   RICHARD, 119
   THOMAS J, 55
   WILBY J, 13
   WILLIAM, 20, 29,
      38, 40, 45, 49,
      55, 67, 102,
      119, 125, 126
   WM, 64

BROYLE
   ABRAHAM, 18, 82, 122
BROYLES
   ABRAHAM, 76
   JOHN, 95
   REUBEN, 95
   THOMAS, 77
BROYLS
   THOMAS, 98
BRUMBELOW
   ISAAC, 114
BRYAN
   ANDREW, 13, 17, 26,
      76, 126
   JACOB, 17
   JAMES R, 26, 30,
      31, 36, 45, 56,
      65
   JOHN, 1, 2, 17, 18,
      31, 36, 39, 41,
      45, 50, 76
   MORGAN, 34, 42, 45,
      53, 92, 106
   SIMON A, 21
   WILLIAM, 13, 16,
      17, 36, 45
   WILLIAM M, 13, 32,
      36, 76, 124
   _AMES R, 18
BRYANT
   JAMES, 84
   JOHN, 11
BUBRICK
   BENJ F, 22
BULLOCK
   JAMES P, 110
BURDEN, 101
   JOHN, 91
   WILLIAM, 27, 28,
      35, 112
BURDIN
   BENJAMIN, 34, 44, 55
   ELISABETH, 44
   JOEL, 67
   WILLIAM, 29, 44
BURGAN
   THOMAS, 100
BURGESS
   THOMAS, 104, 118
   THOMAS H, 118
BURK
   ANDREW, 55, 57, 67,
      93, 106, 110, 114
   HARRIS, 110
BURKS

RILAND, 54
BURRALL
  THOMAS S, 111
BURTINTON
  WM, 32
BURTON
  C, 105
  HENRY, 95, 111, 119
  O, 17
  ROBERT, 30, 32, 36,
    73, 85, 102
  WM, 98
BUSBY
  BRYAN, 61
BUTCHER
  DAVID, 64
BYNUM
  GRAY, 52, 118
BYRD
  JESSE, 100
BYRNE
  BRICE, 108, 110
BYRUM
  GRAY, 63
CAKE
  ROBERT, 69
CALDWELL
  SAML, 13
CALLAS
  JOHN, 114
CALVIN
  JOHN, 22
CAMERON
  WILLIAM, 80
CAMPBELL
  DAVID, 1, 3, 13
  ELIZABETH M, 88
  JAMES M, 88
  JNO, 91
  JOHN, 85, 103, 115
  MARIA W, 88
  SOPHIA M, 88
  W H, 125
  WILLIAM H, 110
  WM H, 126
CANADY
  CHARLES, 30
CANNADY
  DAVID, 21, 22
CANNON
  ARCHIBALD, 125
  ROBERT, 10
CANTWELL
  JAMES, 125
  JERAMIAH, 125

CANY
  WILLIAM, 22
CAPE
  ANDREW, 114
CAPLIN
  JOSEPH, 49
CARBON
  JAMES, 6
CARDIN
  JOSEPH W, 115
CARMICHAEL
  ALEXR, 100
CARNEY
  PATRICK, 38, 47
CAROLINA
  NORTH, 2
  STATE OF NORTH, 1
CARREL
  EDMUND, 102
CARRICK
  BETSY, 23
  GEO, 82
  JNO, 30
  JOHN, 28
  JOHN M, 11, 12, 18,
    24, 26, 27, 31,
    32, 35
  MAJOR, 12
  MOSES, 24
  SALLY L, 82
CARROLL
  WILLIAM, 102
CARRUTH
  JOHN, 13
CARTER
  BALEY, 87
  BAYLY, 97
  DAVID B, 74, 101,
    104
  EDWARD, 45
  JAMES, 81, 84, 113,
    115
  JOHN, 10, 80
  LANDON, 4, 5
  SAMUEL, 61
  THOMAS, 97
CARY
  THOMAS M, 102
  WILLIAM, 22
CAR_STON
  JAMES, 35
CASH
  HOWARD, 35, 39, 82
  JAMES, 53
  SIMPSON, 120

CASSO
  PETER, 11
CATE
  ROBERT, 126
CATES
  ISAAC, 101
  JAMES, 68
CATHEY
  RICHARD, 8
CATRON
  CHRISTOPHER, 57,
    65, 68, 89, 94,
    95, 104, 108, 118
  ELISABETH, 108
  ELIZABETH, 89, 104
  JACOB, 19, 55, 89,
    95, 104, 108
  JOHN, 21, 98, 99,
    102, 104, 107,
    111
  S, 98
  SOLOMON, 89, 95,
    104, 108
CATTRON
  JACOB, 122
CHAMBERS
  JAMES, 111
  REUBEN, 69
CHANY, 18
CHARLES
  JAMES, 76
  STEPHEN K, 82
CHATARD
  SARAH F, 92, 93
CHESNUT
  JOSEPH, 60
Chiefs
  Cherokee, 5
CHILDRESS
  THOS, 30
CHILDS
  THOMAS, 16
CHIRLY
  THOMAS, 122
CHISM
  ELIJAH, 106
  WILLIAM, 111
CHISOM
  ELIJAH, 10
CHISUM
  ELIJAH, 1, 4, 10,
    13, 15, 24, 26,
    28, 30, 31, 32,
    33, 37, 39, 41,
    44, 48, 50, 53,

JOHN, 124
COPE
  ANDREW, 51, 86,
    106, 117
  JAMES, 81
  RICHARD, 105
COPELAND
  STEPHEN, 4, 6
COPHER
  JOSEPH, 107
CORRES
  THOMAS M, 47
CORRY
  THOMAS M, 31, 32,
    50, 53, 122
COTTON
  JOHN, 99
COUNTS
  ISACK, 124
COVENER
  TIMOTHY, 62
COWAN
  DAVID, 80, 82
  JAMES, 2, 3, 9, 12,
    28
  JOHN, 35
COX
  MAY, 84
  SOLOMAN, 118
  SOLOMON, 23, 31,
    40, 46, 95, 105,
    107
CRABB
  BONAPARTE, 82
  JOSEPH, 30, 66, 79,
    82
  STEPHEN, 66
CRADOCK
  RICHARD C, 124
CRAIGMILES
  JOSEPH, 68
CRAIN
  DARBER T, 126
  DOSIER T, 20, 29
CRANE
  ABIJAH, 58, 126
  ALIJAH, 49
  STEPHEN, 47
CRAUCH
  WILLIAM, 75
CRAWLEY
  THOS, 113
CRELLEY
  WM, 14
CRIM

WILLIAM, 107
WM, 102
CRISP
  RIDING, 110
CRIS__
  JOHN, 30
CROOK
  JOHN, 46, 98, 105,
    107, 117
CROWDER
  RICHARD, 115
CRUM
  WILLIAM, 78
CRUTCHER
  THOMAS, 23, 28, 31,
    33, 35, 36, 39,
    40, 46, 57, 82,
    89, 94, 95, 104,
    110
  THOS, 26
CUMMIN
  JAMES, 2
CUMMING
  JOHN, 76
CUMMINGS
  DAVID, 48
  DAVIS, 79
  JOHN, 93, 102
  JOSEPH, 32, 48, 50,
    80, 93, 119
CUNNINGHAM
  EDMOND, 113
  JOHN, 114
CURTER
  JOHN, 89
CUSHING
  CHAS, 12
DADSAN
  JESSE, 111
DALE
  JOHN, 41, 56, 83,
    125
  JOHN E, 115
DALL
  JOHN, 122
DALTEN
  TALB__, 24
DALTON
  TOLBET, 114
  WILLIAM, 73
DAMLOT
  HUGH, 18
DANFORTH
  JOSIAH, 5, 10
DANIEL

DAVID M, 41
EPHRAIM, 40
WILLIAM, 57
DANIELS
  DAVID M, 39
DAN__
  LEVI, 48
DARE
  WILLIAM L, 3
DAUGHERTY
  JNO, 26, 102
  JOHN R, 102
DAVIDSON
  D, 11
  DAN, 109
  DANIEL, 109
  WILLIAM, 14
DAVIS
  ARCHIBALD, 17
  BAIRD, 20
  DARCUS, 105
  DARIEN, 68
  DARIUS, 69
  DAVID, 19
  EDWARD, 80
  FREDERICK, 89, 109
  H, 116
  J C, 121
  JAMES, 67, 68, 69,
    89, 95, 105,
    119, 124
  JESSE, 126
  JNO, 69, 105
  JOHN, 68, 89
  JONATH C, 122
  JONATHAN C, 82, 124
  JOSHUA, 6, 7, 68,
    69, 70, 89, 105,
    109
  NATHANIEL, 18
  SETH, 68, 69, 105
DAVISON
  DANIEL, 11
  DANL, 8
DAWSON
  GEO, 99, 125
DAY
  JESSE, 66
DEAKINS
  TOWNLEY, 1, 11
DEARING
  AUSTIN, 85
  JOHN W, 95, 98, 122
  S__, 35
DEDSON

JESSE, 82
DEFR__
　GEORGE, 81
DEHART
　J, 50
DELANEY
　MICHAEL, 61
DENCALE
　GEORGE, 35
DENEALE
　GEORGE, 32
DENNEY
　WILLIAM, 102
　WM, 102, 103
DENNISON, 50
DENNY
　WILLIAM, 67
(DENTON)
　MARY, 58
DENTON
　ABRAHAM, 53, 91
　ABSALOM, 53
　BENJAMIN, 113
　MARY, 112
　SAMUEL, 2, 3, 4,
　　12, 19, 22, 29,
　　36, 53, 58, 63,
　　88, 96, 105,
　　111, 112
DEPREESE
　GEORGE, 110
DEPRENE
　GEORGE, 81
DEWEESE
　MORGAN, 96, 110
　WILLIAM, 116
DIBRELL
　A, 113, 119, 122,
　　124
　ANTHONY, 77, 93,
　　98, 99, 101,
　　103, 104, 108,
　　112, 113, 116,
　　123, 125, 126
　CHARLES, 97, 113,
　　125
　CHAS, 123
DIBRILL
　H, 84
DICKSON
　JOHN, 8
DILDINE
　EZAHIAL, 114
　EZAKIAH, 114
　EZEKIAH, 108

JAMES, 105, 108, 114
JONATHAN, 22
DILLAN
　THOMAS, 108
DILLARD
　THOMAS, 29
DILLIAN
　ALEX, 123
DILLIARD
　JOSIAH, 76
　MERRITT, 76
DILLIN
　THOMAS, 13
DILLION
　ALEX, 123
　JAMES, 123
DILLON
　THOMAS, 3, 9, 17,
　　20, 21, 22, 24,
　　31, 32, 33, 35,
　　38, 39, 41, 45,
　　47, 49, 50, 52,
　　55, 63, 65, 66,
　　80, 88, 123
　THOS, 92
　WM, 30
DINSMORE
　JAMES, 92
DIRGA
　JOHN, 1
DIRGAN
　JNO, 36
　JOHN, 1
DOAK
　JNO, 10
DODSON
　JESSE, 80, 86
　JOHN, 97, 125
　JOSEPH, 117
　NIMROD, 1
　SOLOMON, 106
　WILLIAM, 91, 106,
　　115
DOLLAR
　JOHN, 66
DONAHO
　PATRICK, 79
DONALDSON
　STOKELY, 17
DONALSON
　STOCKLY, 17
DONELSON
　JOHN, 8
　STOCKELY, 15
　STOCKLEY, 2, 3, 7,

9, 10, 11, 16,
　18, 19, 20, 23,
　75, 83, 86, 87
STOCKLY, 1, 15, 32
STOKELY, 5, 14
WILLIAM, 2
DONNELSON
　STOCKLEY, 31, 45, 55
DONNILSON
　STOCKLEY, 30
DOUGHERTY
　JN, 98
　JNO, 26
DOWNING
　ROBERT, 88
　ROBT, 92
DOYLE
　SIMON, 90
DRAKE
　ELIJAH, 117, 124
　ISAAC, 88, 117,
　　123, 124
　JACOB, 52, 53, 96,
　　117, 123, 124
　JONATHAN, 8
DRIBRELL
　A, 126
DRUMMOND
　DAVIS, 87
DUDLEY
　JOHN, 63
　MATTIAS, 25
　SAMMIE, 84
DUDLY
　MATTHIAS, 120
DUEL
　MATTHIAS, 120
DUFEARN
　JAMES, 74
DUFF
　DUNN, 72
　THOMAS, 72, 93
DUGGIN
　JOHN, 59
　WILLIAM, 7
DUGLAS
　JAMES, 14
DUNBAR
　JOHN, 58
　R, 92
DUNCAN
　MARSHAL, 57, 81
　SOLOMON, 81
　WILLIAM, 70
DUNLAP

HUGH, 5, 10
DUNNAM
 JOHN, 50
DUNNISTON
 JOHN, 123
DURHAM
 ZECHARIAH, 20
DYER
 JAMES, 28
 JOHN, 84
 ROBERT H, 27
 SAMUEL, 34, 35, 39,
  57, 65
 WIDOW, 30
 WILLIAM, 12, 23,
  46, 65, 84
 WM, 30
DYRE
 WILLIAM, 12, 57
DYSON
 JOHN, 112
EADS
 SAMPSON, 2
EARLES
 NATHAN, 113
EARLS
 PLEASANT, 91, 110
EASON
 JAMES, 119
EASTHAM
 JAMES, 126
EASTLAND
 JAMES, 57
EASTON
 J, 9
 JAMES, 11, 21, 22,
  23, 24, 25, 30,
  31, 36, 39, 40,
  46, 48, 56, 78,
  82, 91, 106,
  115, 120
EASTOR
 JAMES, 120
EAVES
 JONATHAN, 49
EDGE
 SARAH, 3
ELIZABETH, 126
ELKINS
 DAVID, 123
ELLEDGE
 EZEKIEL, 114
ELLIOTT
 JONAS, 78
 ___, 82

ELLIS
 JOHN, 127
ELLISON
 HAMBLETON, 111
 JAMES, 87
 JOSEPH, 74, 84
 WILLIAM, 111
ELSEY
 JOHN, 15
EMERSON
 THOS, 11
EMMERY
 STEPHEN, 61
ENGLAND
 AARON, 27, 39, 42,
  46, 48, 68, 77,
  96, 100, 108
 ARON, 95
 ELIJAH, 100, 105,
  107, 120
 JAMES, 55
 JESSE, 95
 JOHN, 73, 74, 75,
  105
ENGLISH
 ROBERT, 50
 SAMUEL, 44, 87
ENRIGHT
 JOHN, 17
ERVIN
 WM, 121
ERWIN
 WILLIAM, 103, 111,
  114, 118
ETHERIDGE
 EDWARD, 22
EVANS
 GEORGE, 2
 JAMES, 98
 PHILIP, 60
 RICHARD, 62
 WALTER, 14
EVINS
 RICHARD, 121
EWING
 ANDREW, 17, 30
 NATHAN, 68, 69, 105
FAIN
 JESSE, 104
FARLEY
 PLEASANT C, 93
FARROW
 WILLIE, 114
FERGUSON
 JNO, 36

JOHN, 30
FINDLEY
 ALEXR, 30
 CONNALLY, 126
 ELIZABETH, 126
 NANCY, 126
FINN
 JESSE, 79
FINNEY
 REUBEN, 30
 W, 30
FISHER
 WILLIAM, 50
FISK
 MOSES, 2, 3, 4, 22,
  29, 30, 36, 37,
  63, 70, 85, 93,
  104, 105
FITCH
 WILLIAM C, 94
FITTSGERALD
 GARRETT, 110
FITZGERALD
 JABAN, 40
 JASBAR, 29
 TABER, 93
 WILLIAM, 66
FITZGEREL
 GARRET, 102
FITZGERRAL
 GARRET, 109
FITZGERREL
 GARRETT, 96
 MARY, 96
 WILLIAM, 96, 102
FLEMING
 JOSEPH, 24, 26
FLETCHER
 JOHN, 60
 LEWIS, 106
 THOS H, 102
FOOCHEE
 JOHN, 121
FORBECK
 DANIEL, 10
FORSTERS
 WILLIAM, 2
FOSTER
 EDWARD, 42, 43, 51,
  65
 JOEL, 64, 77
 JOHN R, 112
 WILLIAM, 72
FOUSHEE
 JOHN A, 121

FOX
    GEORGE, 52
    JOHN, 23, 24
    WILLIAM, 78
FRALEY, 73
    CALEB, 24, 28, 28,
        29, 30, 31, 32,
        34, 36, 39, 40,
        44, 64, 112
FRALY
    CALEB, 28
FRANK
    JOSEPH, 50
    THOMAS, 54
FRANKS
    HENRY, 114
    JOSEPH, 49, 95
    LEMUEL, 114
FRASER
    ALEXANDER, 54
    THOMAS, 54, 126
FRASIER
    JEREMIAH, 60
FRAZER
    ALEXANDER, 3
    ALEXR, 3
    WM, 3
FRAZIER
    DANIEL, 11
FRISBY
    JAMES, 116
FRYER
    JOHN, 93
FULHERRON
    JAMES, 39
FULKERSON
    JAMES, 13, 27, 31,
        33, 35, 46, 49,
        55, 68, 78, 96,
        108, 119
FULKINSON
    JAMES, 42
FULTON
    ANDREW, 100
    JOHN H, 101
    SAMUEL, 100
    WILLIAM, 30
GAINA
    JOHN, 78
GAINES
    JAMES, 8
GAIRY
    WILL, 44
GALDERS
    GEORGE, 9

GALE
    JOHN, 9, 13
GALLINTINE
    NICHOLAS, 85
GALLOWAY
    JAMES, 126
GAMBER
    ANDREW, 68
GAMBLE
    ANDREW, 98, 122
    JOHN N, 45, 47
    ROBERT, 52, 126
GAMMELL
    ROBERT, 49
GANOR
    WILLIAM, 90
GARDNER
    OBED, 30
GARNER
    FAUCHE, 119
GARNETT
    JOHN, 32, 49
GARRET
    JOHN B, 120
GARRIS
    SETH, 63
GARRISON
    DANIEL, 70
GARVER
    WM, 97
GASS
    WILLIAM, 28
GATE
    GEORGE C, 9
GAW
    THOMAS, 78, 83
GELSTON
    DAVID, 2, 4, 63
GEORGE
    THOMAS, 44, 53, 61
GIBB
    BENJN, 124
GIBBS, 125
    BENJAMIN, 97
    BENJN, 90, 109,
        118, 122, 125
    CASON, 96, 105,
        109, 118, 125
    G W, 74
    GEO M, 53
    GEO W, 65, 84
    GEORGE W, 30, 31,
        33, 34, 43, 45,
        67, 77, 81, 104,
        112, 113, 119,

    123
    JASON, 127
    JESSE, 109
    URIAH, 118, 125
GIBS
    BENJAMIN, 82
GIBSON
    ABRAHAM P, 112
GILLENLEND)
    NICHOLAS, 46
GILLENTINE
    JOHN, 125
    NICHOLAS, 27, 38,
        39, 42, 44, 55,
        67, 68, 78, 90,
        96, 98, 100,
        108, 111, 118
    _____, 79
GILLIAM
    DEVERIN(?), 10
    WILLIAM, 18
GILLINTINE
    NICHOLAS, 50, 78
GILLS
    BENJN, 125
GILMORE
    SAMUEL, 35
GILPIN
    GEORGE, 32, 35
GIST
    THOMAS, 38, 79, 91
    WILLIAM, 30, 31,
        34, 51, 52, 85,
        87, 125
GLASCOCK
    ISRAEL, 86
GLASGOW
    J, 4, 8
GLEASON
    EDWARD, 44, 71, 77,
        81
    JAMES, 44, 77, 104
    JOHN, 44
GLEESON
    EDWARD, 41
GLEN
    WILLIAM, 124
GLENN
    ALEXANDER, 56, 67,
        110, 117, 120,
        121
    EDWARD, 41
    ISAAC, 87, 91, 121
    JESSE, 110
    JOHN, 42

JOSEPH, 103
ROBERT, 51, 103
ROBERT B, 64
ROBERT R, 103
SAMUEL, 114, 116
WILL, 34, 40, 49
WILLIAM, 16, 27,
42, 44, 51, 64,
67, 68, 77, 78,
84, 85, 86, 96,
98, 100, 103,
108, 112, 113,
117, 121, 125
WM, 23, 72
GLESON
WILLIAM, 84
GLINN
WILLIAM, 103
GOAD
ISHAM, 51
GODARD
MOSES, 94, 95, 117
GOODLETT
JOHN H, 92
GOODPASTURE
JOHN, 17, 30, 124
GOODWIN
NATHAN, 45
WILLIAM, 25
GOOLSBY
JANE, 30, 98
JOHN CRELEY, 46
PETER, 98
GORDON
GEORGE, 36, 67
JAS, 1
MARTIN, 92
GORHAM
JAMES C, 11
GOW
HENRY, 86
GOWN
JOHN, 13
GRACE
GEORGE, 124
JAMES, 124
GRACEY
JAMES, 64
JOHN, 64
GRACY
WILLIAM, 64, 113
GRAHAM
JOHN, 118
WM, 113, 118
GRANT

DAVID, 41, 47
GILBERT, 62
GRAY
JAMES, 97
JOHN, 8
JOSEPH, 97
GREEN
ISAAC, 4
JNO E, 101
JOHN, 40, 93
ROBERT, 51
S(HERWOOD), 101
SAMUEL, 60
SHADRACK, 85
TIMOTHY, 2, 63
GREENE
MARY, 4
TIMOTHY, 4
GREER
AQUILA, 45
EQUILLO, 124
GRIFFING
ROBT, 109
GRIFFITH
BENJAMIN, 44, 68
GEORGE, 19, 39
HENRY, 59
SAMUEL, 14
WILLIAM, 39
GRIGGS
JOHN, 43, 54, 111
GRIGSBY
JOHN, 27, 33, 65, 77
GUEST
MOSES, 1, 4, 6
GUINN
DANIEL, 6
GUION
JAS LEE, 2
GUIST
MOSES, 1
GUM
HARDY, 61
GUTHERIDGE
LEWIS, 50
GUTHRIE
SAMUEL, 11
GWIN
CHRISTOPHER, 15
HACKETT
JOHN, 14
HADDOCK
ANDREW, 63
HADLEY
JOSHUA, 69, 90

HADSON
JOEL, 58
HAGGARD
NATHAN, 48, 94, 110
HALL
JOHN C, 95
HALLEMAN
JOHN, 86
HAMBLET
GEORGE C, 84
HAMBLETT
BENJMAN, 99
HAMILTON
JOHN C, 36
HAMLET
BENJAMIN, 69
HAMLETT
BENJAMIN, 70
BERRYMAN, 66, 72
GEORGE, 80
GEORGE C, 79, 86,
107
POLLY, 111
WILLIAM, 105
HAMLITT
BENJ, 82
BERRY, 111
HAMMOND
WILLIAM, 72, 78, 86
WM, 121
HAMMONDS
WILLIS, 60
HAMMONS
P, 96
HANCOCK
J B, 88, 112
HANE
JACOB, 34
HANKS
ZACHARIAS, 34
HANNAH
JOHN M, 112
HARBERT
JAMES, 99
JOHN, 99
NANCY, 99
SARAH, 99
THOMAS, 42, 67, 83,
91, 99
WILLIAM, 99, 119
HARBIN
R, 16
HARBUT
THOMAS, 53, 76
HARDESON

HARDY, 51
HARDESTER
   SAMUEL, 120
HARDISON
   HARDY, 49
   HENRY, 19
HARDISTER
   SAMUEL, 120
HARGIS
   JAMES J, 122
   W H, 64
   WILLIAM, 90, 122
   WM, 119
HARRIS
   EDWARD, 2, 58, 60,
      62, 63
   EDWIN L, 41, 52, 85
   HOWEL, 39
   HOWEL G, 39, 41,
      55, 55, 113
   JONATHAN, 79
   SILAS, 120
   THOMAS, 55
   THOMAS H, 11, 87
   THOMAS K, 9, 12,
      13, 24, 27, 39,
      41, 42, 44, 51,
      67, 71, 108,
      116, 121
   THOS H, 82
   THOS K, 79, 87, 107
HARRISON
   AUGUSTINE, 7, 70
   EDMOND, 43
   EDMUND, 27, 39, 42,
      51, 52
   EDW, 66
   EDWARD, 43
   EDWD, 40
   WILLIAM, 109
HARRISS
   JOHN, 32
HARRITT
   HOLLAND, 7
   JOHN, 7
HART
   PEGGY, 73
   THOMAS, 73
HARTIN
   DANIEL, 85
HARTY
   DANIEL, 72
   DENNIS, 68
   JACOB, 24
HARTZ

   JACOB, 93
HASH
   JOHN, 111
HASTIN
   DAVID, 21, 23, 29
   JOSEPH, 21, 23
HASTING
   JOSEPH, 29
HASTINGS
   DANIEL, 67
   JOSEPH, 20, 92
HASTON
   DAVID, 44, 48, 50
HATRON
   JULIANNA, 57
HAVESHAW
   GEORGE, 15
HAWES, 100
   JAMES, 40
HAWKINS
   BENJAMIN, 52, 56,
      63, 64, 66, 73,
      90, 91, 97, 98,
      103, 111, 120
   ELIZABETH, 123
   JAMES, 97, 103, 120
   JOHN, 73, 77, 91,
      103, 111, 115,
      123
   JOSEPH, 103, 111
   WILLIAM, 64, 70,
      73, 77, 79, 91,
      98, 115
HAYES
   WILLIAM, 48
HAYNES
   ADAM, 23
   STEPHEN, 9, 75
HAYS
   ROBERT, 17
   WILLIAM, 41, 54,
      65, 77, 82, 98
HEARD
   JOSEPH, 99
HEATH
   JOHN, 67, 89
HELVY
   JACK, 31
   JACOB, 31
HEMBREE
   JAMES, 122
HENDERSON
   BURRELL, 119
   JAMES, 74
   JOHN, 11, 92, 119

LAWSON, 74
LILBOURN L, 126
LILBURN L, 85
HENDRY
   ABRAHAM, 23
HENERY
   JOHN, 102
HENRY
   JOHN, 8
   MICAJAH, 24
   WILLIAM, 54
   WM, 83
HERAN
   JOHN, 10
HERBERT
   NATHANIEL, 41
   RICE &, 102
   THOMAS, 41, 102, 113
   THOS, 32
HERD
   JOSEPH, 96
HERON
   JAMES, 29, 39, 40,
      42, 44, 45, 50,
      64
HERRIN
   WILLIAM, 89
HERRING
   WM, 89
HERRON
   JAMES, 26, 28, 31,
      33, 35, 39
   WILLIAM ROBINSON
      and JAMES, 32
HESLEY
   W B, 107
HICKMAN
   BENJAMIN, 89, 122
   EDW, 13
   THOMAS, 68
   THOS, 5, 6
HICKS
   HENRY, 63
   JOHN, 124
HIGBEE
   CHARLES, 32
HIGGINS
   RICHARD, 116
HILL
   ABNER, 64, 66, 74,
      103, 109, 110,
      120, 121, 122,
      123, 124
   ELIJAH, 103, 116,
      119, 120, 121,

122, 124
ELY, 116
JAMES, 56, 57, 82,
    98
JOHN, 69, 91, 92
REBEKAH, 56, 57
RICHARD, 12, 16,
    32, 33, 46, 57
SOLOMON, 13
THOMAS, 103, 120,
    123
WILLIAM, 13, 56,
    57, 65, 86, 109
WINKFIELD, 120,
    121, 122
WM, 1, 57, 79
HILLAYBOURN
DAVID, 70
HILTON
EDWARD, 77
HINDS
ANDREW, 61
HINES
THOMAS, 61
HINTON
JOSEPH, 80
HITCHCOCK
BETSY, 74
ELIJAH, 74
EZEKEIL, 81
HENRY, 74
JOHN, 81
NANCY, 74
POLLY, 74
REBEKAH, 74
SALLY, 74
SUSANNA, 74
WILLIAM, 81
WM, 74
HITCHCOFF
ELIJAH, 41
HOBBERT
ANTHONY, 59
HOBBS, 103
HODSON
THOMAS, 85
HOGAN
EDWARD, 31
HOGG
DAVID, 9
WILLIAM, 45
HOLLAND
HARRIS, 88
HARRISON, 57, 95,
    121, 122, 124

JAMES, 120, 124
JOHN, 88, 95
HOLLOWAY
CHARLES, 79
JAMES, 126
HOLMAN
JAMES, 124
HOLMES
JAMES, 53
HONEYCUTT
HARDY, 89
HOOPER
EDWARD, 63, 64, 115
HOPKINS
THOMAS, 97, 107, 123
THOS, 15
HORDIAN
HENRY, 12
HORN
JACOB, 33
RICHARD, 3, 81
SHARAD, 116
SHAROD, 116
THOMAS, 122
WILLY, 81
ZACHEUS, 81
HORNE
JOHN, 102
THOMAS, 35, 64, 102
HORTON
DANIEL, 54
HOUND
JOHN, 1
HOUSE
UNION MEETING, 120
HOUSTON
R, 16, 28
HOWARD
GEO D, 96
GEORGE D, 102
ISAAC, 74
JAMES, 39, 61
JAS D, 91
JOHN, 119
ROBERT, 13, 22, 39,
    48, 66, 76, 98,
    108, 118, 121
WILLIAM, 39, 46, 74
WM, 30, 39
HOWEL
CALVIN, 57
JOHN, 57
HUDDLESTON
CHARLES, 121
DAVID, 92, 97

JOHN C, 121
HUDELLSTON
CHARLES, 122
HUDGINS
JAMES, 124
HUDSON
ABEL, 40
BURREL, 122
BURRELL, 63, 95, 99
BURRIL, 85
DAVID, 113
JAMES, 90, 95
JOHN, 122
PINK, 12, 19, 23,
    24, 86, 87
HUGGINS
JAMES, 68
JON, 7
PHILLIP, 50
HUGHES
JAMES M, 3
HUGHS
SAMUEL, 10
HUMTSMAN
ADAM, 77, 126
HUNT
HARDY, 69
JAMES, 4
HUNTER
CHARLES, 68, 105
JOHN, 119
JOSEPH, 80, 97, 100
JOSIAH, 57
WILLIAM, 79, 97
___, 68
HUNTSMAN
ADAM, 99, 100
HUSTON
R, 105
HUTCHINGS, 105
AARON, 118
BETSEY, 126
CHARLES, 118
J, 104
JOHN, 2, 30, 56,
    79, 80, 90, 91,
    92, 93, 97, 98
JOSEPH, 81
SMITH, 97, 98, 126
SMITTS, 90
WILLIAM, 76
___, 81
HUTCHINS
JOHN, 115
HUTCHISON

ANDW, 75

HUTRON
ABEL, 57
HENRY, 77
ISAIAH, 57
JULIAN, 89
PINK, 89

HUTSON
ABEL, 69, 79, 88,
116, 117, 125
ARCHABAL, 90
ARCHIBALD, 79, 117
BENJAMIN, 99
ISAAC, 126
ISAIAH, 79, 116,
117, 125
JULIA, 108
JULIAN, 104
JULIANNA, 104
MATTHEW, 116, 117
MATTHIAS, 125
PINK, 95, 98, 104,
108

HYDE
JACOB, 64

INGLAND
JESSE, 57

INGRAM
THOMAS, 115, 121,
122
WILLIAM, 115, 121,
122
WM, 115

IRVIN
BASHFORD, 121

IRWIN, 47
ALEXANDER, 21, 40,
70, 74
BASHFORD, 122
THOMAS, 104
WILLIAM, 40, 47,
53, 64, 70, 74,
87

ISH
JOHN, 54

ISHAM
CHARLES, 39, 46
JAMES, 70, 72

IVEY
ELISHA, 59

JACKSON
ANDREW, 11, 32, 83
DAVID, 109, 111
ISAAC, 10, 16
PHILLIP WHITEHEAD,

17
SAMUEL, 47

JADWIN
JOSEPH, 119

JAMES, 124
JOHN, 81

JARRELL
JAMES, 116

JARVIS
CORNELIUS, 125
ELIPHABIT, 64
HARVEY, 81
SAMUEL, 124

JEFFRIES
JOHN, 94

JENKINS
JOHN, 77, 98, 116,
121

JENNINGS
JOHN, 16

JERENING
THOMAS, 62

JERVIS
JOHN, 124

JETT
JNO, 36, 39, 40,
42, 70, 74, 87,
102, 112
JOHN, 33, 49, 51,
85, 101, 105, 125

JEWELL
SAMUEL, 61

JOB
CALEB, 106

JOBE
CALEB, 118

JOHNS
RUSSELL, 87

JOHNSON
ABRAM, 10
BRITAIN, 111
JACOB, 121
SAML, 71
SAMUEL, 119
SML, 91

JOHNSTON
AMOS, 105, 107
HANNON, 58
HARMON, 58
HARPER, 62
HERRON, 74
LEWIS, 105, 107
SAMUEL, 8, 24, 57,
100
THOS, 32

WM, 15

JOINER
DAVID, 72, 78, 86,
96, 102, 105,
120, 121

JONES
EBENEZER, 40, 126
EDWARD, 12
HARDY, 35, 65, 99,
101, 122
JOHN, 67, 68, 69,
99, 105
P, 14
PRETTYMAN, 24
PROTIMAN, 40
SAMUEL, 3
WILLIAM, 83, 100
ZACHARIAH, 40, 65,
67, 73, 110,
119, 121, 126

JORDAN
JOSEPH, 62
SOLOMON, 39

JORDON
SOLOMON, 38, 71, 76

JOWNSEND
JOHN, 90

JOYNER
DAVID, 72

JR
____ RAWLINGS
, 11

KEANEY
JNO, 4

KEAS
SARAH, 109
WESLEY W, 65, 109

KEATHELY
JESSEE, 93

KEATHLEY
HENRY, 119
JESSEE, 90

KEATHLY
JESSE, 88

KEEN
OLIVER, 116

KEESE
GEORGE, 122

KEITH
DANIEL, 121

KEITHLEY
JESSE, 117
JOHN, 66, 119
WILLIS, 66, 119

KELLEY

DUGALD, 61
KELLY
    JOHN, 88, 111, 115
    WILLIAM, 32
KENNEDY
    DAVID, 21
KENT
    JAMES, 4, 63
KERR
    JOSEPH, 64, 111
KEY
    SPENCER A, 58
KILLION
    WILLIAM, 67
KING
    ANDREW, 62
    ANN, 108
    B L, 75
    EDWARD, 108
    ELIZA, 125
    HENRY, 26
    HERON, 27
    JAMES, 86, 108, 125
    JOHN, 86, 108
    ROBERT, 1, 7, 9,
       11, 12, 14, 16,
       19, 21, 22, 23,
       26, 28, 36, 44,
       45, 55, 66, 67,
       72, 79, 84, 86,
       87, 89, 95, 98,
       100, 104, 108
    ROBERT A, 13, 14
    ROBT, 58, 59, 106,
       108
    SAMUEL, 126
    SARAH, 125
    THOMAS, 2, 125
    THOS, 21, 79
    WILLIAM, 1, 50, 52,
       75, 84, 85, 108,
       113, 125, 126
KINKAID
    JOSEPH, 87
KINKEAD
    ELIZABETH, 116
    JOHN, 116
    JOSEPH, 116
KINNEY
    JAMES M, 38
KIRBY
    WILLIAM, 119
    WM A, 118
KITCHEN
    JESSE, 58

KITTY
    W, 35
KNAPP
    JOSIAH, 19, 22
KNOWLES
    JAMES, 57, 75, 98
    JOHN, 40, 42, 57,
       75, 78, 87, 98
    WILLIAM, 116, 117
KORN
    SHERROD, 65
KUHN
    CHRISTOPHER, 71,
       81, 88
LACY
    AMOS, 89
    AMOS H, 95
LAKER
    AUTRY, 4
LALLER
    JOHN, 100
LAMBARON
    LEONARD, 84
LAMBERSON
    CONROD, 53
    LEONARD, 86, 100
LAMBERTS
    AARON, 17
LAMBERTSON
    LEONARD, 112
LAMPTON
    WILLIAM, 100, 112
LANCE
    HENRY, 68
    SAMUEL, 107
LANE
    A B, 103, 113, 121,
       122, 125, 126
    ALEXANDER B, 118,
       122
    BENJ J, 110
    H, 75
    J A, 49, 79, 81,
       97, 100, 102
    JACOB A, 17, 21,
       23, 29, 30, 31,
       34, 35, 39, 42,
       43, 52, 55, 55,
       57, 65, 66, 70,
       74, 77, 79, 85,
       87, 88, 89, 93,
       103, 110, 112,
       113, 122, 125
    RICHARD, 117
    SALLY, 109

SAML, 30
SAMUEL, 82
TURNER, 13, 16, 17,
    24, 26, 27, 28,
    30, 35, 36, 39,
    40, 41, 42, 45,
    46, 55, 64, 67,
    68, 77, 87, 96,
    97, 99, 100,
    108, 120, 122,
    123, 124, 126,
    127
WILLIAM N, 109
___, 120
LANGE
    GEORGE, 94
LARSON
    JAMES, 123
LAUBAND
    CONRAD, 14
LAURENCE
    JULIANNA, 117
    WILLIAM, 114, 117
    WM, 120
LAWRENCE
    WILLIAM, 116, 125
    WM P, 13
LAXON
    JAMES, 69
LAXRON
    THOMAS, 52, 53
LAXSON
    JAMES, 98
LAXTON, 96
    JAMES, 110
LEAK
    WALTER, 15
LEAKE
    WALTER, 16
LEAN
    JOHN M, 63
LEATHERS
    WILLIAM, 95
LEDBETTER
    ARTHUR, 55
    GEORGE W, 124
    WALTON, 55
    WASHINGTON, 27, 32
LEE
    ROLAND, 42, 78, 82
    ROWLAND, 78
LEEPER
    F, 21
    FRANCIS, 9
    FRANK, 109

142

GEO, 36
GEORGE, 36, 100, 105
GRAGE, 75
MATTHEWS
  RALPH, 90
  THOMAS, 1, 4, 10
  THOS, 6
MAXWELL
  DAVID, 14
MAY
  CHRISTIAN, 67
  DAVID, 1
  JOHN, 57, 78, 103,
    123, 124
  JOS, 12
  POLLY, 57
  REYNOLD, 6
  REYNOLDS, 4
  THOMAS, 1, 4, 6
  WILLIAM, 30, 50, 82
MAYS
  THOS, 124
MCADOE
  JAMES, 48
MCAULEY
  JAMES, 11
  JOHN, 11
MCAULY
  DANIEL, 121
MCBEE
  LEVI L, 119
MCBRIDE
  A, 42
  ANDREW, 68, 94
  J, 48
  JAMES, 42
  JAS C, 78
  JO, 35
  JOHN, 13, 35, 42,
    53, 64, 79, 110
  JOSEPH, 78
  JOSEPH C, 66, 82, 94
  RILEY, 35
  THOMAS, 35, 57, 71,
    85
  THOS, 23, 56, 71, 77
MCBURR
  THOS, 76
MCCANN
  WIL, 81
MCCARRY
  THOMAS, 16
MCCLAIN
  JAMES, 79
MCCLANE

JAMES, 91
MCCLARIN
  JAMES, 121
MCCLARN
  JAMES, 118
MCCLEARN
  JAMES, 114
MCCLELLAN
  WILLIAM, 116
MCCLELLAND
  ELIZABETH, 116
  WILLIAM, 116
MCCLOUD
  DANIEL, 52, 91
  DAVID, 66
MCCLUNG
  CHA J, 75
  CHARLES, 47
  HUGH, 47
MCCLURE
  JAMES, 74
MCCOIN
  WILLIAM, 70
MCCORD
  JOHN, 83
MCCORMACK
  JAMES, 68
  REUBIN, 19
MCCORRY
  THOMAS, 13, 16, 17,
    23, 26, 34, 35,
    64, 66, 83, 123
  THOS, 16
MCCOY
  INGOLD, 25
MCCUTCHEN
  SAMUEL, 89
MCDANIEL
  ARCHA, 125
  ARCHIBALD, 91
  DANIEL, 63
  DAVID, 13, 26
  JOHN, 87
  ROBERT, 87
MCDANIELS
  ARCHABALD, 127
  DAVID, 34, 56
MCDEWELL
  STEPHEN, 28
MCDEWETT
  STEPHEN, 28
MCDEWITT
  STEPHEN, 29
MCDONALD
  DAVID, 17

JOHN, 117
JOHN J ROBERT, 98
ROBERT, 117
MCDONNERD
  JOHN, 78
MCDOWELL
  STEPHEN, 56
MCDU__
  STEPHEN, 80
MCELHANEY
  JOHN, 75
MCELHANIE
  JOHN, 53
MCELHINEY
  JOHN, 111
MCELWEE
  HENRY, 14
MCFARLIN
  HENDERSON, 76
MCGAVAN, 24
MCGAVOCK
  D, 16, 24, 94, 105
MCGEE
  JOHN, 121, 122
MCGILVRAY
  JOHN, 36, 65
MCGOWEN
  AMOS, 120, 122
  JOSEPH, 122
MCGUFFIN
  JAMES, 9
  JOSEPH, 9
MCGUIAR
  ISAAC, 93
MCGUIER
  ISAAC, 106
MCGUIRE
  CHARLES, 34
  WE, 12
MCGWIN
  JESSE, 88
MCIVER
  ANDERSON, 80
  JOHN, 23, 24, 26,
    28, 30, 31, 32,
    36, 48, 49, 56,
    65, 66, 72, 73,
    79, 80, 91, 92,
    93, 94, 95, 99,
    104, 105, 106,
    107, 115
  JOHN M, 30
  WILLIAM, 80
MCKEAN
  THOMAS, 14

MCKEEVER
JOHN, 74, 106
MCKEEVES
JOHN, 82
MCKINNEY
JAMES, 89
WILLIAM, 102, 107
MCLEAN
JOHN, 2, 19, 22
MCLEMORE
JNO C, 70, 109
JOHN C, 73, 80, 89,
93, 101, 126
MCLENON
JOHN C, 83
MCLIMORE
JOHN C, 79
MCMILLIN
JAMES, 84
MCMINN
JOSEPH, 101
MCNAIR
J C, 86
MCNAME
PETER, 10
MCNANCE
__TER, 18
MCNARY
JOHN, 98
MCNEESE
JOHN, 108
MCNEIL
DANIEL, 33
MCNEILL
JOHN, 60
MCPHEETERS
SAMUEL, 73
MCPHEY
MORRIS, 59
MCQUISTEN
WM, 17
MCVICKER
JOHN, 3
MEAD
BENJAMIN, 3
MEBANE
_____, 33
MEDCALF
WILLIAM, 35, 41
MEDLEY
JOHN, 38
JOSEPH, 124
RICHARD, 94
MEDLY
JOHN, 93

MEEK
THOMAS, 54, 111
MEEKER, 103
MEEKS
JAMES, 121
MEIGS
HENRY, 4
MELLER
FREDERICK, 56
MELTON
JOEL, 83, 84, 85, 97
JOSEPH, 97
MELVIN
WILLIAM, 70, 81
MENEFEE
WILLIS, 94, 104, 110
MERCER
FORRESTER, 101
MEREDITH
JAMES B, 53
MERRIL
JOHN, 78
MERRILL
JOHN, 122
METCALF
WILLIAM E, 82
MIDKIFF
ISAAC, 45, 70, 74,
85, 99, 108,
111, 112, 113,
115
P H, 113
PHAROAH H, 114
MIDKILL
ISAAC, 70
MIDKOFF
ISAAC, 110
MIDLY
RICHARD, 94
MIDYETT
CHRISTOPHER, 78,
90, 96, 118
RICHARD, 78, 90,
96, 118, 122, 124
MILES
JACOB, 11
JOHN, 21
WILLIAM, 30
MILLAR
JOHN, 124
MILLER
FREDERICK, 30, 41,
72, 82, 97, 117
JACOB, 38, 48, 77,
82, 96, 113,

114, 117, 120
JAS, 115
JNO, 110, 113, 123
JOHN, 23, 24, 38,
48, 82, 96, 117,
120
ROBERT, 47
SAMUEL, 106
THOMAS, 106
MILLS
CARTER, 30
CURTIS, 48, 78
MILSON
JOEL, 83
MILTON
JOEL, 84, 107, 113
MINOR
HUGH, 46
MITCHELL, 126
CHARLES, 21, 23,
24, 48
DAVID, 29, 48, 49,
55, 64, 70, 81,
91
DAVIS, 70
JACOB, 20, 21, 23,
29
JOHN, 55, 102, 125
RACHEL, 125
RICHARD, 115
ROBERT B, 124
S D, 115
SALLY, 125
SPENCE, 23, 49, 120
SPENCER, 72
WILLIAM, 51, 110,
112, 115, 118,
121, 122
WM S, 125
WM SO, 112
MONFORD
SAML D, 58
MOONEY
WILLIAM, 122, 123,
126
MOONEYHAM
SHADRICK, 99
MOOR
JAS, 92
MOORE
ABNER, 64
ALEXR, 30
AMOS, 13
JAMES, 119
JOHN DAVISS, 56

W, 35
MORGAN
  GIDEON, 91
  RICHARD, 61
MORRISON
  WILLIAM, 38, 67,
    70, 74, 109, 114
MORROW
  ROBT H, 14
MORTON
  JAMES, 50
  JOSEPH, 70
MULHANY
  JAMES, 124
MUNKES
  WILLIAM, 113
MURDOCK
  JAMES G, 101
MURPHREE
  URIAH, 64
MURPHRESS
  URIAH, 52
MURPHREY
  JESSE, 45
MURPHY
  JNO B, 91
  JOSEPH, 91
MURRAY
  JOHN, 83
  JOHN M, 83
NAIL
  MATTHEW, 24
NAILOR
  JAMES, 51
NAPIER
  ARCHIBALD H, 119
NAYLOR
  JAMES, 50
NEAL
  DANNIE, 84
NEIL
  DANIEL M, 33
NEILL
  HENRY, 74, 118, 119
NELSON
  JOHN, 12, 19
  SAML, 29
NETHERTON
  JAMES, 64
NETTLES
  JESSE, 35
NEVER
  DAVID, 59
NEVIL
  WILLIAM B, 78

NEVILL
  JOSEPH, 26, 32
  WILLIAM, 34, 53,
    58, 122
  WILLIAM B, 100
  WM B, 114
NEVILLE
  WILLIAM B, 119
NEWEL
  LAWSON, 81
NEWMAN
  DANIEL, 51, 56, 64,
    91, 97, 98, 99,
    103, 111, 114,
    115
  POLLY, 98
NEWSOM
  MOSES, 34, 66
NICHOL
  JOSEPH, 17
NICHOLAS
  DAVID, 16, 17, 26,
    83
  JOHN, 52
NICHOLDS
  DAVID, 34, 41, 64
NICHOLS
  DAVID, 13, 26, 122,
    123
NOBLETT
  DAVID, 107
NORIS
  DAVIS, 97
NORMAN
  MOSES, 113
NORMON
  MOSES, 107
NORRIS
  DAVID, 87, 108, 121
  DAVIS, 86
NORRISS
  DAVID, 91
NORTON
  SETH, 101, 107
  WILLIAM, 29, 38
  WINNEY, 29
  WINNIE, 38
NOUNE
  LAWSON, 86
NOURSE
  LAWSON, 33, 42, 51,
    88, 96, 113, 125
NULL
  HENRY, 70
NUTT

P W, 13
NUTTING
  DAVID, 68
NYDAM
  JOHN, 29
ODIE
  JOHN, 14
ODLE
  ENOCH, 72, 93
ODOM
  SEABORN, 78
of
  GEORGE COMBS, 111
OFFICER
  JAMES, 122
OGEE
  HERCULES, 48
  JOHN, 48
OGLE
  HERCULES, 20, 92
  HERETUS, 45
  JOHN, 55, 92
  WYATT, 92
OLIVER
  DARRITT, 74
ORAM
  JAMES, 21
ORAN
  JAMES, 21
ORFMAN
  T W, 22
OSBURN
  JAMES, 100
OVERTON
  A R W, 14
  ARCHIBALD W, 13,
    26, 105
  ARON, 110
  GEO, 88
  JIM, 4
  JNO, 1, 3, 11
  THOMAS, 88
OWEN
  JAMES, 96
OWENS
  JAMES, 125, 127
  WILLIAM, 14
P
  WILLIAM, 74
PACKER
  JOSEPH, 23
PARISH
  BOOKER, 94
PARKER
  ARTHUR, 103, 121

JOSEPH, 12, 33, 45, 55, 57, 65

PARKERSON
GEORGE, 84

PARKESON
DANIEL, 87
GEORGE, 87
WASHINGTON, 87

PARKINSON
WILLIAM, 125

PARKISON
GEORGE, 119
MANUEL, 94, 104, 110
WILLIAM, 48, 105

PARNAL
JOSHUA, 21

PARRET
JOHN, 14

PARTON
ALEXANDER, 59
TEMPLE, 112

PASS
JAMES H, 106, 108, 110, 121

PATE
ANTHONY, 79, 119
JARAMIAH, 119
JOHN, 79, 119

PATILLA
GEORGE, 120

PATTISON
STEPHEN, 64

PAYNE
JOSIAH, 6, 68

PEADEN
THOMAS, 14

PEARCE
DAVID, 110, 111, 126
DAVIS, 73
ROBERT D, 50
WALKY W, 121
WALSEY, 105
WILREY, 107
WOOLSEY W, 122

PEARROW
HENRY, 50

PEGRAM
WILLIAM, 74

PEMBERTON
JOHN, 16

PENNINGTON
JOSHUA, 70

PERCE
HALLETT, 24

PERKINS

ABSALOM, 106, 115
EPHRAIM, 115
EPRIAM, 106
LEVI, 97
REUBEN, 120
REUBIN, 78, 104
ROBERT B, 89, 106, 114
STEPHEN, 20, 22, 52

PERKISON
MANUEL, 98

PERREN
AARON, 46

PERRIN
AARON, 46
ROBERT, 44

PERRON
AARON, 92, 97

PERROW
AARON, 46
AAROW, 46

PERRY
AARON, 28
SAML, 6

PERRYMAN
JAMES, 81

PERRYMORE
JAMES, 7

PERSON
NATHAN, 6

PETERS
TITUS, 60

PETTILOR
JOHN, 104

PETTYJOHN
MILLERTON, 89
SAMUEL, 89

PEYTON
FRANCIS, 32, 35

PHELPS
DAVID, 49
LUCY, 49

PHILIPS
WILLIAM, 15

PHILLIPS
CAMPBELL &, 45
MARTHA JERUSHA, 23
RICHARD, 28, 96
WILLIAM, 9, 11, 12, 16, 17, 23, 28, 30, 33, 36, 40, 45, 55, 67
WM, 36

PHILPS
DAVID, 54

PICKETT
J, 100

PICKRELL
HARRY, 75
JOHN, 33, 36, 75
NICHOLAS, 75

PIERCE
HALLET, 35
ROBERT D, 47

PILEAR
WM E, 28

PILLAR
WILLIAM E, 26, 28
WM E, 30, 40, 53

PILLOW
GIDEON, 72, 84, 100

PIRKINS
ROBERT A, 110

PIRTLE
GEORGE, 91, 98, 103

PISTOLE
JOHN, 108, 110

PLUMBLEY
ISAAC, 49

POGUE
JOHN, 2

POLK
WILLIAM, 13

POLLOCK
ELIZABETH, 12

POOLE
D KINNEY, 123
KINSEY, 123

POOT
___, 30

PORTER
JOSEPH B, 79, 81

PORTERFIELD
DENNY, 124
FRANK, 33
JAMES, 124
RICHARD, 47, 121

POSTON
TEMPLE, 67

POTEET, 71

POTTS
GEORGE, 85
GEORGE W, 85

POUNDS
DAVID, 10
JARED, 16
JARREL, 10

POWEL
LEWIS, 56

POWELL

STAMPS
  SANDFORD, 116
  WILLIAM, 64, 116
STANLEY
  HANCOCK, 62
STEADMAN
  JOHN, 62
STEAKLEY
  CHRISTOPHER, 103
STECKLEY
  CHRISTOPHER, 103
STEDMAN
  W, 11
STEEL
  ALEXANDER, 105
STEPHENS
  JOHN, 62
STEPHENSON
  JOHN P, 20
  WILLIAM, 19
STEWART
  JOHN, 81
  ROBERT, 35
  WILLIAM, 89
STIGAL
  JACOB, 40
STILL
  BOON, 67
STIMPSON
  SAYER, 100
STIMSON
  JAMES, 32, 82
STINSON
  JAMES, 66, 74, 78,
    78, 100, 106
  WILLIAM, 66, 74,
    78, 78, 82, 100
STONE, 13
  CORDEN, 68
  CORDER, 55, 97,
    106, 112
  CORDER C, 66
  CORDER H, 89, 114
  CORDY, 112
  DAVID, 21
  IREBY, 68
  IREBY W, 66, 86,
    87, 89, 105,
    114, 120
  IREBY W B, 45, 53
  THOMAS, 12, 23, 24,
    28, 32, 33, 45,
    53, 57, 65, 66,
    68, 75, 84, 86,
    89, 97, 105,

106, 114, 120
  WILLIAM P, 89
STORIN
  THOMAS, 58
STORM
  THOMAS, 2, 3, 22,
    29, 37, 63, 105
STOWE
  THOMAS, 87
STREET
  ANTHONY, 14
STRIPLIN
  NEWTON, 16
STRONG
  ISAAC B, 3
STUART
  JOHN, 81
STUBBLEFIELD
  ARMISTEAD, 53, 75,
    99, 100
  ARMSTEAD, 105
SUGG
  GEORGE, 54, 106,
    118, 125
  HAREL, 54, 117
  HAYAL, 117
  HAZEAD, 117
  HAZEAIE, 122
  HAZEL, 122
  MARVEL, 118
SULLINS
  ZACHARIAH, 119
SULLIVAN
  CHARLES, 107, 108
  JOHN, 30, 38, 51, 74
SUMNER
  JETHRO, 54, 55, 56,
    65
  JULIAS, 29, 33
SUTTLE
  JOHN, 95, 102
SUTTON
  JAMES, 23
SWAIN
  LEVI, 126
SWANTON
  R, 112
SWEAT
  LEVI, 87, 113, 115
SWEET
  LEVI, 111
SWIFT
  ELISHA, 67
SWINDEL
  CASON, 96

SWINDELL
  CASON, 79
SWINDLE
  CASON, 52
  CHRISTOPHER, 97, 110
SWINEY
  ADAM, 17
TABB
  JAMES, 53
TABOR
  ____, 50
TANHILL
  JOHN, 121
TATE
  JOHN, 41
TATOM
  WILLIAM, 51
TATTON
  THOMAS, 58
TATUM
  HOWEL, 63
TAYLER
  SURANA, 12
TAYLOR
  AND, 40
  ELIZABETH, 109
  GEORGE, 12
  GEORGE G, 109
  ISAAC, 3, 13, 17,
    20, 26, 28, 29,
    30, 31, 32, 33,
    34, 36, 43, 44,
    45, 47, 48, 50,
    55, 56, 67, 70,
    71, 74, 75, 77,
    80, 84, 85, 87,
    88, 95, 100,
    101, 104, 105,
    108, 111, 112,
    115, 119, 125
  J, 23, 24
  JAMES, 74, 75, 86,
    118, 121
  JAMES P, 53, 54,
    84, 90, 101
  JAS, 12
  JAS P, 40, 64
  JOHN, 17, 67, 75,
    84, 86, 104,
    115, 118, 121
  JOS, 17
  NATHANIEL, 40, 41,
    47, 54, 56, 64,
    80, 87, 125
  PEGGY, 20

SAMUEL, 45
THOMAS, 89
W O, 92
W P, 70, 80, 85,
    93, 102, 113, 115
WILL, 8, 21
WILLIAM, 11, 74,
    109, 119, 124
WILLIAM H, 66
WOODSON P, 16, 23,
    26, 41, 44, 54,
    64, 66, 72, 76,
    77, 85, 100, 103
WHITEACRE
    WILLIAM, 97
WHITLEY
    SHARP, 54, 77, 116
WHITTIER
    JOHN, 13
WICKOFF
    HENDRICK J, 2
WILCHER
    THOMAS, 16, 55
WILLARD
    JOHN, 91
WILLHITE
    JAMES, 77
    REUBEN, 121, 122
WILLIAM, 47
WILLIAMS
    BENJAMIN, 11
    CHARLES, 88
    DANNIE, 83
    ELIZA, 6, 7, 8, 93,
        99, 101, 104,
        107, 116, 126
    ELIZABETH B, 93
    ETHELDRED, 14
    ETHELRED, 14
    H W, 14
    ISAAC, 98
    JAMES, 7, 8, 9, 11,
        13, 19, 21, 23,
        44, 45, 66, 68,
        79, 84, 86, 92,
        99, 101, 104,
        106, 107, 110,
        116, 120, 121
    JESSE, 88, 103
    JOHN, 17, 45, 49,
        55, 103
    JOHN M, 121
    JOSEPH, 79, 97, 101
    JOSHUA, 90, 97
    MORRISON, 16

NATHANIEL W, 13
P, 101
S, 4
SAMPSON, 29, 94
SAMUEL, 119
THOMAS B, 93, 99,
    101, 104, 107,
    116
THOS, 121, 122
WILLIAM, 72, 80, 101
WILLIAMSON
    JOHN, 51, 52, 67
    JOHN C, 55
WILLIS
    DAVIDSON, 55
WILLS
    ZEBULEN, 62
WILLY, 3
WILMORE
    WILLIAM, 12
WILMOUTH
    JAS, 118
WILSHIRE
    THOMAS, 11
WILSON
    HARTWELLL, 126
    JESSE, 53, 72
    JOHN, 98
    SAMUEL, 126
    SYLVESTER, 78
    THOMAS, 17, 56, 65,
        77, 126
    WILLIAM, 29, 56, 78
    WILLM, 30, 65
WINDLW
    JOHN, 40
WINKLER
    JEREMIAH, 48
WINOAH
    JOHN, 24
WINTER
    WILLIAM, 38, 48,
        102, 120
WINTON
    JAMES, 4, 6
WITCHER
    THOMAS, 45
WITHROW
    RICHARD, 110
WITMORE
    WM, 19
WITT
    GEO C, 47
    GEORGE C, 49
WM, 71

WOMACK
    DAVID, 71
    JOHN, 39, 46, 48
WOOD
    HENRY, 8, 9, 11, 109
    JOAB, 2, 9
    JOHN, 11
    JONA, 6
    JONATHAN, 2, 6, 7,
        9, 11, 100, 109
    NATHANIEL, 59
WOODARD
    ISAAC, 30, 33
WOODS
    ALFRED H, 53
    BENJN, 2
    GREEN, 53, 55, 67
    HENRY, 109
    MICHAEL L, 53
    NATHAN, 44, 50
    NATHANIEL, 59
    WILLIAM C, 53
WOODSON
    TUCKER, 124
    TUCKER M, 123
WOODWARD
    GEORGE, 63
WORD
    JOAB, 6
WORK
    JACOB, 64
WORSLEY
    JOHN, 62
WOTHERSPOON
    R, 36
WRIGHT
    JOHN, 1, 4, 6
WYCK
    P C VAN, 22
    PIERRE C VON, 3
WYCKOFF
    HENDRICK J, 63
WYCOFF
    HENDRICK J, 30
WYRRELL
    WILLIAM, 30
YAGER
    SOLOMON, 77
YANCEY
    AM, 1
YATES
    THOMAS, 111
YEAGAR
    JOEL, 95
YEAGER

www.ingramcontent.com/pod-product-compliance
Lightning Source LLC
Chambersburg PA
CBHW080241270326
41926CB00020B/4329